CAMBRIDGE LIBRARY COLLECTION

Books of enduring scholarly value

Linguistics

From the earliest surviving glossaries and translations to nineteenth-century academic philology and the growth of linguistics during the twentieth century, language has been the subject both of scholarly investigation and of practical handbooks produced for the upwardly mobile, as well as for travellers, traders, soldiers, missionaries and explorers. This collection will reissue a wide range of texts pertaining to language, including the work of Latin grammarians, groundbreaking early publications in Indo-European studies, accounts of indigenous languages, many of them now extinct, and texts by pioneering figures such as Jacob Grimm, Wilhelm von Humboldt and Ferdinand de Saussure.

Elements of South-Indian Palaeography, from the Fourth to the Seventeenth Century, A.D.

Published in 1874, this groundbreaking monograph on the palaeography of southern India gained great scholarly acclaim. Arthur Coke Burnell (1840–82) served in the Indian Civil Service and as a judge, also building up a large collection of original or copied Sanskrit manuscripts. Originally intended as an introduction to his vast and pioneering *Classified Index to the Sanskrit Manuscripts in the Palace at Tanjore* (1880), this work won Burnell an honorary doctorate at the University of Strasbourg. Replete with documentary evidence, it contains copies and explanations of numerous texts, the decipherment of which threw new light upon an obscure chapter in the history of writing, offering new theories for dating the introduction of writing into India and the origin of southern Indian alphabets and numerals. Although Burnell's work has since been built on and sometimes superseded, this is still a much-cited resource in South Asian palaeography and epigraphy.

T0382484

Cambridge University Press has long been a pioneer in the reissuing of out-of-print titles from its own backlist, producing digital reprints of books that are still sought after by scholars and students but could not be reprinted economically using traditional technology. The Cambridge Library Collection extends this activity to a wider range of books which are still of importance to researchers and professionals, either for the source material they contain, or as landmarks in the history of their academic discipline.

Drawing from the world-renowned collections in the Cambridge University Library and other partner libraries, and guided by the advice of experts in each subject area, Cambridge University Press is using state-of-the-art scanning machines in its own Printing House to capture the content of each book selected for inclusion. The files are processed to give a consistently clear, crisp image, and the books finished to the high quality standard for which the Press is recognised around the world. The latest print-on-demand technology ensures that the books will remain available indefinitely, and that orders for single or multiple copies can quickly be supplied.

The Cambridge Library Collection brings back to life books of enduring scholarly value (including out-of-copyright works originally issued by other publishers) across a wide range of disciplines in the humanities and social sciences and in science and technology.

Elements of South-Indian Palaeography from the Fourth to the Seventeenth Century A.D.

A.C. Burnell

Cambridge University Press

CAMBRIDGE UNIVERSITY PRESS

Cambridge, New York, Melbourne, Madrid, Cape Town,
Singapore, São Paolo, Delhi, Mexico City

Published in the United States of America by Cambridge University Press, New York

www.cambridge.org
Information on this title: www.cambridge.org/9781108046107

© in this compilation Cambridge University Press 2012

This edition first published 1874
This digitally printed version 2012

ISBN 978-1-108-04610-7 Paperback

This book reproduces the text of the original edition. The content and language reflect the beliefs, practices and terminology of their time, and have not been updated.

Cambridge University Press wishes to make clear that the book, unless originally published by Cambridge, is not being republished by, in association or collaboration with, or with the endorsement or approval of, the original publisher or its successors in title.

The original edition of this book contains a number of colour plates, which have been reproduced in black and white. Colour versions of these images can be found online at www.cambridge.org/9781108046107

DISTRIBUTION OF S·INDIAN ALPHABETS UP TO 1550 A.D.

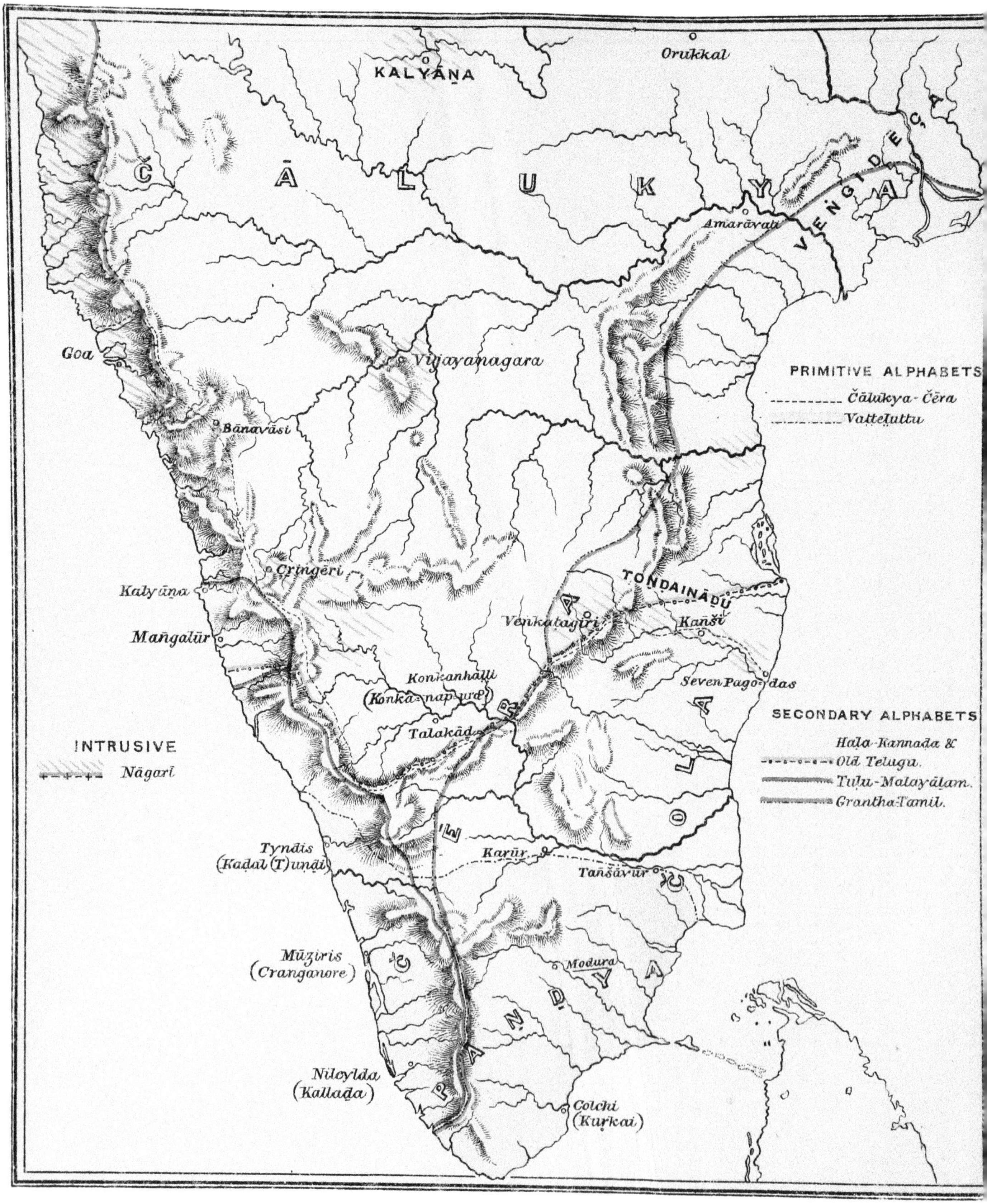

DRAWN BY GUNNOO KASSINATH

ELEMENTS

OF

SOUTH-INDIAN PALÆOGRAPHY

FROM THE FOURTH TO THE SEVENTEENTH CENTURY A. D.

BEING

AN INTRODUCTION TO THE
STUDY OF SOUTH-INDIAN INSCRIPTIONS AND MSS.

BY

A. C. BURNELL
HON. PH. D. OF THE UNIVERSITY OF STRASSBURG;
M. R. A. S.; MEMBRE DE LA SOCIÉTÉ ASIATIQUE, ETC. ETC.

MANGALORE
PRINTED BY STOLZ & HIRNER, BASEL MISSION PRESS
1874
LONDON
TRÜBNER & Co. 57 & 59 LUDGATE HILL

Der

Philosophischen Facultät

zu

Strassburg

widmet

als Zeichen der Dankbarkeit für die ihm verliehene Doctorwürde
diese Erstlings-Arbeit auf einem bisher unbebauten Felde

der

Verfasser.

INTRODUCTION.

I trust that this elementary Sketch of South-Indian Palæography may supply a want long felt by those who are desirous of investigating the *real* history of the peninsula of India.

From the beginning of this century (when Buchanan executed the only archæological survey that has ever been done in even a part of the South of India) up to the present time, a number of well meaning persons have gone about with much simplicity and faith collecting a mass of rubbish which they term traditions and accept as history. There is some excuse for Buchanan, but none for his followers; the persistent retailing of this "lying gabble" (as Genl. Cunningham aptly terms it) has well-nigh ruined the progress of Indian research, and caused the utter neglect of a subject that evidently promises much[1]. The Vedic literature will always remain the most attractive object of study in relation to India, but there is much besides to be studied. The history of Indian civilization does not cease (as some appear to think) with the early period of Buddhism. About the

1) It must be obvious that these traditions are merely attempts at explanations of the unknown through current ideas, which in S. India amount to the merest elements of Hindu mythology as gathered from third rate sources. Mouhot the illustrious discoverer of the Cambodian temples, though a naturalist and not an archæologist, saw this very plainly. He says ("Travels in the Central Parts of Indo-China", vol. ii. pp. 8, 9.): "All traditions being lost, the natives invent new ones, according to the measure of their capacity." The Mâhâtmyas are equally worthless with the oral legends, for they are modern compositions intended to connect particular places with events entirely mythical and belonging to modern or even foreign religious systems. How worthless tradition is in S. India, a few examples will easily prove. The chain of rocks from India to Ceylon is (as is well known) connected with the myth of Râma's conquest of Lankâ, but this localization of the mythical event must be quite recent; for, *firstly*, whatever may be the age of the Râmâyaṇa, the worship of Râma is quite modern. *Again*, had there been any such myth current in the place during the early centuries A. D., we might expect something about it in the Periplus or Ptolemy, especially as the former gives the legend then current about Cape Comorin; but there is nothing of the kind to be found. *Lastly*, there is nothing whatever (Mr. D'Alwis assures us) known of the legend in Ceylon. Again, the localization of the events of the Mahâbhârata is endless; every few miles in S. India one can find the place where some battle or other event occurred, and so it is also in Java. Such legends therefore are absolutely worthless, for they prove no more than that the Mahâbhârata and Râmâyaṇa are or were favourite stories over a large part of the East. But the traditional practice in respect of ceremonies is worth little more; though in this case religious prejudices can hardly interfere. Thus for the S'o m a many different plants are used. The Brahmans on the Coromandel Coast take the 'Asclepias Acida', those of Malabar the 'Ceropegia Decaisneana' or 'Ceropegia Elegans'. How different in appearance these three plants are, may be readily seen by a comparison of the figures of them given by Wight in his "Icones" ii., 595 ("Ascl. Acida) and his "Spicilegium Neilgherriense" pl. 152 and 155. From Dr. Haug's description ("Aitareya Brâhmaṇa" ii., p. 489) I am inclined to think that a fourth plant is used at Poonah. Which then, if any of them, is the original Soma? And this loss of tradition must (apart from the obvious development of rites) have begun very early; for otherwise, it is impossible to account for the variations in the details of the same ceremony as described, *e.g.* by the different Çrautasûtras. Thus we find, in the Cayanas, that Âpastamba directs the construction of the altars in a different way to that prescribed by Bodhâyana. So again the great difference in the way of uttering the Vedic accents and the singing of the Sâma Veda, must strike every one who hears them. These differences, at all events, cannot be original; for they occur among followers of the same Çâkhâ of the Veda. The Açoka tree of S. India is the Guatteria longifolia; that of the North, the Jonesia açoka. Tradition is worthless all over the East in exactly the same way. Once, when crossing in a boat from the Nubian bank of the Nile to the temple of Philae, I asked the native boatman what he knew of the Temple? He replied directly: "It is the Castle of Ânas Alwajûd". This personage is the hero of a popular Arabic fairy-tale! Had the boatman been a native of India, he would have answered: "Râma's (or the Pâṇḍava's) palace", and backed up his story with an endless legend.

early centuries of the Christian era, we find the Buddhist-Brahmanical civilization extending from its home in the North over alien races inhabiting the peninsula of India, and in the course of some few centuries it had already extended over Burmah, the Malay Islands, and even to the forests and swamps of Cambodia. But this immense progress was not a mere reception of stereotyped forms and opinions by uncivilized peoples; it was on the contrary (and herein lies the interest of the subject), a gradual adaptation[1] to circumstances, including the creation of national literatures in many languages, which were then first reduced to writing and system. In South-India, at all events, new sects rapidly arose, which have reacted powerfully on Northern India. Books containing the various religious opinions that have prevailed more or less in these Hinduized, or rather Brahmanized, countries, are yet easily accessible; but the chronological framework is almost entirely wanting, and this can only be supplied from the inscriptions still existing in large numbers. If an outline of the historical events of the last fifteen centuries of S. Indian history could be gained from these inscriptions, the wearisome dry dogmatic treatises would begin to possess some human interest, and the faint outlines of a long obliterated picture would reappear; faintly at first, but with time and patient research, they would (like fossils in the hands of the geologist) present a living picture of a past, if not attractive, at all events strange. The prospect of such a result should attract the few European students of Sanskrit in S. India who at present, in the hope of learning something of Indian matters, devote their attention to mechanical poems which repeat themselves with "most damnable iteration," or to plays composed by pedants during the worst times of India. This real history of S. India can only be gathered from inscriptions.

A manual of Palæography like the one I have here attempted has a double object in view— to trace the gradual development of writing by means of documents of known date, and thus also to render it possible to assign a date to the larger number of documents which do not bear any. For this purpose I have given a chronological series of alphabets traced (with two exceptions[2]) from impressions of the original documents; these are by no means perfect, as I have selected only the most usual letters, as these only can assist in determining the date. Unusual letters are often formed after analogy or capriciously, and thus have, in Indian Palæography, but little value.

Indian, and even S. Indian, Palæography is hardly a new subject, though much that is really new will, I believe, be found in the following pages, which were originally intended to form part of an introduction to a Descriptive Catalogue of Sanskrit MSS. at Tanjore, now nearly ready for the press. As, however, I found that that work would necessarily be of considerable size, I have preferred publishing these pages separately. The foundations of Indian Palæography were laid by J. Prinsep some forty years ago[3], when he showed that the Indian alphabets then known to him were probably derived from the S. Açoka character which he first deciphered; since then, little or nothing has been done except Sir W. Elliot's lithographic reproduction of the Hala Kannada

1) Cfr. W. von Humboldt's remarks on the Kawi (old Javanese) literature in his treatise on the Kawi language. ii. p. 4.
2) Plates xi. and xii.
3) *Bengal As. Soc. J.* vi. pl. xiii.

alphabet, at Bombay about 1836[1]. Dr. Babington had already given an old Tamiḻ alphabet[2], and Harkness republished both with some unimportant additions[3]. The materials I have used have been collected by myself during several years and in very different parts of the country, and are (I have every reason to believe) fairly complete.

Many attempts have been made by Mackenzie, Sir W. Elliot, Mr. C. P. Brown, Mr. H. J. Stokes and others to collect the inscriptions of S. India; but, though the importance of this work has been often acknowledged, few results have followed, as no individual (except perhaps Sir W. Elliot) could hope to be able to finish such a task. When the greater part of the plates and text that follow were already printed (between one and two years ago), this important subject was still viewed with indifference; since then, the *Indian Antiquary* in Bombay, and the labours of Profr. Kern at Leiden and Profr. Eggeling in London raise hopes that will not be disappointed. The treatment of parts of the Açoka edicts by the former[4] marks the epoch of a real scientific study of Indian inscriptions, and his knowledge of Indian antiquities and ways of thought has cleared up what seemed likely to remain for ever obscure. Profr. Eggeling is the first to publish the W. Câlukya documents, and to show what they really mean. But the subjects of these researches present many difficulties. If S. Indian inscriptions present comparatively few puzzles, as far as the characters used are considered, they can only be satisfactorily explained by a knowledge of Sanskrit and the Dravidian languages which rests upon a more certain foundation than is now usual. If the absence of notes and abbreviations render transcription easy and certain, there is much in the language of the documents that will create serious difficulties. The earliest and most important grants for historical purposes are nearly all in Sanskrit, but the scribes were seldom content with leaving the names of places untranslated, and to restore these names to their Dravidian forms, and thus render identification possible, is often a task beset with difficulties[5]. A large number of documents are in Canarese and Tamiḻ, but as the orthography fluctuated, and the vocabularies of these languages have been but little studied in a scientific spirit, it is not too much to say that not a single early inscription in either of these languages has as yet been explained in a perfectly

1) The only copy I have seen had no title, hence I cannot give the exact date.

2) Transactions of the R. As. Soc. ii. pl. xiii.

3) London, 1837. ("Ancient and Modern Hindu Alphabets, by Capt. H. Harkness" 37 pp.)

4) "Over de Jaartelling der Zuidelijke Buddhisten", 4° Amsterdam, 1873.

5) The Sanskritizing of Dravidian names by official scribes seems to have happened in the following ways:

A. Alteration of the whole name.

1. *Correct translation.* *e. g.* Tâlavṛinda=Paṇaikkâḍu; Vaṭâraṇya.
2. *Mis-translations.* *e. g.* Bâlâ(purî)=Koššì (Cochin); Kânsi(pura)=Kaṇsi (Conjeveram).

B. *Partial translation* of the last part of a compound word, and which=town, village, mountain, etc. *e. g.* Koṅkaṇa-pura=Koṅkaṇa-haḷḷi or rather Koṅkaṇi-haḷḷi; Kolâcala=? Golkoṇḍa.

C. *Mythological perversions* of Dravidian names the meaning of which was early lost. *e. g.* Pâṇḍiyan into Pâṇḍya hence derived from Pâṇḍu; Râshṭra from Raṭṭa=Reḍḍi; Taṅšâvûr; Mahâbalipura from Mâmallaipura; Çrîbali from Çivaḷḷi. Such perversions are generally intended to localize the N. Indian mythology.

D. *Substitution* of an entirely new name, the first part of which is the name of the God worshipped and the second part S t h a l a or some equivalent word.

I hope some time to be able to bring out a map of S. India in which all such names will be entered, as far as I have been able to identify them.

satisfactory manner[1]. These documents contain the earliest specimens of the Dravidian languages (beyond single words), that we possess; they are, therefore, of capital importance for the comparative study of the S. Indian dialects, but have not as yet been used at all, except by Dr. Gundert.

These grants will again by their local irregularities of spelling throw great light on the history of the literary dialects of those languages, and especially of Canarese and Telugu. It is certain that the earliest literary culture in the Deccan was purely Sanskritic, and that compositions in the vernacular scarcely existed before the 10th century A. D.; but these were artificial to the last degree, and contained Sanskrit words in profusion, they were in short Kâvyas[2]; hence for specimens of the language as actually used we must depend on the earlier inscriptions. The Tamiḻ literature has also fallen under Sanskrit influences, but to a less degree; yet as it is scarcely probable that the grammarians had ended their work at the date of the earliest documents, these will furnish important information illustrating the history of the language.

I have thus briefly pointed out what we may hope to gain by a study of the S. Indian inscriptions, and, to all aware of the utter uncertainty attending all Indian researches, the prospect must be a very attractive one. But there are many difficulties as I have also pointed out, and there is one obstacle that I must not omit to notice. From the beginning, Indian studies have been infected by a spirit of vague sentimentalism, the cause of which it is difficult to find, and which has reasonably caused prudent enquirers to doubt the value of much that has been done. To all students of Indian literature one can only repeat the words of advice addressed by M. Chabas to the Assyriologists. "Nons invitons les Assyriologues sérieux à pousser de leur côté le cri d'alarme, et à maintenir leur science au-dessus de la portée des enthousiastes qui en abusent[3]." If an eminent Egyptologist finds it necessary to address his cautious fellow-labourers in this manner, how much more does the warning apply to Indianists. If Egypt and Assyria present merely ruins and broken fragments, these are at least real, whereas Indian literature is mostly but a fata-morgana of ruins that have disappeared ages ago.

I owe my best thanks to the Rev. G. Richter of Mercara for a loan of the Cêra grant in his possession. To the Rev. F. Kittel I owe many important references and suggestions, as will be seen by the text and the "Corrections and Additions" at the end. The Basel Mission Press at Mangalore has spared no pains to bring out this Monograph in a complete form; and I especially am indebted to my friend Mr. C. Stolz and the other authorities there for the trouble they have taken, I hope, not in vain.

Tanjore,
22nd December 1874.

A. B.

[1] Dr. Gundert's labours on Malayâḷam, and more recently, those of Mr. Kittel on Canarese will soon remove this obstacle; a really good Tamiḻ Dictionary is yet, however, to be written. The best now existing is that printed at Pondicherry in 2 vols. 8° ("Par deux missionaires Apostoliques").

[2] Cfr. Āndhraçabdacintâmaṇi i., 1. "Viçvaçreyaḥ Kâvyam" which sûtra gives the object of the work. The analogy between the S. Indian artificial poems in the Dravidian languages and those in the old Javanese called Kawi are complete, and there can be no doubt that the last thus got their name.

[3] Etudes sur l'Antiquité' historique d'après les sources Egyptiennes." 2nd ed. p. 128.

ELEMENTS

OF

SOUTH-INDIAN PALÆOGRAPHY

CHAPTER I.

THE DATE OF THE INTRODUCTION OF WRITING INTO INDIA.

THAT the art of writing was imported into India is now allowed by most Orientalists who can claim to be heard, but how and when this occurred is by no means clear[1]. The earliest written documents that have been discovered in India are the proclamations of the Buddhist king Piyadasi or Açoka which are written in two different characters; and the silly denunciations of writing in which the Brahmans have always indulged, render it excessively improbable that they had anything to do with the introduction of the art. The inscriptions of Açoka are of about 250 B. C., but it seems probable that writing was practised to a certain extent in Northern India nearly half a century before that period.

Nearchus (B. C. 325) expressly states that the Brahman laws were *not* written[2]. Megasthenes a few years later (c. 302 B. C.) mentions that they had no written books, and that they did not know letters (grammata)[3] or use seals, but he also mentions milestones at a distance of ten stadia from one another, "indicating the bye-roads and intervals"[4]. It is difficult, though not impossible, to suppose that these indications were made by the stones merely, and that there were not any marks on them to tell more than the mere position of the stones could do[5]. The inscriptions of Açoka

1) Kopp (in 1821) first suggested a foreign Semitic source of the Devanāgarī alphabet. Dr. R. Lepsius followed in 1834: and then with much stronger arguments came Prof. A. Weber (Z. D. D. M. G. x. pp. 389 and ffg. "Indische Skizzen" pp. 127—150). He has always been the strongest supporter of this theory. But many consider it probable: Prof. Th. Benfey ("Orient und Occident" iii, 170); Prof. Max Müller (A. S. L. 2nd Ed. p. 521). Prof. N. L. Westergaard ("Ueber den ältesten Zeitraum der Indischen Geschichte" p. 37) hesitates. He considers it likely that writing was, originally, in India a secret known to the traders only. I am not able to refer to Böhtlingk's article on the age of writing in India mentioned by Lassen. Prof. Pott ("Etymologische Forschungen, Wurzel-Wörterbuch" ii., 2 p. liii.) is not however satisfied (1870). Mr. E. Thomas (1866) suggested a Dravidian origin of the Indian alphabets. Prof. Lassen repudiates a foreign origin for the Indian alphabets (I. A. K. Vol. I. 2nd Ed. p. 1008) altogether. Prof. Whitney ("Studies" p. 85) considers a Semitic origin probable.

2) Frag. F. in "Reliqua Arriani et Scriptorum de rebus Alexandri". Ed. C. Müller, Paris, 1846 (p. 60.)

3) "Megasthenis Indica" ed. Schwanbeck, Frag. xxvii. (fr. Strabo. xv. 1. 53—56) p. 113.

4) Do. Frag. xxxiv. (from the same source). pp. 125,6.

5) It is however singular that, as yet, none of these milestones have been discovered.

are also in themselves proofs that writing was about 250 B. C. a recent practice, for they present irregularities of every kind[1]. That these inscriptions are of a period immediately after the introduction of writing has been insisted on by Prof. Wassiljew, who also remarks that it is not long after their date that the Buddhists refer to their scriptures as written[2].

On the other hand Nearchus is also represented as stating that the Indians wrote letters on a sort of cotton cloth or paper[3].

Again, passages in Megasthenes have been understood by Schwanbeck to imply the use of writing at the period when he visited India. These are: (1) some passages which describe the proclamation at the beginning of the year of a sort of astrological calendar for the coming seasons[4]; again, (2) the statement that births were considered for astrological purposes[5]. But it is obvious that such usages afford but a faint presumption that writing was necessarily employed to enable them to be practised. There are many savage tribes still existing which are utterly ignorant of writing, and nevertheless do exactly the same things. Thus the description given by Megasthenes might apply to the 'Medicine men' of America, and the Fetish priests of parts of Africa at the present day who are utterly ignorant of any art at all like writing. The Aztecs who, at the best, had only an imperfect hieroglyphic character, were great astrologers. Megasthenes also mentions (3) songs in honour of gods and deceased persons[6]; but there is no necessity to assume that these were written. The (4) milestones that he describes, I have already mentioned. On the other hand it is expressly stated by Megasthenes that the Indians had no *written* laws, and strangely enough this is quoted by much later writers like Strabo, who must have been able to correct this statement if wrong at their time.

The next point for consideration is: whence did these two alphabets come that we find in use in India in the third century before our era?

During several centuries before that time, the natives of India had opportunities of becoming acquainted with many different systems of writing then current in the West and in Persia.

---

1) Thus in the third tablet we find aṅapitam, and in the fourth aṅapayisati, but in the sixth âṅâpi°. The reduplication of consonants is universally omitted where it should be found (*e. g.* piyasa, janasa, ârabhisante, dukaram, svagam, dighâya, etc.). Nor is the orthography uniform; we find in the Southern inscriptions: etârisam and etâdisam also. Again in the Southern inscriptions we have anathesu, but in the Northern (at Kapurdigiri) anaṭhesu. Again the Southern inscriptions have both dasanam and dasaṇa. The insertion of nasals before consonants is also excessively irregular. But this may perhaps be attributed more properly to the carelessness of the masons who carved the text on the rocks. The existence of inscriptions like the Açoka edicts proves that writing was more or less commonly understood, but it is impossible, looking at the above irregularities and the numerous others that occur, to suppose that writing was then used to express the minute distinctions that we find in the grammarians' rules. Hitherto, these irregularities have been generally considered to be dialectic!

2) "Der Buddhismus" p. 30 (28). It is much to be regretted that this admirable work, which marks an epoch in Indian studies, is not known by an English translation. The author's immense learning has not prevented him from giving his result in the clearest way, and he has evidently worked without any prejudice.

3) u. s. p. 64, a.

4) "Megasthenis Indica" ed. Schwanbeck Fr. I. 42 (p. 91).

5) Do: Fr. xxxiv., 5 (p. 126).

6) Do: Fr. xxvi., 1 (p. 112).

The Phœnicians who voyaged for Solomon came to Southern India at least, and exported from thence peacocks which were called in Hebrew by a Tamil name[1]. The Persians about 500 B. C. conquered India (that is probably, the Punjab and part of India Proper or Northern India), under Darius; and in the Inscriptions at Persepolis and Naksh-i-Rustam India occurs as the 21st and 13th province, respectively, of that monarch's empire[2]. According to Herodotus India was the 20th satrapy, and paid as tribute 360 talents of gold. To pay such a very large sum a great extent of the country must have been subject.

Still earlier conquests by Semiramis and Sesostris are mentioned, but the former is certainly mythical[3], and the latter rests on the assertion of Diodorus Siculus alone. As his statement is not as yet, corroborated by Egyptian monuments, little weight can be attached to it, but that the Egyptians traded with India, and that from very early times can hardly be doubted.

Thus before the conquests of Alexander the natives of India had ample opportunities to learn the art of writing from others, or to invent a system for themselves, and thus it must be held that they copied, for there has not been found as yet the least trace of the invention and development of an independent *Indian* Alphabet[4], while of the two characters in which the inscriptions of Açoka were written, the northern has been conclusively identified with an Aramaic original, and a number of letters in the Southern Alphabet point clearly to a similar source. I shall also show, further on, that there is a third alphabet of use only in S. India, the Vaṭṭeḻuttu, which must also have been derived from the same or a Semitic source; but which is not derived from, nor is the source of the southern Açoka Alphabet though in some respects very near to it. Perhaps the most important proof of the Semitic origin of these two last alphabets is the imperfect system of marking the vowels which is common to them both. They have, like the Semitic alphabets, initial characters for them, but in the middle of words these letters are marked by mere additions to the preceding consonant. In the Vaṭṭeḻuttu it is difficult to avoid the conclusion that the initial i and u are anything more than the consonants y and v. These points are intelligible only on the supposition that the Indian Alphabets are derived from the Phœnician, which was formed to suit languages in which the vowels are subsidiary to the consonants, a condition which is not met with either in

---

1) That the Hebrew tuki is the Tamiḻ toγai seems to be finally determined. The identification is due to Dr. Caldwell ("Comparative Grammar" p. 66) and is in every way satisfactory. The remaining foreign terms in the same Hebrew passage appear however to have not been fairly considered as yet, and all proposed identifications of "almug" or "algum" would present the greatest difficulties. What has been proposed is to be found in Prof. Max Müller's "Lectures on the Science of Language" I. pp. 224-5. The word Tukiim appears to have been last discussed by M. Vinson in Hovelacque's "Revue de Linguistique" VI. fasc. 2; but I regret not to be able to refer to his article.

2) On the Empire of Darius see Menant 'Les Achéménides' pp. 167-9. Kossowicz ("Inscriptiones Palæo-Persicæ Achæmenidarum" pp. 72-3 and 76—7.) translates the passages as follows: (Inscription of Persepolis) "2. Edicit Darius rex: Voluntate Auramasdae hae *sunt* provinciæ, quas ego tenui cum isto Persiae populo . . . . mihique tributum afferebant: Susiana . . . . India" etc.

(Inscription of Naksh-i-Rustam) 3. Edicit Darius rex: "Hae *sunt* provinciæ quas ego capi extra a Persia (extra Persiam). Ego eas meae ditionis feci, mihi tributum afferebant quodque eis a me edicebatur hoc obsequentissime faciebant, lex quae mea est, haec *ab iis* observabatur: Media . . . . Indi" etc. The original Persian word is 'Hi(n)dus'.

3) La Legende de Sémiramis, par F. Lenormant. (1872) p. 11 etc.

4) Max Müller, Sanskrit Grammar (2nd Edition) p. 3.

the Sanskritic or Dravidian languages. The character in which the Northern Inscription of Açoka (at Kapurdigiri) is written, is from right to left, like all the Semitic characters; and the character of the Southern Inscriptions which runs in the contrary direction, yet shows traces of once having been written the same way.[1]

Mr. E. Thomas[2] has lately propounded a theory that the southern Açoka alphabet is originally Dravidian, and then adapted to the N. Indian languages. This could only be the case if we assume the Vaṭṭeḻuttu to be the prototype, but as this is an imperfect expression of the Dravidian sound-system[3], it cannot be an indigenous invention, and the theory presents many other objections. One insuperable difficulty is the entire absence of traces of any alphabet having existed in S. India before the Vaṭṭeḻuttu, and that all written monuments now known to exist prove a gradual invasion of the South by Buddhist and Brahmanical civilizations which brought more complete alphabets (derived from the Southern Açoka character) with them in historic times, and meeting the old Tamiḻ alphabet or Vaṭṭeḻuttu gradually supplanted it. It is especially remarkable that this last never had separate signs for the sonant letters (g etc.) which must have existed if Mr. Thomas's theory is correct, but though as I shall afterwards prove, the Tamiḻ language had these sounds in the third century after our era, the earliest monuments do not exhibit any marks or letters for them.

Very few Sanskrit books are nowadays even supposed to belong to a period when writing did not exist in India, and the only early ones that appear to mention writing are the Grammars attributed to Pâṇini and to Çâkaṭâyana. But the age of these works is by no means clear[4]; and even if it be supposed that the Mahâbhâshya (or great commentary on Pâṇini by Pata*n*jali) has not been

1) The Southern Inscriptions of Açoka have *e.g.* yv where vy must be read, (*e.g.* in katavyo) and the v is put under the right end of the y. Again the vowel e precedes the consonant which in reading it must follow. The peculiar way of marking r to be read before or after the consonant above which it is marked (as was first pointed out, I believe, by Prof. Westergaard) appears to me also to point to the same conclusion. So also the marks which qualify the sign for 100 in the cave character, and which are affixed to the *right* side of the sign.

2) In the Journal of the R. Asiatic Society, New Series V. pp. 420—3, p. 420 *n.* "The Aryans invented no alphabet of their own for their special form of human speech, but were, in all their migrations, indebted to the nationality amid whom they settled for their instruction in the science of writing: (4) The *Devanâgarî* was appropriated to the expression of the Sanskrit language from the pre-existing Indian Pâli or *Lât* alphabet which was obviously orginated to meet the requirements of Turanian (Dravidian) dialects." Mr. Thomas goes on to connect the advance of Sanskrit Literature and Grammar "with the simplified but extended alphabet they (*i. e.* the Arian invaders of India) constructed in the Arianian provinces out of a very archaic type of Phœnician, and whose graphic efficiency was so singularly aided by the free use of birch bark." On the p. 423 he appears to consider that the Dravidians were taught by Scythian invaders who preceded the "Vedic Aryans". It is not clear if Mr. Thomas considers that the primitive alphabet which he assumes to have existed, was invented in Indian or an importation. 3) Below, App. B.

4) Prof. Goldstücker considered Pâṇini to have lived before Buddha ("Pâṇini's Place" pp. 225-227) chiefly on the ground that the sûtra viii., 2, 50 ("nirvâṇo 'vâte) does not provide for the peculiar Buddhist sense of nirvâṇa, and that therefore it is subsequent to Pâṇini. The same identical sûtra, however, occurs in the Grammar attributed to Çâkaṭâyana (iv., 1, 249), and is explained by the commentator (Yaxavarman) in a manner that makes it appear as if Goldstücker's interpretation were too strict—avâte kartari | nirvâṇo muni*h* | nirvâṇa*h* pradîpa*h* | 'avâta' iti kim | nirvâto vâta*h* | nirvâta*m* vâtena |

Prof. Benfey ("Geschichte d. Sprachwissenschaft" p. 48 *n.* 1.) puts Pâṇini's Grammar at about 320 B. C. The latest authority is Prof. Aufrecht who says ("Annual Address" by A. J. Ellis Esq. as President of the Philological Society, 1873, p 22) "Sanskrit Grammar is based on the grammatical aphorisms of Pâṇini, a writer now generally supposed to have lived in the fourth century B. C. at that time Sanskrit had ceased to be a living language." Cfr. Whitney "Studies" pp. 75-7.

since worked over again and again and tampered with (a supposition it is very difficult to avoid), this commentary would only prove the existence of Pâṇini's Sûtras in the second century before our era, a time when writing was certainly in common use in India.

Pâṇini implicitly mentions (according to the Mahâbhâshya) the writing of the Yavanas. It has not yet been fully determined what was intended by this term, nor is it clear whether it was in use in India or not[1]. It can mean either Persian or Greek writing. If the date of Pâṇini and Çâkaṭâyana is put before 350 B. C. the first would be the probable meaning, as has been assumed by Prof. Goldstücker[2]; if later than that, it could not possibly mean anything but Greek, for which Prof. Weber has decided[3].

But Pâṇini's sûtras show that writing was known in his time, and many expressions render it impossible to doubt that he used writing, and that to express minute details[4]; and one of his Sûtras (vi., 3, 115) shows that the figures for eight and five were then used for marking cattle. That

1) The passages (text and C. Mahâbhâshya) are: (P. iv., i, 49) "Indravaruṇabhavaçarvarudramṛiḍahimâraṇyayava-yavanamâtulâčâryâṇâm ânuk." On this sûtra the Mahâbhâshya ("Benares edition, p. 27 of Ch. iv. in Vol. iii.) remarks: "Himâraṇyayor mahattve" | 'Himâraṇyayor mahattva' iti vaktavyam | mahad dhimam himânî | mahad araṇyam araṇyânî || "yavâd doshe" | 'Yavâd dosha' iti vaktavyam | dushṭo yavo yavânî || Yavanâl lipyâm | 'Yavanâl lipyâm' iti vaktavyam | yavanânî lipi*h* || etc.

The other Grammar gives the substance of this sûtra in several (Çâkaṭâyana I., 3, 52—57):—

52. Mâtulâcâryopâdhyâyâd ân ca |
53. Varuṇendramṛidabhavaçarvarudrâd ân |
54. Sûryadevatâyâm |
55. Âḍ | (This allows sûryâ also).
56. Yavanayavâl lipidushṭe |

On this last sûtra Yaxavarman's C. runs: Yavanayavâbhyâm yathâkrama*m* lipau dushṭe câ 'rthe striyâm ânpratyayo bhavati yavanâna*m* lipi*h* yavanânî | yavanânyâ | dushṭo yavo yavânî | yavânyâ || 57 Himâraṇyâd urau | etc.

The word lipi (which occurs in a sûtra of Pâṇini—iii., 2, 21, corresponding to Çâk. iv., 3, 132, *i. e.* divâvibhâniçâprabhâ-bhâskarârushkartrantânantâdinândilipibalicitraxetrajanghâbâhvahardhanurbhaktasankhyâṭ ṭa*h* ||) is in some respects remarkable. The Açoka edict (where it first occurs) is called a dhammalipi and is said to be lekhitâ or lekhâpitâ. As in every case writing originally consisted of scratches or incisions on a hard substance (bricks were used in Assyria; bamboos in China, and stone in Egypt *primitively*), one would expect instead of a word from √ lip (= smear), a derivative of √ likh (= scratch); especially as the last is always used in India to express the act of writing on *any* substance (*e. g.* in the Mânavadharmaçâstra). Now in the cuneiform inscriptions of the Achaemenides d̓ipi is the term used for those edicts. Thus in the Behistan inscription of Darius we find (iv. 15) "tuvm kâ hya aparam imâm d̓ipim vainâhy." Thou whoever beholdest afterwards this *writing*! It seems to me, therefore, not unlikely that lipi has been introduced into India from the Persian d̓ipi. Both Kossowicz and Spiegel refer d̓ipi to the Sanskrit √ lip, but I see by a note that Dr. Hincks took this word to be Semitic. I have lost the reference, so cannot give his derivation, but the root ktb will occur to every one. With an admittedly Semitic *ultimate* origin of the Indian alphabets, it is natural to expect a foreign term for the art of writing, and I would, therefore, suggest that lipi is not a derivative of √ lip, but, a corrupt foreign term. The primâ facie derivation from √ lip assumes that 1) writing is indigenous to India, and 2) that it originally began there with marks not scratched on a hard substance but *painted* on the prepared surface of a suitable stuff; both which assumptions are strongly negatived by facts. (*contra* Pott's W. W. v. pp. 180—1).

2) "Pâṇini's Place" p. 16. "It would seem to me that it denotes the writing of the Persians, and probably the cuneiform writing which was already known, before the time of Darius, and is peculiar enough in its appearance, and different enough from the alphabet of the (17) Hindus, to explain the fact that its name called for the formation of a separate word."

3) "Indische Studien" iv., 89. In the Berlin "Monatsbericht" for Dec. 1871, p. 616 *n.* he says: der Name...Yavana... ist übrigens jedenfalls wohl schon vor Alexander's Zeit, durch die früheren Perser-Kriege nämlich, in denen ja auch Inder als Hülfstruppen gegen die Griechen mit im Felde standen, den Indern bekannt geworden." Prof. Westergaard is also of opinion (Ueber den ältesten Zeitraum p. 33) that Greek writing is intended.

4) "Pâṇini's Place" pp. 34—61 Prof. Westergaard appears to have arrived independently at the same conclusion.

writing must soon have come into general use in India for literary purposes cannot be doubted, for without it, it is impossible that the systematic *prose* treatises which form so large a share of the Sanskrit literature, could ever have been composed[1].

In all the earlier Sanskrit works there is very little, if any, reference to writing, and the preference for oral teaching exhibited by them is very marked; in fact the Brahmans seem to have regarded the writing of any of their sacred or grammatical works as a deadly sin. But in the mediæval treatises it is evident that this most useful of arts had gained recognition in spite of priestly fanaticism and exclusiveness. Thus the earliest Sanskrit treatise on prosody which is attributed to Pi*n*gala contains nothing that can be held to imply the use of writing; the later imitation which describes the Prakrit metres, however, contains a sûtra which proves the use of writing at the time it was composed[2]; so also does the recent (13th century) grammar the Mugdabodha.

That a literature of considerable extent can exist without being written has been conclusively shown by Prof. Max Müller in his "Ancient Sanskrit Literature," but it could not possibly include scientific and systematic treatises, though the oral transmission of long epics is quite probable[3].

The foregoing facts will, I think, prove that the art of writing was little, if at all, known in India before the third century before the Christian era, and as there is not the least trace of the development in India of an original and independent system, it naturally follows that the art was introduced by foreigners.

I have already mentioned the numerous indications that point to a Semitic original of the Indian alphabets, and which are generally received as sufficient; the immediate original is, however, as yet uncertain. Three probable sources may be suggested. The first is that the Indian alphabet came direct from Phœnicia, and was introduced by the early Phœnician traders[4]. The second is that the original of these alphabets is to be sought in the modified Phœnician alphabet used by the early Himyarites of Arabia, and this has been lately put forward as an ascertained and certain fact[5]. As a third possibility I would suggest that the Indian alphabets may be derived from an Aramaic charecter used in Persia or rather in Babylonia.

---

1) Cfr. Haug's "Essays on the Religion etc. of the Parsees" p. 129. "In the fragments of the Ancient Literature as extant in the Zend-Avesta, nowhere a word of the meaning 'to write' is to be found. That it merely fortuitous; because systematical books on scientific matters can never be composed without the aid of writing." Whitney "Studies" p. 82.

2) "Prâkrit Piṅgala" I., 2. Dîho sa*m*juttaparo bindujuo etc. Here bindu can only refer to a written mark o. It is explained by Laxmînâtha (in his "Piṅgalârthapradîpa"): 'bindujuo' binduyukta*h* sânusvâra*h*.

3) Cfr. Grote's "History of Greece", ii., pp. 144—148 on the long period during which the Homeric poems were recited before they were committed to writing.

4) "Orient und Occident" iii., p. 170. "Dass es einen uralten Zusammenhang zwischen Indien und dem Westen gab, wissen wir mit Entschiedenheit durch König Salamon's Ophirfahrten. Sicherlich waren diess nicht die ältesten. Die Phönicier waren gewiss schon lange vorher Vermittler des Handels zwischen Indien und dem Westen und wie sie, höchst wahrscheinlich, die Schrift nach Indien brachten, mochten sie und vielleicht Ægypter selbst auch manche andre Culturelemente hinüber und herüber bewegt haben."

5) By F. Lenormant ("Essai sur la propagation de l' alphabet Phénicien" Vol. I., pt. I., Table vi.) The author makes the "alphabet primitif du Yémen" the source of both the Himyaritic and Mâgadhi (!!) alphabets.

As regards the first possibility, it seems altogether inconsistent with the evidence regarding the scanty use of writing in the fourth century B. C. already given; for, as Phœnician communications direct with India must have ceased full five-hundred years, if not more, before that date, it is almost incredible that the art should not have arrived at perfection as applied to the Indian languages in that time, and have been in common use; but this is (as has been already shown) far from being the case. Again it is difficult to understand how the forms of the letters could be retained with so little modification for such a long period as this view would require; for, from the date of the inscriptions of Açoka (250 B. C.), documents with undisputed dates show that changes were marked and rapid, and the progress of adaptation no less so[1].

As regards the second possibility, that the southern Açoka alphabet came from the Himyarites, the great difficulty is to show that the people of S. W. Arabia were in a position to furnish India with the elements of an alphabet so early as the 4th century B. C. It is very remarkable that the Himyaritic character was written from left to right, and that this was an innovation made by the people of Arabia is proved by the boustrophedon Himyaritic inscriptions that have been recently discovered[2]. The difficulty of direction of the southern Açoka character being from left to right would disappear if the Himyaritic character be assumed to be the original; but it remains to be proved that the civilization of S. W. Arabia had advanced so far already in the fourth century before the Christian era, as to be able to furnish India with a system of writing. It must also be recollected that the Himyaritic alphabet did not mark the vowels, as its derivative, the Æthiopic alphabet does. It is to be hoped that the intrepid explorer M. Halêvy will be able to clear up the very interesting question of the date of the Himyaritic civilization.

The possibility and probability that the Indian alphabets are derived from an Aramaic type used in Persia, seems not to have been yet considered. The Persian or Assyrian cuneiform characters cannot be thought of, though the last remained in use up to the first century of our era[3] for many purposes; but it is certain that a cursive Aramaic character was already long used, before (in the third century A. D.) it became (in the form of Pahlavi) the most generally used character for the official languages of Persia. The researches of Layard and Fresnel brought to light bricks with inscriptions in cuneiform and also in Egyptian and Semitic characters[4], and these go back, probably, to the time of the Achæmenides[5]. Whichever of these three probable

1) It is also worthy of notice that all the Southern Açoka Inscriptions from Gujarat to Ganjam (in the Bay of Bengal) are in precisely the same character. This looks as if the art of writing had then first spread over Northern India from the place where it was first used, perhaps Gujarat. In the course of a few hundred years, however, the alphabets used in Gujarat and Bengal had already become so different as to be very little alike in appearance.

2) The discovery was originally made by a French traveller some years ago, but has been only recently confirmed. (Letter by von Maltzan in the Allg. Zeitung for March 1st 1871, pp. 10-11.)

3) Oppert in "Mélanges d'Archéologie Égyptienne et Assyrienne" fasc. I. p. 27.

4) Cfr. Renan, "Histoire des langues Sémitiques", p. 115 etc.

5) Spiegel, "Grammatik der Huzvaresch Sprache", p. 26: "die späteren Alphabete Erâns verrathen einen Semitischen Ursprung, und mögen daher vielleicht aus einem früheren aramäischen Alphabete stammen, das bereits unter den Achämeniden neben der Keilschrift im Gebrauche war."

sources of the Indian alphabets may be accepted, there is a difficulty which seems to have escaped the notice of palæographists—the origin of the manner of indicating vowels in the body of a word. All the three primitive Indian alphabets possess this peculiarity with comparatively unimportant differences, but though the system closely resembles the vowel points used by the Semitic races, it seems that there is not the least evidence for believing that it was used by these last earlier than at a time when it was already in use in India.

A cursory inspection of the alphabet used in the Southern Açoka inscriptions will satisfy any one accustomed to such enquiries, that the character from which it is derived did not comprise a sufficient number of letters, and that new signs were made by altering some of the old ones[1]. This is, in itself, sufficient proof that the Indian alphabet was adapted, and not an indigenous invention. Other facts point to an adaptation from a Semitic character, but in the absence of further evidence than already exists, it is useless to attempt to decide authoritatively as to how and when this occurred. The question is one of the greatest importance, but except new discoveries are made of inscriptions older than any yet known, it must remain open. The reasons, however, for believing that writing was but little known or practised in India before 250 B. C. are tolerably conclusive.

In considering the question of the age and extent of the use of writing in India, it is important to point out that the want of suitable materials in the North at least, before the introduction of paper, must have been a great obstacle to its general use. The best material for writing on to be found in India is the palm leaf; either of the Talipat (Corypha umbraculifera), or of the Palmyra (Borassus flabelliformis). But the former appears to be a recent introduction from Ceylon into S. India and it is there by no means common even on the West Coast. The Palmyra also appears to have been introduced from Ceylon or Tinnevelly into the rest of the Peninsula; it is by no means common out of the South[2]. The materials mentioned at an earlier date (excluding lotus leaves and such fancies of poets) almost preclude the existence of MSS. of books or long documents. The 'bhûrjapatra' which is understood (apparently on philological grounds) to mean the bark of the birch-tree, could not have been available in large quantities, nor would it be very suitable[3]. The supposition of those who with Whitney and Böhtlingk assert that writing was, in India, long used only *esoterically* for composition and the preservation of texts, while the instruction was entirely oral, is, on these grounds almost certainly correct.

Arrian[4] (quoting Megasthenes) calls the palmyra palm by its proper name (tala[5]), but its leaves are not mentioned anywhere by classical writers as affording writing materials used in India.

1) Mr. Thomas has proved this clearly by his figures on p. 422 of the fifth volume of the New Series of the *R. As. Society's Journal.* The letters čh, ṭh, ḍh, th, ph show their origin very clearly.

2) Voigt. "Hortus Suburbanus Calcuttensis" p. 640. Roxburgh, however, states that it is "common all over India". (Flora Indica, III. p. 790.) It requires the leaves of *many* trees to make an ordinary *grantha.* Palm leaves (there called *lontar*) were and are used for writing the Kawi or Old Javanese in Java and Bali.

3) MSS. written on this substance are said to be in existence, but I have not seen or even heard of any in India. It is remarkable that this 'bhûrja' has not been botanically identified.

4) "Indica" ed. Dübner, ch. VII., 3 (p. 209). 5) In S. India the palmyra is called 'tâla'; the talipat, çrîtâla.

Pliny[1] indeed mentions palm leaves as used for this purpose, but he refers the practice to Egypt before the discovery of papyrus.

Paper was probably introduced by the Muhammadans; in all parts of India it appears to be called by some corrupt form of the Arabic name 'kâgat'. Its use in S. India is at all events very recent, and even now scarcely ever occurs except among the Mahrâṭhî colonists. I have seen a Telugu MS. of a Sanskrit work written about the end of the 17th century, and Paulinus à St. Bartholemæo notices MSS. on paper of the Bhâgavata (in Travancore 18th century); but the bigoted Hindus of the South consider this material to be unclean and therefore unfit for writing any book with the least pretence to a sacred character.

CHAPTER II.

THE SOUTH-INDIAN ALPHABETS AND THEIR DEVELOPMENT.

THE Açoka inscriptions written in the Southern alphabet are found at numerous places in India Proper, (which is North of the Vindhya range), from Girnar in Gujarat, to Jogada Naugam in Ganjam[2], the northernmost province of Madras on the Bay of Bengal; but not to the south of the line extending from the one place to the other. What the state of civilization was in the Deccan and Tamil̤ country in the third century B. C. it is impossible to say, but Piyadasi addresses his proclamation to kings in the Peninsula in the same sentence with the Greek sovereigns to whom he appeals[3]. It is therefore most improbable that the South of India was Buddhist at that time, and it is almost certain that it was not Brahmanized. It is possible to show, historically, how the Brahmans gradually supplanted the old Buddhist-Jain civilization of the Peninsula, the earli-

1) Ch. XIII., 21.

2) 19° 13' 15" N. and 84° 53' 55" E. The description of the place is given in a report to the Madras Government reprinted in the *Indian Antiquary*, I., pp. 219-221. It was first discovered by Sir W. Elliot (Madras J. VI. N. S. p. 103).

3) Tablet II. "Evam api sâmanteṣu yathâ Coḍa Pâ(ṇ)ḍâ Satiyaputo Ketalaputa etc. The third word is read pačantesu by H. H. Wilson, and taken to be for pratyanteshu a word which is not supported by authorities. As p and s, and č and m only differ in a very trifling degree, I venture to read sâmantesu which is far preferable. Prinsep suggested, and no doubt rightly, that Coḍa refers to the Côḷa kingdom in S. India; Prof. H. H. Wilson, however, (pp. 14-15 of his article on the Inscriptions, separately printed from J. R. As. S. xii.) seems to think that these names refer to the North of India; but as the Côḷa kingdom of the South was always famous, it does not appear necessary to assume another Cōḷa kingdom in the North as yet unknown.

est historical civilization of which there is any record in that part of India; and the fact that the Vedas of the South are the same as those of the North, proves conclusively that this was done at a time when the Brâhmaṇas and Sûtras had been definitely reduced to their present form, or at a time, at all events, not before the Christian era. There is not much historical evidence to prove that there were Brahmans in Southern India before the seventh century A. D., and there is very little to indicate that there were Buddhists or Jains there before that date[1]. The exodus of members of both sects from the favoured North to the unattractive South, was, probably, the result of political events in the former country. The Jains as heretics were most likely driven out by the orthodox Buddhists[2], and the Brahmans followed some centuries later, owing to the ceaseless conflicts that had disturbed their original friendliness with the Buddhists, and to foreign invasions. In the South they got the mastery perhaps sooner than in the North.

At all events the oldest inscriptions that have been found in Southern India are far from being as old as the Açoka edicts, and the paucity of them—for the only place where they occur is Amarâvatî—shows that Buddhism cannot have advanced to any considerable extent. The cave hermitages, peculiar to the Buddhists, appear to exist in many other parts of S. India; in the Deccan[3] and even near Madras. In a hill about a mile to the east of Chingleput there is a cave now made into a Linga temple, but which was evidently intended for a Buddhist hermit's cell, and many of the curious caves and monolith temples at Seven Pagodas appear to have been originally made for the same purpose[4]. At Amarâvatî and at Seven Pagodas[5] there are inscriptions of a few words each, which are written in a character precisely similar to that used in the cave inscriptions near Bombay. It is tolerably certain that these last belong to the first century before and the first and second centuries after the Christian era. There is not, however, a S. Indian inscription which can be accepted as genuine with a date before the 5th century of the Christian era, though one or two (without dates) exist which may be safely attributed to the fourth century A. D. The earliest inscriptions belong to three dynasties, the Câlukya of Kalyâṇapura in the Deccan, to a nameless dynasty which ruled the country (Ve*n*gî) between the K*r*ishṇâ and Godâvarî before the middle of the seventh century A. D., and to the Cera dynasties which ruled the modern Mysore, Salem, Coimbatore and part of the Malabar coast. These three classes of inscriptions present alphabets which, though well marked, are merely varieties of the Cave and Sah character, and it is, therefore, impossible to suppose that the civilization now prevailing in S. India but which took its rise in the North originally, can have commenced to work on the South before the earlier centuries of the present era.

1) Fa-Hian (A. D. 400) mentions only one Buddhist establishment (? Ellora) in the Deccan, and mentions that it was very difficult to visit S. India in his time. (Beal's "Travels of Buddhist Pilgrims," pp. 139-141).

2) Dr. Bühler has ascertained that the Jains are the heretical Buddhists excommunicated at the first Council.

3) J. As. Soc. of Bombay. V., pp. 117 ffg.

4) Hiouen-Thsang appears to have considered Conjeveram (Kien-tchi=Kañci, which inscriptions prove to be more correct than the Brahmanical fiction Kâñci) to have been the Southern limit of Indian Buddhism in his day (c. 640 A. D.). As the Brahmanical system of Çankara sprung up in the next half century, this must have been near the most flourishing period of S. Indian Buddhism, yet Hiouen-Thsang's lamentations over the decayed state of his religion are perpetual.

5) V. Tripe's "Photographs of the Elliot Marbles etc." (obl. Fo., Madras, 1858), and Trans. R. As. S. ii.

In the tenth and eleventh centuries northern influences commenced again to prevail in parts of the Deccan, and introduced the Devanâgarî alphabet which has there assumed forms peculiar to the South of India.

In this chapter I shall consider the different forms of the letters in use at different periods as proved by inscriptions, confining myself entirely to the forms of the letters. But as the history of the expressions of the phonetic elements of the Dravidian languages is a matter of importance even in palæographical questions, all material that could be discovered relating to this subject will be found collected in an Appendix (B).

The derivation of the South-Indian Alphabets (except the Vaṭṭeḷuttu) may be represented as follows in a tabular form:

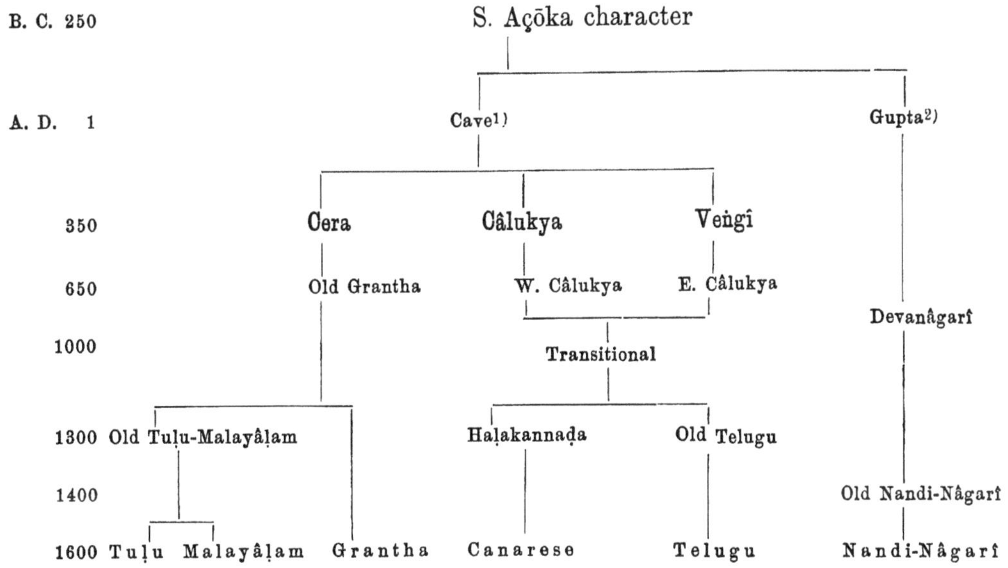

The names that I have given to the different characters in use in S. India at different periods, are mostly derived from the names of the dynasties under which they obtained currency; for a change of dynasty in S. India generally brought about a change of even such details as the form of official documents, and these constitute almost the entire palæographic material existing from the earlier times.

1) The Cave inscriptions and the character used for them etc. are discussed in the *Bombay Journal:* I. pp. 488-443 (Caves of Beira and Bajah near Karli, by Westergaard); II. pt. ii., pp. 36-87 (General Description of all the Caves, by Dr. J. Wilson); III. pp. 71-108 (Bird); IV. pp. 132-4 (Inscriptions at Salsette, by Stevenson); pp. 340-379 (Second Memoir, by Dr. Wilson); V. pp. 1-34 (Kâṇheri Inscriptions, by Stevenson); do: pp. 35-57 (Nâsik Cave Inscriptions, by the same); do: pp. 117-123 (Cave-temples etc. in the Nizam's Dominions, by Bradley); do: pp. 151-178 and 426-428 (Sahyâdri Caves, by Stevenson); do: pp. 336-348 (Caves at Koolvee in Malwa, by Impey); do: pp. 543-573 (Caves of Bâgh in Râth, by the same); VI. pp. 1-14 (Kânheri Inscriptions, by E. W. West); do: pp. 116-120 (Kânheri Topes, by the same); do: pp. 157-160 (Excavations at Kânheri, by the same); VII. pp. 37-52 (Nâsik Cave Inscriptions, by E. W. and A. A. West); do: pp. 53-74 (Ajanta Inscriptions, by Bhau Dâji); do: pp. 113-131 (Junagar Inscriptions, by Bhau Dâji); VIII. pp. 222-224 (Bedsa Cave Inscriptions, by A. A. West); do: pp. 225-233 (Cave and Sah Numerals, by Bhau Dâji); do: pp. 234-5 (Inscription at Jusdun, by the same).

2) Specimens of this character are to be found in the *Bengal Journal* and in Cunningham's "Reports." (I. p. 94 etc.)

§ 1. TELUGU-CANARESE ALPHABETS.

Of the South-Indian alphabets, the most important from every point of view are the Tĕlugu and Canarese. The parts of the Peninsula where these characters have been developed have been of the greatest importance in the political and literary history of the South, and chronologically they are the first.

The earliest documents existing belong to the Telugu Country comprising the deltas of the K*r*ishṇâ and Godâvarî, where also, at Amarâvati, the most important Buddhist remains in the South, have been found. The origin of this kingdom does not probably go back beyond the second century A. D., for it is not mentioned in Ptolemy or by the Periplus of the Red Sea by the name found in the inscriptions—Ve*n*gîdeça—or even by the later name Āndhra used by Hiouen-Thsang (7th century[1]). The names and dates of the kings are quite uncertain, for only two grants of this dynasty appear to be in existence, and one of these is almost entirely illegible. The dates they bear, are also, like those of all early inscriptions, merely the year of the king's reign, and this is not referred to any era. This dynasty was supplanted in the latter half of the seventh century A. D. by a branch of the Câlukyas established at Kalyâṇa about the beginning of the fifth century A. D. and which is the first *historical* dynasty of the Deccan.

Taking Fa-Hian's account of the Deccan (400 A. D.) it is excessively improbable that the history of that part will ever be traced back to an earlier date.

A. *The Vengî alphabet.* (*Plates* i., ii. *and* xx., xxi.)

Compared with the Cave character the Ve*n*gî alphabet presents little development, and I think that this fact justifies the date I have assigned to the Specimen given in Plates xx. and xxi.[2]

In â the curl at the foot which distinguishes this letter from the short a is extended, and this is a peculiarity which appears only in this character.

---

1) There is not the least mention of any Telugu kingdoms in the Açoka inscriptions. Probably that part of India was not then civilized at all, but inhabited by wild hill-tribes.

2) That the dynasty, to which the inscription given in Plates xx. and xxi. belongs, preceded the Câlukyas was first pointed out by Sir W. Elliot in the *Madras Journal* (Vol. xi. pp. 302-6). The capital (Veṅgi) appears to have entirely vanished; it is said to have been the place now called Pedda Veṅgi or Vegi in the Kṛishṇa District, but there are several places of the same name in the neighbourhood. As in the Telugu Mahâbhârata which belongs to the twelfth century A. D. Rajahmundry is called the Nayakaratnam of Veṅgideça, the old capital must have been deserted long before that time. Hiouen-Thsang (iii., pp. 105-110) calls the small kingdom that he visited ''Ān-ta-lo' (Andhra) and the capital—'P'ing-k'i-lo'. It appears to me that this is intended for Veṅgî; the 'lo' being merely the locative suffix '-lô' of the Telugu nouns, naturally mistaken by the worthy Chinese pilgrim monk for a part of the word. Julien's suggestion 'Viṅkhila' only fails in there'not being the slightest trace of such a place. The -î in Ve*n*gî is uncertain; it occurs both short and long in the inscriptions.

'Āndhra' is properly the name of the country between the two rivers, and only became synonymous with 'Telugu' owing to that kingdom being the native place of the writers in and on Telugu in the twelfth and following centuries.

The perpendicular strokes on the left sides of j and b are here curved, as are the top and bottom lines of ṇ.

v in the second inscription to which I have referred, is represented by a triangular form disproportionately large compared with the other letters, and thus very near the Cave form.

The suffixed forms of the vowels differ somewhat from those in the Cave character.

i which is in the last represented by a semicircle open to the left is here open towards the top of the consonant which it follows or is united to it; î which was originally represented by a semicircle open above and attached to the consonant, or by a semicircle open to the right is here represented by a curl which marks the long vowel very clearly.

û which was originally marked by a semicircle open at the bottom, and under the consonant it follows, is here represented by a highly characteristic curved form which does not appear in any other alphabet.

In the compound consonants the second and third letters still retain their complete original form. The superscript r still preserves the straight line of the original r of the Açoka inscriptions.

r is here represented by a form that occasionally occurs in the inscriptions of the W. Câlukyas up to the end of the sixth century, viz., with a short loop turned to the *left*. In the E. Câlukya deeds the loop is generally turned to the *right*, if it is not complete.

Final m is represented by a small m less than the other letters, which is also peculiar to the Ve*n*gi character. The existence of a distinct sign for upadhmânîya (ꀀ) is especially worthy of notice, as proving that the Sanskrit alphabet was in the fourth century A. D. already adapted to suit the niceties of the Grammarians.

As in the Cave inscriptions, so also here, we find that a small cross-stroke or thickening of the end of the line is made in all cases where the letters begin with a perpendicular stroke downwards.

This has, no doubt, arisen from the necessity of marking clearly the end of the line, especially in inscriptions on stone, but developed in the course of time it has become the angular mark √ above some Telugu and Canarese consonants which has been strangely imagined to be the short vowel a. This error was started by the first Telugu Grammar by A. D. Campbell[1], but has been constantly repeated down to the present time without any reason at all[2].

B. *Western Câlukya.* (*Plates* iii., iv. *and* xxii.)

The earliest specimen of the Western Câlukya character is a grant by Pulakeçi dated ç. 411 (or A. D. 489), and of which an abstract is given in the Journal of the R. Asiatic Society[3]. The earliest I can give are, however, two grants on copper plates dated 608 and 689 A. D. respectively.

1) Second edition (1820) p. 3. The error is probably of native origin as this mark is called in Telugu—talakaṭṭu.
2) See the last published Telugu Grammar by the Rev. A. Arden (1873) p. 7 where it is called a '*secondary*' form of *a*.
3) Vol. v. pp. 343 flg.

The first of these presents in the cursive forms of the letters unmistakable traces of a much wider use of writing than had occurred previously, and such as might be expected in a kingdom so flourishing and important as was that of the Câlukyas in the beginning of the seventh century A. D.[1] There is every reason to believe that Buddhism was then more vigorous in the Deccan than perhaps any other part of Southern India.

---

[1] The defeat of Harshavardhana the King of Kanoj by a Câlukya which is satisfactorily established by Cunningham ("Reports" i., pp. 280-282), shows the rapid growth in power of the Câlukyas of Kalyâṇapura. This defeat was not, however, by Vikramâditya (as Genl. Cunningham states) but by Satyâçraya his father, as is proved by several inscriptions. For the first (608 A. D.) see pl. xxii. The second (in possession of a Jain âcârya at Hyderabad) has: Çrî-Pulakeçimahârâjasya prapautra*h* . . . . Çrî-Kîrtivarmap*r*ithivîvallabhamahârâjasya pautra*h* samarasa*m*saktasakalottarapatheçvaraÇrî-Harshavarddhanaparâkramopalabdhaparameçvaranâmadheyasya Satyâçrayaçrîp*r*ithivîvallabha . . . . priyatanaya*h* etc. The 3rd (photographed in the Mysore collection) has *nearly the* same phrase: . . . . Çrî-Harshavarddhanaparâjayopalabdhaparameçvarâparanâmadheya*h* Satyâçrayaçrîp*r*ithivîvallabhamahâdhirâjaparameçvaras etc. This defeat must be put near the end of the 6th century. The genealogy of the dynasty of these kings was first given by Sir W. Elliot in the *London Asiatic Society's Journal;* and his paper was afterwards reprinted with corrections in the *Madras Journal* (Vol. vii., pp. 193-211). With a few additional corrections required by inscriptions since discovered, and some of which were pointed out by Lassen (I., A. K. iv.), the table is as follows:—

Jayasi*m*ha
|
Raṇarâja
|
Pulakeçi-Vallabha or Pŏlakeçi appears as reigning in Ç. 411 (489 A. D.)
|
Kîrttivarmâ-P*r*ithivîvallabha I. — Mangalîça (ascended the throne 566 A. D.)
|
Satyâçraya-Çrîp*r*ithivîvallabha (or S. vallabhendra) — Kubja-Vishṇuvarddhana (Eastern Câlukyas. See next table, pp. 19-20) was probably reigning in 622 A. D.
|
Vikramâditya I.? began to reign Ç. 514 (592-618 A. D.)[1]
|
Vinayâditya-Yuddhamalla I.
|
Vijayâditya began to reign Ç. 617 (695 A. D.)
|
Vikramâditya II. began to reign Ç. 655 (733 A. D.) — ****
|
Kîrttivarmâ II.. — Kîrttivarmâ III.
|
0

So far the flourishing older dynasty of the Câlukyas, which after Vikramâditya II. appears to have been for a time almost overthrown by feudatories such as the Râshṭrakûṭa, Kâlabhurya, and Yâdava chiefs, and the history of this kingdom is, thus, very obscure for the eighth and ninth centuries. With Tailapa the restorer of the Câlukya power in the later dynasty, all once more becomes tolerably certain, especially as regards the dates of the reigns.

---

[1] *Bombay Journal*, iii., 206. He appears also to have been called Vikramâditya-Satyâçraya.

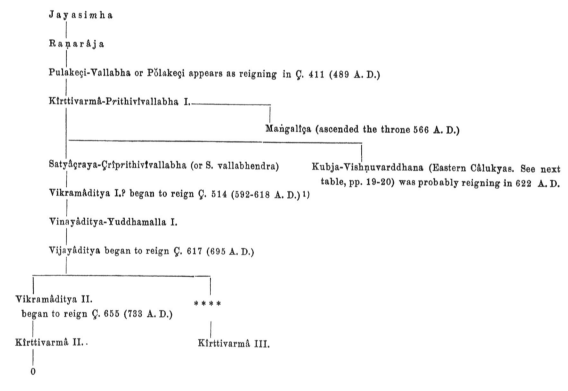

The first of the two alphabets given (Pl. iii.) shows greater development than the second (Pl. iv.) which is nearly a century later in date. It, however, represents a different hand to the other; the first being from the north (southern Mahraṭha country)[1] whereas the last is from the extreme south of the Câlukya kingdom (the Karnûl district), and is therefore influenced by the Cêra character as a comparison with Pl. ii. will show[2].

It is, however, to be remarked that inscriptions in an older, square type of character which belong to this dynasty and are of the end of the sixth or beginning of the seventh century, are still in existence. The character given by plates iii. and xxii. may therefore be taken as the later hand used in the Deccan in the seventh century. Both hands present a feature common to all the inscriptions of the western Câlukyas (cfr. Pl. iv.) but which does not occur in any others, a marked slope of the letters to the right. The eastern Câlukya character is, on the other hand,

---

Tailapa

Bhîmarâja

Ayyana

Vijitâditya (Vikramâditya, Satyâçraya) *m.* Bonta Devî (ç. 895-919=973-997 A. D.) Restorer of the dynasty.

Tailabhûpa-Vikramâditya III.

Satyâçraya *m.* Ambikâ Devî (? ç. 919-930=997-1008 A. D.)

Dâsavarmâ *m.* Bhagavatî Devî.

Vibhuvikrama-Vikramâditya IV. (? ç. 930-940=1008-1018 A. D.)

Ayyana

Jayasi*m*ha (Jagadekamalla) (? ç. 940-962=1018-1040 A. D.)

Someçvara Deva (Trailokyamalla, Ahavamalla) I. (? ç. 962-991=1040-1069 A.D.)

Someçvara Deva II. (Soyi or Sovi Deva) (? ç. 991-298=1069-1076 A. D.)

Vikramâditya V. (Kalivikrama) (ç. 998-1049=1076-1127 A. D.)

Someçvara Deva III. (Bhûloka-malla) (ç. 1049-1060=1127-1138 A. D.

Jagadekamalla (ç. 1060-1072=1138-1150 A. D.)

Tailapa II. (Trailokyamalla) (ç. 1072-1104=1150-1182 A. D.)

Vîrasomeçvara IV. (Tribhuvanamalla) (ç. 1104-1111=1182-1189 A. D.)

1) *Madras Journal*, vii. p. 198 and *n*. This grant is now, apparently, in possession of the Royal Asiatic Society of London.

2) Cfr. especially the subordinate forms of â, û, ê as affixed to consonants.

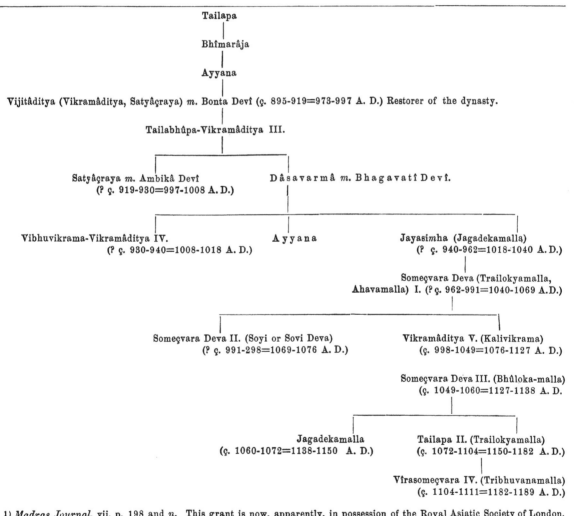

remarkably square and upright; this distinction is quite sufficient, after 600 A. D., to show the origin of an inscription.

The alphabet given in Pl. iii. shows the beginning of the change in writing subscript vowels which afterwards formed the chief difference between the Telugu-Canarese alphabets on the one hand, and the Grantha on the other—a tendency to bring the marks for â, ê and ô from the side of the consonant to which they are attached to the top, and again to bring the mark for a subscript form from underneath the consonant to its right side. Thus in Pl. iii. there are two forms of e, o (cfr. bho, yo) and also of u. The character in Pl. iv. uses almost universally the older form (cfr. ku, pu, ru in Pl. iii. and ku, tu, etc. in Pl. iv.).

Only the cursive forms of a and â occur in the inscriptions of the western Câlukyas as far as they are known to me, and this again distinguishes them from those of the eastern dynasty which preserve most generally the older forms of these letters up to the middle of the tenth century, though we find both forms co-existing in inscriptions of the eighth and ninth centuries.

In Pl. iii. we find the cursive form of kh which does not occur in the Kali*n*ga inscriptions till at least a century later. So again the same remark holds good of j and l. The cursive form of the last letter seems to have prevailed in all the S. Indian alphabets by the tenth century.

Ch. appears at the time of the oldest South Indian inscriptions to have had the form of ⋈ (cfr. pl. iv. ččh); in the modern alphabets this is quite lost, and this letter has the ordinary form of č with the addition of a small stroke underneath, such as marks the aspirate in ಧ, ಫ etc.

Interesting as the inscriptions of the western Câlukyas are historically, owing to the synchronisms with events in the history of northern India that they exhibit, they are but of little importance in the literary history of the south of India; for it is certain that the kings of Kalyâṇapura always favored the culture of the north.

With the temporary fall of this dynasty the western Câlukya alphabet appears to have gone entirely out of use[1].

C. *Eastern Câlukya. (Plates* iv.*, v. *and* xxiv., xxv.)

In the early history of the Dravidian part of India, this dynasty is of the greatest importance, but as yet no account of it has been published. It succeeded the Ve*n*gî kings some time in the seventh century, not long after the famous defeat of Harshavardhana by Satyâçraya of Kalyâṇapura, and was founded by his younger brother[2].

1) Several of the Inscriptions of this earlier dynasty have already been published in the *Journal* of the *R. Asiatic Society of London*, and in the *Bombay Journal*. (See for the last: Vol. ii., pp. 1-12, pp. 263-2; Vol. iii. pp. 203-213. The first of the grants described belongs to the reign of Vijayâditya, and is dated, ç. 627=A. D. 705. The second is dated in the tenth year of Vijayâditya; the third appears to belong to a feudatory). Facsimiles of some from the sixth to about the fourteenth century are given in the "Collection of Photographic Copies of Inscriptions in Dharwar and Mysore" published by the Committee of the Architectural Antiquities of Western India.

2) The dynasty is given as follows in a number of inscriptions which I have been able to consult; nearly all of which (an unparalleled circumstance in India) give the number of years that the several kings reigned. A. (from Masulipatam) *d.* 5th

The earliest inscription I have seen, is a grant by the first sovereign Vishṇuvardhana; it is on copper-plates and was found in the Vijayanagaram Zamindary in 1867 (Pl. xxiv.). Except in regularity and neatness, the character of the writing of this document differs very little from that already described as the Ve*n*gî character, and does not exhibit any cursive forms; these first appear in the latter part of the seventh century.

---

year of Vishṇuvardhana II. B. (in the Nellore Sub-Collector's Office on five plates) contains a grant by Yuddhamalla (about 950). C. on five plates (? the Godâvarî Collector's Office) *d.* ç. 867=945 A. D., being in the reign of Ammarâja. D. a grant of Kulottu*n*ga-Coḷa-Deva, *d.* ç. 1001=1079 A. D. E. a grant by Kulottu*n*ga son of Vikrama-Coḷa-Deva, *d.* ç. 1056=1134 A. D.

The number of years each king reigned follows in ( ) his name. Those names which are not of actual sovereigns of Ve*n*gi are in spaced type.

K î r t t i v a r m â (see above, p. 16 *n.*)

S a t y â ç r a y a v a l l a b h e n d r a

Kubja-Vishṇuvardhana I. (18) about 630 A. D.

Jayasi*m*havallabha I. (30)[1]

Indrabhaṭṭâraka (Indrarâja D.)

Râjanandana-Vishṇuvardhana II. (9)[2]

Ma*n*gi(-yuvarâja D.) (25)

(1) Jayasi*m*havallabha II. (13)

(2) Kokkili (Kaikkili) (6 months)

(3) Vishṇuvardhana III. (37)[3]

(Çaktivarmâ-) Vijayâdityabhaṭṭâraka I. (18)

Vishṇuvardhana IV. (30)[4]

Vijayâditya-Narendra-Mṛigarâja II. (48)

Kali-Vishṇuvardhana V. (1 year 6 months)[5].

Guṇâṅka-Vijayâditya III. (44)

V i k r a m â d i t y a Y u v a r â j a

Y u d d h a m a l l a

---

1) B. D. E. make Jayasi*m*ha reign 33 years.

2) A. "Çrîkîrttivarmaṇa*h* pranaptâ.....Çrîvishṇuvarddhanamahârâjasya napt(â).....Çrîjayasi*m*havallabhamahârâjasya priyabhrâtur anekayuddhâlaṅkṛitaçarîrasye 'ndrabhaṭṭârakasya priyatanaya*h* çrîmân Vishṇuvarddhanamahârâja*h*" etc. D. makes Indrabhaṭṭâraka reign for seven days.

3) D. has: "tasya (*i. e.* Kokkile*h*) jyeshṭo bhrâtâ tam ucchâṭya saptatri*m*çat.

4) D. E. make his reign last 36 years.

5) C. E. have: dvyardhavarshâṇi; B.—Ashṭâdaça mâsâ(n); D.—dvyardhavarsham..

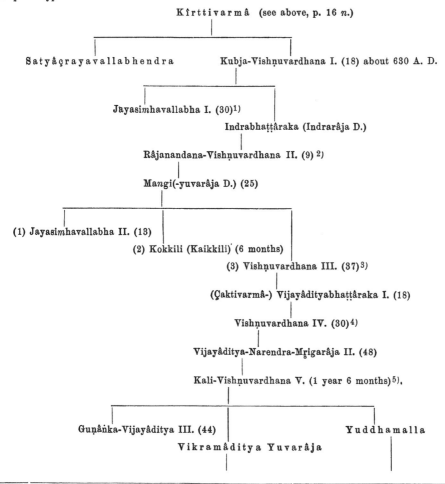

The chief distinctions between the characters used for the Western and Eastern Kal*i*nga[1] inscriptions have already been given. As the two countries were under branches of the same royal family about the same periods, it is convenient to call the respective characters after the two dyna-

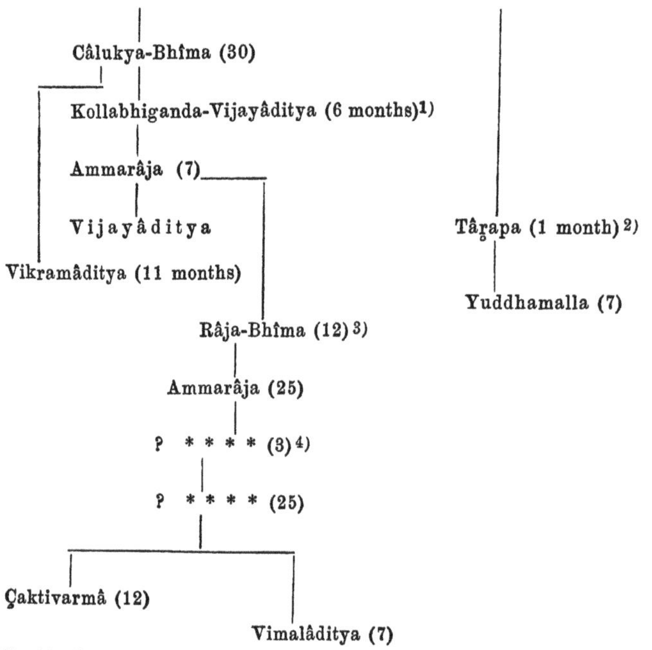

Vimalâditya was succeeded by Râjarâja Coḷa owing (it is stated) to an intermarriage of the Coḷas and Kal*i*nga Câlukyas, which is perhaps the fact. His son Kulottu*n*ga succeeded him in 1064 A. D. (*Madras Journal*, xiii., Pt. 2, p. 40), and as Râjarâja reigned 41 years (D. and E.) this makes the date of the end of Vimalâditya's reign to be 1023 A. D. Both D. and E. *explicitly* term Râjarâja son of Vimalâditya.

C. carries the genealogy down to Ammarâja, and it is dated 945 A. D. in his reign. The grants D. and E. would make the beginning of his reign four and six years respectively after this date. The discrepancy is not, however, sufficient to throw doubts on the list given above, and is probably owing to the uncertainty of the Çaka era. It is obvious that the number of entire years of most reigns only being given, the list cannot be *absolutely* correct.

The total of the reigns of sovereigns of this dynasty amounts to above 393 years, which brings the first year of Kubja Vishṇuvardhana to about 630 A. D., and as his elder brother Satyâçraya reigned in Kalyâṇapura about 600 A. D., this date is by no means improbable. It is nevertheless impossible to suppose that the Kal*i*nga Câlukyas were established in the old Vengi kingdom for some years after that date. Thus the grant printed in pl. xxiv. was found far north (in Vizagapatam), and it seems probable that the Câlukyas first seized the northern part of the Telugu sea-coast, and then conquered the south. The best initial date, at present, for this dynasty will thus be the latter part of the seventh century A. D.

1) Kal*i*nga, or rather Tri-kal*i*nga is a very old name for the greater part of the Telugu Coast on the Bay of Bengal. The latest mention I know, is in the grant of Yuddhamalla (already referred to as B.), which says of this king (about 950 A. D.) "Ve*n*gibhuva*h* patir abhû(t) Trikal*i*ngakoṭṭe*h*" (4 line 3). Hiouen-Thsang also mentions Kalinga (7th cent.). Pliny (vi., 67 of the edition published by Teubner) says: "Insula in Gange est magnæ amplitudinis gentem continens unam, nomine Modogalingam." Dr. Caldwell (Comp. Gr. pp. 64-5) has strangely taken this to be for the old Telugu 'Modoga and l*i*nga' and to mean "three-lingas", and has, thus, accepted the native etymology of 'Telugu.' There can be no doubt that it is merely Mûḍu-

1) E. has eleven months.

2) D.—Tâḍapa.

3) D. tam ucchâtya diçâd Ammarâj(â)nujo Râjabhîma*h* dvâdaça varshâṇi.

4) In D. only the years are clearly legible. E. has after Ammarâja: ta(j)jyeshṭo Dânâ * * as tri*m*çat; tatputra (*h*) Çaktivarmâ dvâdaça; tadanujaVimalâdityas sapta; tatputro Râjarâjadeva ekacatvâri*m*çat; tatputra(*h*) çrîKulottuṅgacoḍadeva ekonapañcâçat etc.

sties of the Câlukyas; but it must be recollected that there is no real connection between them palæographically, except so far as their common origin through the 'Cave character' is in question.

The decided tendency of the eastern Câlukya character to preserve archaic forms, clearly distinguishes it from the character used under the western dynasty. This last seems to have been affected by the North-Indian early Devanâgarî, as it almost copies the horizontal stroke at the top of letters used in the latter. It also uses cursive forms to a large extent.

The Plates iii., iv., xxii. and xxiv. if compared, will show how correct is the account by Hiouen-Thsang (about 640 A. D.) of the writing used in his time in the Deccan and on the sea-coast. He says[1]: "La langue et la prononciation différent beaucoup de celles de l'Inde centrale; mais la forme des caractères est en grande partie la même".

All unquestionable grants by kings of both the Câlukya dynasties that I have met with are in Sanskrit. The later they are, the greater is the neglect of the minute rules for orthography laid down by the Sanskrit grammarians, especially as regards the use of the *bindu.* I shall give a summary of the results that I have ascertained, further on in describing the modern alphabets used in the Telugu and Canarese countries. (p. 24.)

D. *Transitional. (Plates* vi., vii. *and* xxvi.*)*

What I have termed the transitional period, or from 1000—1300 A. D. marks the rise and most flourishing period of the North-Dravidian literatures. During the whole of this time the older kingdoms decayed rapidly, feudatories became more or less independent, and changes in the limits of territory subject to the different sovereigns were perpetual. The encouragement of literature was, however, general, and this period is also marked by the rise of several religious sects. The result, palæographically, was that by 1300 A. D. the old Telugu Canarese alphabet which was in use from the coast of Canara to Rajahmundry, presented scarcely any varieties or differences of form of the letters sufficient to justify a distinction being made. From 1300 A. D. up to the present time, however, a marked divergence has arisen between the alphabets used by the Telugus of the coast and the Canarese people; and this divergence has been much increased since the introduction of printing in the course of the present century.

The feudatories which overthrew the western Câlukya kingdom appear to have been partial to

Kali*n*ga or Three Kali*n*gas, and has nothing to do with li*n*ga. The native etymology of 'Telugu' first occurs, I believe, in the Kârikâ of Âtharvaṇâcârya who copied and *quotes* Hemacandra, and therefore could not have lived before the thirteenth century.

'Telugu' is evidently from a common Dravidian root √tel which means 'to be clear or bright', and the Trili*n*ga theory is certainly not supported (as Dr. Caldwell appears to think) by Ptolemy's Triglypton or Trilingon (vii., 2, 23), which is most probably a copyist's error for Trikalingon. At all events a derivative of 'glypho' could never mean *linga.* Cunningham ("Ancient Geography of India," p. 519) recognizes three Kali*n*gas, and rightly doubts the name having anything to do with li*n*ga.

1) "Voyages des Pélerins Bouddhistes," iii., p. 105.

the N. Indian culture, and used the Devanâgarî character for their grants[1]. The Cô|as (who succeeded the Eastern Câlukyas) preserved the indigenous character and used Sanskrit for the northern part of their territories, but soon gave these up for Tamil̤. Thus, at the time of the Muhammedan invasions and settlements in the peninsula about the beginning of the fourteenth century, the use of the South Indian alphabets was confined to the extreme south of the peninsula, and did not extend much beyond the present northern limits of the Madras Presidency. That the Telugu and Canarese alphabets and literatures did not become entirely obsolete, is owing to the considerable power of the Vijayanagara dynasty in the 14th, 15th and early part of the 16th centuries, and to the steady patronage of South-Indian Hinduism by the kings of this dynasty during that period of time[2]. It is owing to this influence that many inscriptions from about 1500 to 1650 A. D. in the North-Tamil̤ country and even still further south are in the Telugu character. This is especially noticeable in the old Toṇḍainâḍu (or neighbourhood of Madras), and it is to the same influence that must be attributed the numerous settlement of Telugu Brahmans over greater part of the Tamil̤ country, and especially in Tanjore.

The transitional type of the Telugu-Canarese alphabet differs from the Kali*n*ga-Câlukya by the admission of a number of new forms which eventually became permanent; they are used, however, concurrently with the older forms except in a few instances.

The exclusive new forms of letters are: 1) ŏ; in this the top is opened out. 2) *dh;* in which the old square form is now provided with a ˇ at the top, 3) and *bh.* This last was evidently written in the alphabet of 945 A. D. by two strokes, the second being made from the first, and prolonged down in a curved form; in the transitional alphabet which began in the next century these two strokes are separated. 4) *ç* has a more cursive form than in the alphabet of the previous century.

As in the alphabet of 945 A. D. there is little distinction between the long and short i superscript. In the older alphabets the long î is marked by a curl in the left end of the circle which marks this vowel, *e. g.* ∩(i) and ൭(î), but from the tenth century this distinction is almost lost.

In the eleventh century the modern form of the subscript u begins to appear, and is used far oftener than the old form written underneath the preceding consonant; but the reverse is the case with the long û which rather preserves the old form. In the next century the modern form of û (to the right of the preceding consonant) prevails nearly universally, but the old form of the short u is by no means entirely disused. The secondary forms of e and ui and ai are very nearly the same as in the alphabet of 945 A. D., *i. e.* written at the top of the preceding consonant, whereas in the earlier forms they are on the left side. O and au are also very little changed in form.

It is necessary also to notice the changes in the way of distinguishing ph from p. In the earliest form (pl. i.) this is done by the upper end of the stroke on the right side being curled round to the left; in the later alphabet of the tenth century there is a loop on the middle of the inner side of

1) I shall for this reason notice them when describing the varieties of the Devanâgarî character used in the South of India.

2) The Telugu poet Bhaṭṭamûrti was encouraged by Narasaraya, and Allasanni Peddaṇṇa by Krishṇaraya. ("*Madras Journal,*" v. pp. 363, 4.)

this stroke. In the alphabet of the next century this loop has become a slanting stroke across the upright stroke, and finally about a century later this is underneath the middle of the letter.

The transitional stage continued till the end of the thirteenth century A. D., and includes a period of great literary activity not only as regards the Telugu and Canarese languages, but also in Sanskrit. The reforms of the Vedântist Râmânuja belonged to the twelfth century, and he obtained great influence in Mysore where he converted the sovereign (a Yâdava of the southern dynasty of Dwârasamudra) from the Jain persuasion. This king appears to have encouraged Telugu literature (because, no doubt, it was thoroughly brahminical and orthodox), as much as his immediate predecessors had encouraged the Canarese[1]; and Nannaya Bhaṭṭa (a native of the east coast) composed under his patronage (about 1180 A. D.) a Telugu Grammar in Sanskrit, and began a translation of the Râmâyaṇa which was finished by another Brahman, also a native of the east coast, a little later[2]. These events are nearly contemporaneous with the final ruin of the western Câlukya dynasty which fell in 1182, and then the Yâdavas became independent both in the north (Devagiri) and south, and thus shared the greater part of the territory of the old Cêra and Câlukya kingdoms.

E. *The old and modern Telugu-Canarese Alphabets (Plates* viii., ix. *and* xxviii.*)*

The next stage in the development of the northern Dravidian alphabets is the Haḷa-kanaḍa and old Telugu, between which it is impossible at present to establish any distinction. This alphabet dates from the end of the thirteenth century, and the distinction between it and the character I have termed transitional consists merely: 1) in the disuse of the few remaining older forms which I have described in the last section as being found in that alphabet, and the exclusive use of the new forms; 2) in the absence of distinction between *d* and *dh*, *p* and *ph* and some other aspirates; 3) in the absence of marks to distinguish *i* and *î*.

As will be easily understood in the case of an alphabet like this which was in use from the Canara coast to the mouths of the Krishṇâ and Godâvarî, there were several slight varieties or hands, but it would take far too much space to notice here more than a few points, even though such details are of interest as partly subsisting up to the present time.

The earliest important variation, I have noticed, is in the form of *t*. About 1300 this letter appears in inscriptions on the west (or Canara) coast with a double loop ಟ, whereas on the east coast, and the central territory between the two, the form ట with a single loop is preferred. In the modern Telugu and Canarese alphabets, this is exactly reversed. Again the Canarese

1) See Mr. Kittel's preface to his edition of Keçirâja's Canarese Grammar.

2) This poet (?) was named Tikkaṇṇa; he died in 1198 A. D. (Brown's "Cyclic Tables" Madras edition, p. 58). Nâgavarmâ the author of the Canarese Prosody was also a Telugu from Vengi; his date is, however, uncertain. (Mr. Kittel.)

form of *k* (ಕ) was originally the most general one[1], whereas the modern Telugu క was confined in the fourteenth, fifteenth and sixteenth centuries to the northern part of the present Nellore district, where a very *round* hand has always prevailed. Owing to that part of the Telugu country having been one of the earliest British possessions in Southern India, this hand was adopted as the model, on the introduction of Telugu printing in the beginning of this century at Madras. At present, the Canarese is especially distinguished from the Telugu alphabet by the method of marking the long vowels î, ê and ô, by the addition of a separate sign (—ೕ) following the consonant with the usual short vowel affixed; this is entirely wanting in Telugu. The earliest instance I have noticed is in a palm-leaf MS. of the first half of the sixteenth century A. D., but it does not occur in any old Sanskrit MSS. in the Canarese character at all, nor commonly in Canarese MSS. till much later. The Telugu method of marking the short and long e and o does not appear till the seventeenth century. About this period apparently owing to the revival of Sanskrit studies for a time, the distinction between aspirated and unaspirated letters becomes again usual, and has continued up to the present, though really alien to the Dravidian languages. It began much earlier in Telugu than in Canarese, and even in the Sanskrit MSS. on grammar written in the latter character, it is but seldom made; a fact, which, by itself, proves the prevalence of oral teaching[2].

From the earliest inscriptions down to the latest, the gradual extension of the use of the bindu (○) is very remarkable, and appears a tolerably safe test of the age of a document. I shall therefore give briefly the results I have gathered.

In the early inscriptions the Cêra bindu is *above* the line, the Çâlukya *on* the line; but after the twelfth or thirteenth century it is always, and in all S. Indian characters, written *on* the line. This is even the case in the Nandi-nâgarî, though here, it, by being in this position, renders the writing unsightly.

As regards the employment of the *bindu*, the broad rule is: the later the inscription, the more incorrect and indiscriminate is its use. In the earlier inscriptions it is seldom used for *n*, ṇ, n, and m before a consonant of the same class *in* a word; but it is used for all these nasals except ṇ, by the fifteenth century; and from that time to the present one occasionally finds *m*ḍ. The common practice of using the bindu to express all the nasals, even including a final m, which editors in Europe have copied from the more modern MSS. from N. India, is, therefore, a very old practice in the south, though it is most certainly erroneous according to the chief grammarians, and, therefore, as Profr. Whitney contends, is to be rejected, though convenient in practice[3]. It is hardly necessary to remark that the *bindu* is properly the sign of the unmodified nasal or anusvâra.

---

1) See pl. xxviii.

2) Cfr. the alphabet given in pl. ix. I have already given a facsimile of a Canarese Sanskrit MS. of about 1600 A. D. in my edition of the Vaṃçabrâhmaṇa. The difference between the writing of MSS. of the fifteenth and sixteenth centuries is very slight; the body of the letters in the latter is not so large, or so round and close together.

3) Profr. Max Müller (Hitopadeça, p. viii. and S. Gr. pp. 6-7) allows it as a convenient way of writing.

I have not noticed in any inscription the nasalized semi-vowel; it sometimes occurs in Telugu Vedic MSS. and then has the form of ꣳ. Nor have I met with the ardhânusvâra to which some Telugu grammarians allude[1]. The ఱ (ṟ) of the Telugu inscriptions is now disused[2].

The use of visarga is generally incorrect in the inscriptions; it is seldom converted according to rule. In S. India the alternative allowed by the grammarians of assimilating visarga to a following sibilant is almost universally accepted, and the reduplication of the sibilant then omitted. This is a common source of error in reading S. Indian inscriptions and MSS. The separation of the superscript r from the following consonant (as pronounced) above which it is written, begins about 1300 A. D. After 1350 it is always on the right hand, *e.g.* rka is written ర్క (kr). By 1550-1600 A. D. the modern secondary form of e is always used, *e.g.* ve is written వె. (For the older form see pl. viii.) In the fifteenth century both forms co-exist; in the fourteenth the modern form begins to appear.

Allusions to the current alphabets are almost as rare in the S. Indian mediæval works as in the Sanskrit. Âtharva*n*âcârya (who cannot be earlier than the end of the twelfth or beginning of the thirteenth century) describes the transitional alphabet just as it was changing into the earliest modern form ("Kârikâ*h*" 29-32)[3]:

29. *b.* paṅčavargâdayo varṇâ*h* ça*n*kha-(*a* అ)çâr*n*gâ-(*g* గ)disa*m*nibhâ*h* ||
30. tiryagrekhâyujaç čo 'rdhva*m* daṇḍarekhânvitâ adha*h* (✓ *and* ı) |
ta eva ca dvitîyâ(*h*) syur ûrdhvam . . . . ||
31. prathamâs tu t*r*itîyâ(*h*) syus t*r*itîyânte čaturthakâ*h* |
rekhâdvayâdhodaṇḍena yuktâ(*h*) syur anunâsikâ*h* ||
32. miladdaṇḍadvayopetâ*h* prathamâ paya*sm*r*itâ*h* |
pûrṇendusadr̥iça*h* pûrṇas tv ardhendus tv ardhasannibha*h* ||

There is much here very unintelligible, but the description of some of the letters clearly points to about 1200 A. D. The Canarese "Basavapurâṇa" (of 1369 A. D.) mentions the Telugu, Canarese, Grantha, Tamiḻ (Drâviḷa), Lâḷa (*i.e.* Lâṭa or Gujarat) and Persian alphabets[4].

Nor is it quite clear what letters the mediæval grammarians considered to belong to the alphabet. Al-Birûnî (who lived from 970-1039 A. D.)[5] puts the number of Sanskrit letters at fifty; Nannaya Bhaṭṭa, in his Telugu Grammar (of the twelfth century), also puts the Sanskrit letters at fifty, the Prakrit at forty, and the Telugu at thirty-six[6]. The commentators are, however, not agreed as to whether both x (ksh) and ḷ are intended to be included among the Sanskrit letters[7]. Lassen ("Indische Alterthumskunde" iv. p. 796) takes the *R*igveda ḷ to be the fiftieth letter of

1) v. App. A.

2) This letter is etymologically of significance; and, therefore, cannot be neglected.

3) I follow a transcript of the unique MS. in Mr. Brown's collection at Madras.

4) I owe this reference to Mr. Kittel; it occurs in ch. v.

5) Elliot, "Muhammedan Historians of India" (by Dowson) I. p. 42.

6) "Āndhraçabdacintâmaṇi", I. 14. âdyâyâ*h* paṅcâçad varṇâ*h*. 15. Prak*r*ites tu te daçonâ*h* syu*h*. 16. Shaṭtri*m*çad atra te. 17. Anye câ 'nupraviçanti çabdayogavaçât. (*i.e.* in Sanskrit or Prakrit words used in Telugu).

7) Ahobala (18th century) says in his C. on the first of the Sûtras quoted in the last note: "Atra kecid a, â . . . . xaḷavarṇasahitâ ûshmâṇaç ca hala ity učyante | militvâ paṅčâçad varṇâ bhavantî 'ti vadanti | . . . . keshâ*n*cin mate . . . . . ḷavarṇasyâ 'grahaṇa*m* ca sammatam || (MS.)

Al-Birûnî; it may reasonably be doubted if that was the view held in India. The Canarese Grammar includes both x and ḷ[1].

The Vajrâkṛiti and Gajakumbhâkṛiti of Vopadeva (*i e. h* before k and kh, and before p and ph) very rarely occur in modern MSS.; they have the form of ⧖ and ∞. The last occurs in only one inscription, as far as I know. (Pl. i.) The northern form (ᵕ) is also used sometimes.

§ 2. THE GRANTHA-TAMIL ALPHABETS.

A. *Cêra.* (*Plates* ii., x., *and* xxiii.)

The Grantha, Modern Tamiḻ, Malayâḷam and Tuḷu alphabets all have their origin in the Cêra character, a variety of the 'Cave character' which was used in the Cêra kingdom during the early centuries A. D. From the third to the seventh century appears to have been the most flourishing period in the modern history of this kingdom; it then extended over the present Mysore, Coimbatore, Salem, Toṇḍainâḍu, South Malabar and Cochin. It was, however, one of the three great old Dravidian kingdoms and existed already in the third century B. C. What civilization it had before the period referred to, there is no information; nor is there the least trace as yet of any inscription before the early centuries A. D.[2] The existing inscriptions show that about the fourth or fifth century A. D., the rulers of this kingdom received the Jains with great zeal, and made most liberal endowments to them in the territory that constitutes the modern province of Mysore. There is much reason to believe that the alphabet found in the inscriptions of this kingdom is the source also of the alphabets of the inscriptions left by the mysterious Hindu civilization that once was powerful in Java and Sumatra and also in Indo-China. Who the first Indian missionary to Java was, does not appear, but it is historically certain that Buddhaghosa (fifth century) was the first who preached in Indo-China. It also seems excessively probable that the original Indian civilization of those countries was kept up by constant emigration there from S. India, owing to the bitter religious quarrels[3] that arose in the seventh and eighth centuries on the preaching of Kumârilasvâmin and Çaṅkarâcârya, and which ended in the entire destruction in India of modern Buddhism, one sect of by far the noblest religion that country ever produced.

---

1) "Çabdamaṇidarpaṇa" (by Mr. Kittel) p. 11.

2) The history of the Cêra kingdom is excessively obscure, and will probably, always remain so. Like in most Indian kingdoms that have preserved an existence for several centuries, there were, in all probability, many revolts of feudatories and changes of dynasty; it is thus very little use to accept the "KoṅYudesarâjakkal" as an authority, for it bears evident signs of being a very recent compilation from grants and local traditions most clumsily put together. It is translated in the *Madras Journal*, vol. xiv. pp. 1—16. The most important investigation (as yet) respecting the Cêra kingdom is by Profr. Dowson (in Journal of the R. A. S. of London, vol. viii. and also printed separately).

3) Kumârila and Çaṅkara were both reactionary, and (if such summary judgments be allowed), the best explanation of the early decay of Buddhism in the South of India and Indo-China and Java is one which the Positive Philosophy supplies, that the countries in question were not advanced sufficiently to allow of their receiving such a religion as Buddhism, and that the premature reception of it thus led at once to deterioration rather than progress.

The Cêra alphabet changed but little during a considerable time; the earliest and latest authentic inscriptions which are in existence, and which belong to a period of about four centuries, show very few innovations. Two varieties of this character must be distinguished; the first, which was in use in that part of the Cêra country which constitutes the modern Mysore and Coorg up to the final end of the kingdom which was conquered by the Côḷas about 877 A. D., and which then fell into disuse being soon supplanted by the western Câlukya and Transitional characters; and the second which was used in Toṇḍainâḍu (the neighbourhood of Madras) which formed part of the Cêra kingdom till about the end of the seventh century when it fell under the Côḷas. This last alphabet then became under the new dynasty the medium if introducing brahmanical culture to the Tamiḻ country[1].

The earliest unquestionable inscription as yet known is that of which the alphabet is given in Pl. ii., and which has been published in facsimile in the *Indian Antiquary*[2]; the date is about 466 A. D. A later inscription of the same dynasty is also given in the same Journal[3]. Its date is, though not clearly put, as there is an obvious error of the engraver in omitting a letter in the date, beyond doubt. This runs (v. *l.* 8): "ashṭanavatyuttareshu ṭchateshu çakavarsheshv atîteshu". The ṭ in ṭchateshu is clear, and though 'sha(ṭ)' is entirely wanting, yet as 'shaṭ' is the only possible numeral it must be read 698 (= 777-8 A. D.) The difference in character between the alphabets of the two inscriptions is so slight that I have not thought it worthwhile to give both.

1) In the third century B. C., the Açoka Edicts show that Keraḷaputra (*i. e.* the Cera sovereign) was one of the great powers of the South. Ptolemy (2nd century A. D.) and the Periplus of the Red Sea (3rd century A. D.) prove that this was still the case. Hiouen-Thsang (about 640 A. D.) does not mention this kingdom, but under the name of the kingdom of Koṇkaṇapura (the present Ko*n*kaṇa-haḷḷi) he describes a part of it ("Pélerins Bouddhistes" iii. pp. 146-9). The dynasty which the inscriptions mention extends from the early centuries A. D. down to the ninth, but it was probably established by a feudatory revolted against the older dynasty to which Açoka, and the classical authors refer. The Mercara grant (Mr. Richter's) gives the kings as follows:

1. Ko*n*gaṇi (i.) (The eighth king of the so-called chronicle!)
2. Mâdhava (i.)
3. Ari-(*i. e.* Hari)varmâ (The grant d. 247 A. D. is attributed to him!)
4. Vishṇugopa
5. Mâdhava (ii.)
6. Ko*n*gaṇi (ii.) in 466 A. D.

This would place Ko*n*gaṇi (i.) about 350 A. D.

The Nâgama*n*gala grant continues:

7. Durvinîta
8. Mushkara
9. Çrî-Vikrama
10. Bhû-Vikrama
11. Pṛithivî Ko*n*gaṇi (? A. D. 727—777)

There is a grant on stone in Kiggatnâḍ (in Coorg) which mentions Satyâditya-Ko*n*ginivarmamahârâjâdhirâja; it is dated Îçvara year. The çaka date is not clear.

There are however, many difficulties about the genealogy and succession which remain to be cleared up. It would be well to term this 'the later Cêra dynasty'.

2) Vol. I. The transcript needs some corrections. Jinâlakke is clearly, "for the Jinâlaya" (Jain temple) and not "for the destruction of the Jains," as the whole inscription is Jain in style (cfr. the mention of the Vasus). I have been able to examine the original plates of this very valuable document, through the kindness of the Rev. G. Richter of Mercara.

3) Vol. II. 155 ffg. See especially Dr. Eggeling's remarks (iii. pp. 154-2).

that alphabet; it is, therefore in origin, very near the Cave character; and the introduction of this alphabet into Toṇḍainâḍu is, probably, to be placed about the fourth century. In the second century A. D. (as we know from Ptolemy) this country was inhabited by nomads; and its settlement and the formation of a kingdom there was due to Cêra influences. In the seventh century Hiouen-Thsang found a small kingdom of which Ka*n*çi (or Conjeveram) was the capital. He calls it Ta-lo-pi-tcha or Draviḍa. The name of the family of kings of which inscriptions occur at Seven Pagodas (Mâmalaippuram, the old port of Conjeveram) was Pallava, and they appear to have been formidable enough to have been attacked by the Western Câlukyas about the beginning of the seventh century. Still later (about the eighth or ninth century) the country was conquered by the Côḷas who had revived again after a long eclipse.

There can be no question that the caves and monoliths at Seven Pagodas, and in the neighbourhood, are of Buddhist-Jain origin[1]; the sculptures on the so-called *rathas* (monoliths) show (if any thing at all) a slight admixture of Çaiva notions, such as appear in the later Buddhism. Over several of the figures are, however, Vaishṇava names (*e.g.* çrî Narasi*m*ha*h*) which ill-agree with the representations. In some of the caves are pure Vaishṇava and Çaiva mythological scenes. Taking into consideration the fact that this place is not mentioned by Hiouen-Thsang together with the nature of the sculptures, the original work is to be attributed to Jains of about the fifth century, and the alphabet of the inscriptions corresponds with this date. But as the caves now exist, they have been subsequently extended and adapted to the worship of Çiva, or to the combined worship of Vishṇu and Çiva in the same temple, which is so remarkable a feature in the older and unaltered temples in the neighbourhood of Madras[2], and which can only be attributed to the influence of the Vedânta doctrine as preached by Ça*n*karâcârya[3]. It is to the period of this adaptation that the dedicatory inscription, from which the alphabet in pl. xi. is taken, belongs. The king under whom it was done is termed 'lord of the Pallavas' (Pallaveçvara) with the epithets "victorious in battle" (raṇajaya*h*), or "very fierce in battle" (atiraṇacaṇḍa*h*), and had, therefore, come under the northern brahmanical influence[4].

---

with whom he associated intimately, and his kind and playful disposition endeared him to his own countrymen among whom he was distinguished no less by his capacity as a public servant than by a mind fraught with intelligence and alive to every object of interest or utility. The College of Fort St. George which owes its existence to him is a lasting memorial of his reputation as an Oriental Scholar, and this stone has been erected as a tribute of the affectionate regard of his European and Native friends."

So little interest in science is there in S. India, that this eminent man is chiefly recollected among the native Roman Catholics by some quasi-devotional poems in Tamiḻ which are attributed to him.

1) Mr. Fergusson long ago stated this ("*History of Architecture*," ii. pp. 502 ffg.)

2) An often engraved temple of this description is the one at Seven Pagodas on the sea-shore, and washed by the waves at high tide; another is on the northern bank of the Pâlâṟu also near the sea and a few miles south of Seven Pagodas. There are the best examples that I know, but there are many others (often more or less altered) in the same neighbourhood. In the first the Vishṇu cell is behind that in which the Linga is found; in the others I know, the two cells are side by side. There is a correct plan of the first temple in No. 6 of the large map in Major Carr's book, and an incorrect one in pl. xxiii.

3) Ça*n*karâcârya must be put at about 650-700 A. D. See my "Sâmavidhânabrâhmaṇa" vol. I. pref. p. ii. *n*. He preached at Conjeveram, it is said.

4) The Çambhu of these inscriptions is shown by the sculptures to be Mahâdeva-Çiva; one inscription mentions Pârvati.

that alphabet; it is, therefore in origin, very near the Cave character; and the introduction of this alphabet into Toṇḍainâḍu is, probably, to be placed about the fourth century. In the second century A. D. (as we know from Ptolemy) this country was inhabited by nomads; and its settlement and the formation of a kingdom there was due to Cêra influences. In the seventh century Hiouen-Thsang found a small kingdom of which Ka*n*çi (or Conjeveram) was the capital. He calls it Ta-lo-pi-tcha or Draviḍa. The name of the family of kings of which inscriptions occur at Seven Pagodas (Mâmalaippuram, the old port of Conjeveram) was Pallava, and they appear to have been formidable enough to have been attacked by the Western Câlukyas about the beginning of the seventh century. Still later (about the eighth or ninth century) the country was conquered by the Côḷas who had revived again after a long eclipse.

There can be no question that the caves and monoliths at Seven Pagodas, and in the neighbourhood, are of Buddhist-Jain origin[1]; the sculptures on the so-called *rathas* (monoliths) show (if any thing at all) a slight admixture of Çaiva notions, such as appear in the later Buddhism. Over several of the figures are, however, Vaishṇava names (*e.g.* çrî Narasi*m*ha*h*) which ill-agree with the representations. In some of the caves are pure Vaishṇava and Çaiva mythological scenes. Taking into consideration the fact that this place is not mentioned by Hiouen-Thsang together with the nature of the sculptures, the original work is to be attributed to Jains of about the fifth century, and the alphabet of the inscriptions corresponds with this date. But as the caves now exist, they have been subsequently extended and adapted to the worship of Çiva, or to the combined worship of Vishṇu and Çiva in the same temple, which is so remarkable a feature in the older and unaltered temples in the neighbourhood of Madras[2], and which can only be attributed to the influence of the Vedânta doctrine as preached by Ça*n*karâcârya[3]. It is to the period of this adaptation that the dedicatory inscription, from which the alphabet in pl. xi. is taken, belongs. The king under whom it was done is termed 'lord of the Pallavas' (Pallaveçvara) with the epithets "victorious in battle" (raṇajaya*h*), or "very fierce in battle" (atiraṇacaṇḍa*h*), and had, therefore, come under the northern brahmanical influence[4].

with whom he associated intimately, and his kind and playful disposition endeared him to his own countrymen among whom he was distinguished no less by his capacity as a public servant than by a mind fraught with intelligence and alive to every object of interest or utility. The College of Fort St. George which owes its existence to him is a lasting memorial of his reputation as an Oriental Scholar, and this stone has been erected as a tribute of the affectionate regard of his European and Native friends."

So little interest in science is there in S. India, that this eminent man is chiefly recollected among the native Roman Catholics by some quasi-devotional poems in Tamiḷ which are attributed to him.

1) Mr. Fergusson long ago stated this ("*History of Architecture*," ii. pp. 502 ffg.)

2) An often engraved temple of this description is the one at Seven Pagodas on the sea-shore, and washed by the waves at high tide; another is on the northern bank of the Pâlâṛu also near the sea and a few miles south of Seven Pagodas. There are the best examples that I know, but there are many others (often more or less altered) in the same neighbourhood. In the first the Vishṇu cell is behind that in which the Linga is found; in the others I know, the two cells are side by side. There is a correct plan of the first temple in No. 6 of the large map in Major Carr's book, and an incorrect one in pl. xxiii.

3) Ça*n*karâcârya must be put at about 650-700 A. D. See my "Sâmavidhânabrâhmaṇa" vol. I. pref. p. ii. *n*. He preached at Conjeveram, it is said.

4) The Çambhu of these inscriptions is shown by the sculptures to be Mahâdeva-Çiva; one inscription mentions Pârvati.

The inscriptions in question are not dated; the earlier ones (which consist of merely a few words in explanation of the figures on the so-called *rathas*) are in a character very near to the Ve*n*gi and early Cêra, but distinguished from them by a few important variations. The first of these is the use to a considerable extent of secondary forms of â, e and o separated from the consonant to which they belong and follow in pronunciation[1] thus râ, vâ, çâ and hâ occur in these words with the â separated only; and kâ, bhâ and râ both united to the consonant and also separate. To and no occur with the o separate. Besides these variations some of the letters, and especially ç, show an approach to the grantha form. The position of the *bindu* (○) shows clearly a Cêra, and not a Ve*n*gi or Câlukya original as I have already pointed out. (p. 24.)

A still further development in the direction of the grantha forms is to be found in the inscription on a monolith at Seven Pagodas now used as a Gaṇeça temple; and also again in a still more developed form at *S*âluva*n*kuppam. There can be no doubt that these inscriptions must be put at about 700 A. D. The first four lines of the Gaṇeça temple inscription describe Çiva in a way that is only possible after Ça*n*kara's development of the Vedânta; and as the rest states that a Pallava king built "this abode of Ça*m*bhu", the inscription cannot be later than the eighth century, for the Côḷas then conquered Toṇḍainâḍu, and rendered such an inscription in praise of a king of the old dynasty, impossible[2]. Again, decidedly archaic forms of letters occur; *e. g.* the secondary form of â which is occasionally turned up instead of down, and which early disappeared in the Câlukya and Cêra characters. That again this inscription is later than those on the so-called *rathas*, follows from the words "atyantakâmapallaveçvara çrî hâ (!?) raṇajaya*h*" being written in this character over a nondescript figure on one of them. Were all these explanatory labels over the figures of one date or of about the same date, such a difference in the writing would not have occurred. There is another circumstance which corroborates the date I have assigned to this inscription — the existence

1) See plates 16, 17 and 18 in R. A. S. Transactions ii. and in Major Carr's Collection of papers relating to the Seven Pagodas (Madras 1869, 8vo.) I put at the editor's disposal my copies of the inscriptions at Seven Pagodas and also at *S*âluva*n*kuppam, as well as the results of excavations which I had made in 1867, and some of these are printed by Major Carr. (pp. 221-225.)

2) Major Carr has given my transliteration of this inscription (in Devanâgarî) on pp. 221-2; as, however, it is not quite correct, I give it again here. (I mark the half-çloka · by ;).

1. Sambhavasthitisa*m*hârakâraṇa*m* vîtakâraṇa*h*; bhûyâd atyantakâmâya jagatâ(*m*) kâmamardana*h* |||
2. Amâyaç čitramâyo 'sâv aguṇo guṇabhâjana*h*; ....jîyâd............
3. Yasyâ '*n*gushṭhabharâkrânta*h* kailâsa*h* sadaçânana*h*; pâtâlam agaman ma*çrînidhis tâ.........|||
4. Bhaktiprahveṇa manasâ bhavam bhûshaṇalîlayâ; doshṇâ ča yo bhûm (au) * * (j jîyât sa çrîbharaç ciram |||
5. Atyantakâmo n*r*ipatir nirjitârâtimaṇḍala*h*; khyâto raṇajaya*h* çambhos tene 'da*m* veçma kâritam |||
6. *prâṇanishkaḷa*h*..................vijayata ça*n*karakâma....na*h* |||
7. Râjarâjo navaraçmaç čakravartijanârddana*h*; târakâdhipati*h* svastho jayatât taraṇâ*n*kura*h* |||
8. Çrîmato 'tyantakâmasya dvishaddarpâpahâriṇa*h*; çrînidhi*h* kâmarâjasya harârâdhanasa*n*ginah |||
9. Abhishekajalâpûrṇe čitraraktâmbujâkare; âste viçâle sumukha*h* çirassarasi ça*n*kara*h* |||
10. Tene' da*m* kârita*m* çambho-(r bhavana*m* bhûtaye bhuva*h* kailâsa-) mandiraçubham prajânâm ishṭasiddhyartham
11. ....shashṭi..............çivam..............yeshâ(*m*) na vasati hṛidaye kupathagativimo—
12. xako rudra*h* ||| atyantakâmapallaveçvara ç î—

See pl. 14 in Major Carr's Collection of Papers, and in Dr. Babington's article (Trans. R. A. S. ii.). The translation given by the last (pp. 266-7) and reprinted by Major Carr, is not satisfactory. For Major Carr's "known as Raṇajaya" (p. 224), I think "tamed, victorious in battle" should be substituted. Line 10 is completed from the *S*âluva*n*kuppam inscription.

of a Devanâgarî transcript of some verses selected from it with additions at *S*âluva*n*kuppam. The Devanâgarî is precisely that of the eighth or ninth century, and it is accompanied by a transcript in old grantha very near to that of the eleventh century as given in Plate xii.

It is from the character of these inscriptions that the Indo-Chinese and Javanse alphabets must, I think, be traced. If this be the case, the civilization of that part of the East cannot be very old, and I think the facts bear out this view.

It is unquestionable that the civilization of Cambodia was Buddhist, and that this was also chiefly the case with Java. As then Buddhaghosa was the apostle of the first country in the fifth century (a fact corroborated by the very advanced form of Buddhism that the ruins there display) and as the Chinese pilgrims Fa-Hian and Hiouen-Thsang (to say nothing of the Açoka inscriptions) make no mention of the first country, which they certainly would have done had Buddhism been long established there at their own periods (400 A.D. and 640 A.D.), it is impossible to assume any considerable civilization there before the eighth century A. D. It is especially noteworthy that Hiouen-Thsang diligently visited the mythical sites of events in Buddha's life which he found in S. India, and had Buddhism been long established in Cambodia, he would have probably visited the places of pilgrimage (*e.g.* the holy foot-print in Siam) which must have in that case existed; but he does not mention anything of the kind. It must, therefore, be presumed that they did not then exist. Now the alphabets current in S. India about the eighth and following centuries up to about 1000 A.D. are obviously nearer the Cambodian and old Javanese than those current in N. India, and in which the characteristics of the Devanâgarî were already settled. But again these two alphabets are more closely allied to the Southern (or Cêra-Grantha) than to the Northern or Câlukya stock, for like the former these alphabets have preserved the subscript u and û, and also have the secondary forms of â, e, ai, o which are separated from the preceding consonant. Thus the eastern Cêra subsequent to 700 A.D. is the most probable source of both the Cambodian and old Javanese alphabets, and the reason of the great exodus of Indian Buddhists which alone could render possible the erection of such temples as those of Maha-Nakhon-Wat (? Mahâ-Nagara) in Cambodia and Boro-Boudour in Java, is then the persecution raised by Kumârila and Ça*n*karâcârya in the last half of the seventh century A.D. That the civilization of Indo-China and Java cannot be later than 1000 A.D. is obvious from the archaic type of many of the letters (*e.g.* a, â, č, dh, *n*, b, bh, m, etc.) in the alphabets of those countries, as by that time the original types were disused in India. As regards the date of the Cambodian civilization this conclusion is confirmed by the way in which that country is mentioned by the Sanskrit grammarians. The gaṇa 'çakâdi' occurs in Çâkaṭâyana (No. 76 in the gaṇapâṭha), and this list of words includes Kamboja (*i.e.* Cambodia) in a connection that is, I think, historically explicable. This gaṇa runs: Çaka, Yavana, Kamboja, Coḷa, Keraḷa, etc. in Çâkaṭâyana; and in Pâṇini (Vârttika to iv., 1,175 according to the Mahâbhâshya)[1]: Kamboja[2] (this word is actually in the sûtra iv., 1, 175), Coḷa, Keraḷa, Çaka, Yavana. By these

1) p. 60, *b.* of the Benares edition (ch. iv.)

2) This word also occurs in Pâṇini's gaṇas 'Kacchâdi' (iv. 2, 133) and 'Sindhvâdi' (iv. 3, 93)

rules these names unaltered, signify the king of each country also; at the time therefore, that these vârttikas assumed their present form there was no Pâṇḍya 'king' but only a people. Of these names, Yavana, Coḷa and Keraḷa occur in the Açoka inscriptions (250 B. C.), but Çaka could and does not; and it is difficult to see how it could occur in a gaṇa before the first century A. D. *i. e.* before the event which gave rise to the Çaka era. Again, if the above reasoning be correct, Kamboja could not occur before about 800 A. D. That this gaṇa is of this late date, I think the omission in it of the word Pâṇḍya is clear proof, for this could only have occurred when that old kingdom existed no longer, as otherwise the rule equally applies to that word. But the Pâṇḍya kingdom existed 250 B. C. (as the Açoka inscriptions prove), and was very flourishing in the second and third centuries A. D. (as Ptolemy and the Periplus prove), and it only fell on the rise of the Côḷas in the seventh century A. D. By the tenth century A. D. *all* the old Pâṇḍya kingdom was under the Côḷas as inscriptions prove. Thus a native of N. India about 850-900 A. D. would not know of a Pâṇḍya king, but he would know of the Çakas historically, the Yavanas (*i. e.* the Persians) by intercourse, and he would also know of the existing kingdoms of the Côḷas, Keraḷas and Kambojas. Again it cannot be later than 900 A. D. because at the end of the ninth century the old Cêra kingdom (Keraḷa) fell not to rise again. The Mahava*m*so (compiled after the fourth century A. D.) also omits all mention of Pâṇḍya in the history of the early centuries A. D., and thus coincides with the gaṇapâṭhas.

If this view be correct, it is then impossible to avoid the conclusion that all the Sanskrit books in which 'Kamboja' occurs have had interpolations made in them in quite recent times; and thus, besides the grammars, the Râmâyaṇa [i. 55 (56)2], Mânavadharmaçâstra (x. 44), Nirukta (Naig: ii., 2) must be held to be interpolated. Profr. Max Müller long ago pointed out that the Pâṇinîya Uṇṇâdi-sûtras must have been interpolated[1], and the few S. Indian MSS. that I have seen prove not only the correctness of this supposition, but also the existence of a distinct recension which differs in many respects from that edited by Profr. Aufrecht.

That two redactions of the Mahâbhâsya have been made, appears from a passage in the Vâkyapadîya[2], which states that the great Commentary was cut up (nilâvita) by Vaiji and others; and again that a text was established by Candra and others from a single MS. under king Abhimanyu[3].

The cause of the interpolations so frequent in all Sanskrit texts is the evident desire to make every independent work encyclopædic, and thus to justify its adherents in putting forward claims to have their favorite text considered as the most important. The endless episodes in the epic poems owe their inclusion to this craving, and the practice was superseded in recent times, rather than prevented, by the sectarian commentaries.

The Javanese alphabet of the inscriptions is exceedingly near the Eastern-Cêra, as a superficial comparison will prove[4].

1) A. S. L. pp. 245—9.

2) Goldstücker's "Pâṇini" sep. impr. pp. 237-8.

3) This is confirmed by the account in the Râjatara*n*giṇî. Abhimanyu is believed to have reigned 45-65 A. D. cfr. Lassen's I. A. K. ii. p. 1221.

4) See the inscription (d. ç. 1265=1343) given by Weber and Friedrich in Z. d. D. M. G. xviii. pp. 494-508.

But besides the resemblance of the old Javanese character to the Eastern-Cêra, the likeness of style of the inscriptions of the two countries is very remarkable. The common and large use of the epithet 'bhaṭṭâraka' or 'bhaṭâra' is an instance of this. It is rarely used in the Kalinga-Câlukya inscriptions, but is excessively common in the Cêra. In old Javanese the word perpetually occurs[1]. On the other hand it seems scarcely ever used in the N. Indian inscriptions[2].

The question of the origin of the Javanese and Indo-Chinese civilizations is very obscure, but of vast importance. The information for its decision is very scanty, and hence palæography may afford not a little help.

B. *Côla-Grantha.* (*Plate* xii.)

The development of the early stages of the Grantha character is very difficult to trace, for the reason that the N. Indian civilization, when it got as far down in the peninsula as the Tamiḻ country, found there a people already in possession of the art of writing, and apparently a cultivated language[3]. Thus Sanskrit did not regulate the Tamiḻ phonetic system, nor did it become more to the people than a foreign learned language; it thus remained almost exclusively in the knowledge of the Brahmans, and the Grantha alphabet is nothing more than the character the Tamiḻ Brahmans used and still use for writing their sacred books in a dead language. As there are no old MSS. written in this character, the records we possess of its early stages are most imperfect, and consist chiefly of Sanskrit words which casually occur in Tamiḻ inscriptions. I am aware of the existence of only two or three Sanskrit inscriptions in the Grantha character more than three centuries old, and these are not dated.

The only interest this character possesses is the proof it affords of the derivation of the modern Grantha alphabet from the Cêra, and thus from the Southern Açoka character. The first traces, I have found of it, are a few words in the grant B. to the Persian Christians, and which are, therefore, to be referred to the early part of the ninth century A. D. The letters are somewhat carelessly formed, but are almost identical with the Cêra of the same period (cfr. Pl. xxiii.). To the fall of the Cêra kingdom in the ninth century must be attributed the sudden appearance of brahmanical culture in the Tamiḻ country and Malabar.

---

1) Cfr. v. Humboldt's "Kawi-sprache" I. p. 190, Batara Guru; 194, Batara Kâla, Batara Sakra; 200, Batara Asmara etc. Even a feminine form occurs: Batari Rati (p. 200), Batari Umâ (p. 203). v. Humboldt (p. 190) took this to be a modification of *avatâra*, but it was rightly explained by Lassen (I. A—K. IV., p. 470).

2) I must, however, point out that Profr. Kern is disinclined to consider the Javanese civilization as derived from S. India. At the end of a notice of the inscription of Pagger Roejong (in Java) he remarks that the Tamiḻ and Telugu words in Javanese could have been introduced through commercial intercourse, and cannot be taken as a proof of S. Indian colonies in Java. That Dravidian words are to be found in Javanese, I pointed out in the preface to my edition of the Vaṁçabrâhmaṇa. Profr. Kern's article is in p. 2 of vol. viii. of the third Series of the "Bijdragen tot de Taal-, Land-, en Volkenkunde van Nederlands Indië;" it is called "Nog iets over't opschrift van Pagger Roejong".

3) This is proved by the entire absence of *old* inscriptions in the Tamiḻ country in the Grantha or Grantha-Tamiḻ characters, all such are in the Vaṭṭeḻuttu. See § 3 (below).

The letters in the upper part of Pl. xii. are taken from two sources: 1. the inscription round the shrine of the great temple at Tanjore (which belongs to the end of the eleventh century A. D.[1]; and 2. an undated inscription near Muruɣamaṅɣalam (in the Chingleput district) which is evidently of about the same date.

The only point to which it is necessary to call attention is the advance made in about two centuries in the separation of the secondary forms of â, ê, ai and ô, as shown by these inscriptions. In 825 A. D. only the ꭱ (e) was clearly separated from its consonant; about 1100 A. D. â is also generally separated (cfr. Pl. xii., kâ, tâ, nâ, pâ, mâ, yâ, râ, hâ); the form in which it is attached being rare (cfr. câ, çâ). The modern Grantha alphabet dates from about 1300 in all probability.

C. *Modern Grantha*[2] *and Tuḷu-Malayâḷam.*

(*Plates* xiii., xiv. *and* xx.)

The materials for the history of this section of the S. Indian alphabets are also excessively defective. These alphabets were up to quite recent times in very limited use, and except in Malabar, are still applied merely to write Sanskrit. The name 'Grantha' by which the E. coast variety has been known for some centuries[3] indicates that it was merely used for 'books' or literary purposes. This being the case, it is hopeless to look for old specimens, as palmleaf MSS. perish rapidly in the Tamiḻ country where they are mostly written on leaves of the 'Borassus flabelliformis', far inferior to the Talipat leaves in beauty and durability. The oldest MS. I have been able to discover is Tanjore 9,594 which must be of about 1600 A. D. Autographs of mediæval authors who must have used this character (*e. g.* Appayya Dîxita in the sixteenth century A. D.) appear to be no longer in existence.

There are at present two distinct Grantha hands. The brahmanical or *square* hand (cfr. pl. xiv.), and the *round* or Jain hand which has preserved the original features of the early Grantha far better than the other. The first is used chiefly in the Tanjore province; the last by the Jains still remaining near Arcot and Madras.

By far the largest number of Grantha MSS. now existing are brahmanical, and the lesser or greater approach of the writing to the angular Tamiḻ forms, is a certain test of the age of a MS. Such a hand as that shown in pl. xxx. became quite obsolete by 1700 A. D. The only modern

1) Letters taken from this are marked *. This immense inscription was photographed by Capt. Tripe in 1859 and published by the Madras Government. There is little Sanskrit in it except an introductory verse (Svasti çrî*h*| etat viçvarûpaçreṇimaulimâlopalâbhitam| çâsana*m* Râjarâjasya Râjakesarivarmaṇa*h* ||) which belongs to a part of the inscription dated in the 25th year of the king's reign (=1089 A. D.), and a few words in the Tamiḻ text.

2) The first complete representation of the Grantha alphabet is in "A Sanskrit Primer" by Harkness and Visvambra Sastri, (*sic*) (4° Madras, College Press, 1827); the letters are, however, badly formed. The type now in use at Madras is very little better in this respect.

3) See the reference to the Basava-purâ*n*a (1369 A. D.) on p. 25 *n*.

MSS. that I have seen at all like it, came from Palghat (Pâlakkâḍu); but Malayâḷam forms of occasional letters show their origin[1].

The Tuḷu-Malayâḷam alphabet is a variety of the Grantha, and like it, was originally applied only to the writing of Sanskrit; it is, therefore, the Grantha of the West, or the original Côḷa-Grantha modified in course of time in a country secluded from all but very little communication with the east coast of the peninsula. The importation of this alphabet into the S. W. coast must obviously have occurred after the Grantha had assumed its characteristic forms, or about the eighth and ninth centuries A. D.[2]

Up to about 1600 A. D. the Tuḷu[3] and Malayâḷam alphabets (as shown by Sanskrit MSS.) are identical, and hardly differ from the modern Tuḷu hand given in pl. xiv. MSS. from Malabar proper are generally written in a very irregular sprawling hand[4], those from the Tuḷu country are neater. This character was termed in Malabar Ārya-eḻuttu, and was only applied to write Sanskrit works up to the latter part of the seventeenth century when it commenced to supplant the old Vaṭṭeḻuttu hitherto used for writing Malayâḷaṁ. In the Tuḷu country it cannot be said ever to have been used for writing the vernacular language—a Dravidian dialect destitute of a literature.

The application of the Ārya-eḻuttu to the vernacular Malayâḷam was the work of a low-caste man who goes under the name of Tu*n*jatta Eḻuttacchan, a native of T*r*ikkaṇḍiyûr in the present district of Malabar. He lived in the seventeenth century, but his real name is forgotten; Tu*n*jatta being his 'house' or family-name, and Eḻuttacchan (= schoolmaster) indicating his caste. It is probable that there was a scanty vernacular literature before his time[5], but it is entirely owing to him that the Malayâḷam literature is of the extent it is. He translated the Sanskrit Bhâgavata, and several similar mythologico-religious poems, leaving, however, a large infusion of Sanskrit, and writing his composition in the ârya character. His translations are often erroneous, and beyond adopting the Vaṭṭeḻuttu signs for ṟ, ḻ, and ḷ, (റ, ഴ and ള) he did nothing whatever to systematize the orthography which till lately was most defective[6], or to supply signs for letters (*e.g.* ụ) which are wanting in most of the other Dravidian languages. The Sanskrit literature was, after this, no longer a secret, and there was perhaps no part of S. India where it was more studied by people of many castes during the eighteenth century.

Tu*n*jatta Eḻuttacchan's paraphrases were copied, it is said, by his daughter. I have seen the

1) MSS. in all these hands, and of different ages occur among those I presented to the India Office Library in 1870.

2) See the words (from the grant to the Persian Christians), given in pl. xii.

3) I have been told by a Brahman of the Mâdhva sect that the founder (Ānandatîrtha, † 1198 A. D.) wrote his works in this character on palm leaves, and that some are still preserved in a brass box and worshipped at Uḍupi. It is probable, but I have not been able to get any corroboration of this story. The MSS. (if still existing) must be reduced by time to the condition of tinder; for the oldest MS. that I have seen in S. India which was of the 15th century, could not be handled without damage to it.

4) The types used in printing the first edition of the Malayâḷam Gospels (at Bombay in 1806) exactly represent it.

5) Dr. Gundert considers the Malayâḷam Râmâyaṇa to belong to a period of perhaps some centuries before the arrival of the Portuguese.

6) The distinction between ĕ and ē, and ŏ and ō was first made within the last thirty years by Dr. Gundert. In a new fount of types used at Kunamâvu (Cochin territory) an attempt is made to separate the secondary forms of u and û.

MS. of the Bhâgavata [1] which is written in a round hand sloping to the left (or backwards), and thus precisely agrees with the current hand used in Malabar proper, and which was imitated in the types cut to print Spring's Grammar in 1836. The modern types vary considerably. The Travancore hand is more angular [2].

The Sanskrit MSS. in this character (inscriptions there are none to my knowledge) present a peculiarity which deserves notice—the substitution of l and ḷ for a final t or ṭ, when these letters *unchanged* precede other consonants, or are final. Thus for tatkâla we find താൽകാല (talkâla), and for tasmât തസ്മാൽ (tasmâl). This practice is totally wrong according to all authorities, and probably arises out of the tendency of the people of Malabar to slur over all surd consonants [3].

Apart from this singular practice, the Sanskrit MSS. from Malabar are among the best that can be had in India. Up to quite recent times the study of Sanskrit literature, and especially of the mathematical and astrological treatises, appears to have been followed in Malabar with more living interest than anywhere else in the South.

It is hardly necessary to remark that the Ārya-eḻuttu or modern Malayâḷam alphabet is necessarily affected by the old Tamiḻ orthography as far as it is applied to the writing of Dravidian words. So in a Malayâḷam sentence ത, except if initial, should be pronounced δ in a Malayâḷam word, but t in one that is Sanskrit; ഗ should also be pronounced γ and g in the same circumstances. This however, is but little observed, and Sanskrit words are commonly Dravidianized.

The Tamiḻ and Canarese Grammars give rules for Dravidianizing Sanskrit words [4], but the subject deserves more attention than has yet been paid to it. These influences unquestionably affect the orthography of Sanskrit MSS. written in S. India.

D. *Grantha-Tamiḻ.* (*Plates* xvi. *and* xxx.)

The earliest inscriptions in which this character occurs are of the tenth century, and belong to the earlier kings of the revived Côḷa kingdom; they are at Conjeveram and in the neighbourhood

1) This is preserved at Puḷakkale a village in the Cittûr Tâlûk of the Cochin territory, and not far to the south of Palghat (Pâlakkâḍu). The MS. was much broken and injured by damp when I saw it in 1865. The author's stool, clogs and staff are preserved in the same place; it thus looks as if Tuṅjatta Eḻuttaččhan was a sannyâsi of some order.

2) There are some MSS. in this hand, among those I presented to the India Office Library in 1870; including one of the Mâdhavîya Dhâtuvṛitti. The types used to print books at Trevandrum follow this model. The first printed specimen of the ârya-eḻuttu that I know of is in the preface of vol. i. of Rheede's "Hortus Malabaricus". The complete alphabet was printed by the Propaganda at Rome in 1772, 8°. "Alphabetum Grandonico Malabaricum."

3) P. Paulinus a St. Bartholemeo followed this practice in his "Vyacaranam." (Sanskrit Grammar), and was in consequence ridiculed, but most unjustly, by Leyden and the Calcutta Sanskrit scholars of the last century.

4) Nannûl, iii. sûtras 19—21. "Çabdamaṇidarpaṇa" pp. 46, ffg. cfr. also the introduction to the excellent Tamiḻ-French Dictionary, published at Pondichery (in 2 Vols. 8vo.) "par deux Missionnaires Apostoliques."

of Madras and the Kâverî delta. South of Tanjore, there are few old inscriptions in this character[1].

The origin of this Tamiḻ alphabet is apparent at first sight; it is a brahmanical adaptation of the Grantha letters corresponding to the old Vaṭṭeḻuttu, from which, however, the last four signs (ḻ, ḷ, ṟ and ṉ) have been retained, the Grantha not possessing equivalents The form of *m* is also rather Vaṭṭeḻuttu than Grantha. Çaṅkarâcârya is said to have preached with much success in the Côḷa kingdom; that it was the seat of a great brahmanical mission in the tenth century is shown by the inscriptions. This alphabet, accordingly, represents the later brahmanical Tamiḻ culture as opposed to the older culture of the Jains of Madura.

Inscriptions in this character abound in all the Northern Tamiḻ country, where there is scarcely a temple of any note which has not acres of wall covered in this way. I need only mention the great temples of Conjeveram and Tanjore. It is, however, very unusual to find any with dates that can be identified, most being only in the year (âṇḍu) of the king's reign (or life?), and genealogical details being very rarely given in them. As the list of the Côḷa and Pâṇḍya kings is quite uncertain, it is thus impossible to procure a series of palæographical standards, and I, therefore, give only two specimens. These will show how very little alteration and development occurred between 1073 and 1600 A. D. The greatest development has occurred in this century owing to the increased use of writing, and to the arbitrary alterations of the type founders[2].

The Grantha-Tamiḻ differs from the Grantha-alphabet in precisely the same way as the Vaṭṭeḻuttu, as far as the reduplication of consonants and the expression of the absence of the inherent vowel (virâma) are concerned. The puḷḷi or dot above the consonant which serves the purpose of the virâma, does not occur in any of the inscriptions I have seen, and it is omitted in the earliest printed books[3]. The famous Jesuit Beschi (1704-174) is the author of a great improvement in Tamiḻ orthography—the distinction between the long and short e and o. This he effected by curving the top of the ெ - used to express the short e, thus ே, and the same sign serves (in the compound for o) to express the long ô[4]. Before then, he states, the short a and o were *occasionally* distinguished by a stroke (the Sanskrit prosodial mark) above them.

The angular form of this Tamiḻ character is owing to a wide spread practice in the South of

1) The old Grantha-Tamiḻ alphabet was given by Babington in Pl. xiii. of vol. ii. of the Transactions of the Royal As. Society of London; he apparently took it from the inscription of *S*âlva*n*kuppam, which is probably of the year 1038 A. D. I have examined this inscription which is very roughly cut, and therefore preferred that at Tanjore which is of various dates from 1073 A. D. to 1089. It includes a large number of grants with many clauses in each. The whole was photographed by Capt. Tripe in 1859 and published by the Madras Government.

2) The first edition of the N. T. in Tamiḻ (4°. Tranquebar, 1714) is printed with type that exactly reproduces the character of the Tamiḻ inscriptions of the fifteenth and sixteenth centuries.

3) It appears to have been known to the Tamiḻ grammarians.

4) "Grammatica Latino-Tamulica, in quâ de vulgari Tamulica lingua" etc. (Tranquebar, 1739 12°). — longis (e et o) nullo notatis signo brevibus superscribendum docent illud signum (-). Attamen nullibi hæc signa praterquam paucis aliquot dictionibus ex inertia fortasse amanuensium superscribi vidi unquam......... addo excogitasse me alium et faciliorem modum distinguendi e et o longa a brevibus: scilicet, cum utrique inserviat littera ெ *combu* dicta; si hæc simplici formâ scribatur, erit e breve et o breve: si autem inflectetur in partem superiorem, ut infra dicam de î longo, sic ே, e at o erunt longa."

India, of writing with the style resting on the *end* of the left thumb nail; in Malabar and the Telugu country the roundness of the letters is to be attributed to the practice of resting the style on the left *side* of the same thumb.

The map shows a great extension of the Grantha Tami̱ḻ alphabet to the North extending over the deltas of the Kṛishṇâ and Godâvarî; this occurred under the Côḻa rule in the eleventh and twelfth centuries. Inscriptions in Tami̱ḻ and in the form of character given in pl. xvi. still exist (or existed till lately) in some of the islands of the Godâvarî delta, and the village accountants were originally all Tami̱ḻ Brahmans. The ritual of many temples was also in this language. This however did not continue long, and in the beginning of the fourteenth century, Telugu inscriptions and grants only appear [1].

§ 3. THE VAṬṬEḺUTTU (*Plates* xv. *and* xxix.)

This is the original Tami̱ḻ alphabet which was once used in all that part of the Peninsula south of Tanjore, and also in S. Malabar and Travancore where it still exists though in exceedingly limited use, and in a modern form. It may, therefore, be termed the Pâṇḍyan character, as its use extended over the whole of that kingdom at its best period; it appears also to have been in use in the small extent of country below the ghats (South-Malabar and Coimbatore of the present day) which belonged to the Cêra kingdom. As it was only gradually supplanted by the modern Tami̱ḻ character beginning about the eleventh century under the Côḻas, it is, therefore, certain that the Tôlkâppiyam, Nannûl, Kuṟal and all the other early Tami̱ḻ works were written in it, under the most flourishing period of the "Pâṇḍya" (or Madura) kingdom, or before the tenth century when it finally fell under the Côḻas[2].

But though it is certain that the beginning of the Tami̱ḻ literature may be safely put about the ninth century, there is nothing to show that there was in any way a literature before that time. The legend of Agastya's settlement in the south is, of course, historically worthless, and though the Pâṇḍya kingdom is undoubtedly one of the three old Dravidian kingdoms[3], we have nothing about its condition till Hiouen-Thsang's visit to the Peninsula about 640 A. D. He says of the inhabitants of Mo-lo-kiu-tch'a (Malai-kkoṭa?): "Ils ne font aucun cas de la culture des lettres, et n'estiment que la poursuite du lucre"[4]. He mentions the *Nirgranthas* or Digambara

1) This remarkable extension of Tami̱ḻ to the north was first pointed out by F. W. Ellis; I was able to verify it for myself in the Nellore province.

2) Caldwell, "Comparative Grammar" pp. 56, 85-88.

3) It is mentioned in the Açoka inscriptions (250 B. C.) by Ptolemy (vii., 1, 11. vol. ii. p. 143. ed. Nobbe) in the second century A. D. and by the Periplus in the third century A. D. The Mahavamso (ed. Turnour) makes Vijayo (543 B. C.!) marry the daughter of the king of Dakkhina Madhura called "Panduwo" (p. 51), I do not find any subsequent mention of the Pâṇḍyas in this very monkish choronicle. I put the date of the Periplus at the third century A. D. following Reinaud.

4) "Voyages des Pèlerins Bouddhistes" iii. p. 121.

Jains (ascetics)[1] as the most prominent sect in the South, and this corresponds with the actual remains of the early Tamiḻ literature which are in fact Jain, but he would have hardly said what he does if the grammars and the Kuṟal then existed. The earliest apparent or probable mention of writing in S. India is the passage in the Periplus of the Red Sea which describes Cape Comorin. Among other facts the author mentions that "it is related (historeîtai) that a goddess bathes there". Considering that this journal was composed in the third century, and that, therefore, the Greek is very late, it is quite possible that this word 'historeîtai' may mean that the legend was written, and the earlier editors and translators of the text took it in this sense[2], but the passage is by no means beyond doubt in this respect[3]. The earliest Tamiḻ Grammar by Aɣattiyan (Agastya) clearly refers to writing if we may trust a quotation (preserved by a commentary on the Nannûl) which compares the relation between a letter and the sound it stands for, with the relation of an idol to the deity it represents. The age of this is unknown.

The Vaṭṭeḻuttu was gradually supplanted by the Modern Tamiḻ after the conquest of Madura by the Côḷas (ninth century), and it appears to have entirely gone out of use in the Tamiḻ country by the fifteenth century. In Malabar it remained in general use up to the end of the seventeenth century among the Hindus, and since then, in the form of the Kôleḻuttu, it is the character in which the Hindu sovereigns have their grants drawn up. The Mâppiḷas of the neighbourhood of Tellicherry and in the Islands used this character till quite recently; it is now being superseded by the modified Arabic character which has religious prestige on its side[4].

1) I proposed the identification of the Nirgranthas with the Jains (in I. A. i., p. 310, *n.*) on the ground that in the Jain Aṭṭhapâhuḍaka (*i. e.* Ashṭaprâbh*r*itaka) Nirgrantha is constantly used as an epithet of the true Jains, and that, therefore, it could not be referred to the Brahmans as had always been done hitherto, and also on the ground of probability, as *e.g.* Hiouen-Thsang's account of the Nirgranthas is much more likely of Jains than of Brahmans; but I have since got additional information which makes my identification certain and can leave no doubt that Jain ascetics are intended by the word 'ṇiggantha' (nirgrantha), though the word is now not understood by the Jains. Thus in the Digambara cosmogony called 'Trilokasâra' the gâthas 848-850 describe the persecution of some Jain ascetics by Kalki (a king said to have lived 394 years after the Çakarâja). These run:

848. So ummaggâhimuho čaümuho sadadivâsaparamâü čâlîsarajjao jidabhûmi pučhaï samattigaṇa*m* ।

C. Sa Kalkî unmârgâbhimukhaç čaturmukhâkhya*h* saptativarshaparamâyushyaç čatvâri*m*çadvarsharâjyo jitabhûmi*h* san svamantrigaṇa*m* pričchati.

849. A*m*hâṇa*m* ke avasâ? ṇigganthâ atthi! kīdisâyârâ? ṇiddanavatthâ bhikkhabhoji jahâsattham idi vayaṇe ।

C. Asmâka*m* ke avaçâ? iti. mantriṇa*h* kathayanti: nirgranthâ*h* santî 'ti. puna*h* p*r*ičchati: kîd*r*içâkârâ? iti. nirdhanavastrâ yathâçâstra*m* bhixâbhojina*h* iti mantriṇa*h* pṛativacana*m* çrutvâ—

850. Ta*m* pâṇiüḍe ṇipaḍitapathamappiṇḍa*m* tu sukka*m* idi geya*m* ṇiyame sa jîvakade čattâhârâ gayâ muṇiṇo ।

C. Teshâ*m* nirgranthâṇâm pâṇipuṭanipatita*m* prathamapiṇḍa*m* çulkam iti grâhyam iti râjňo niyamena jîvena k*r*itena tyaktâhârâ*h* santo munayo gatâ*h*.

Further proof will no doubt, also be given by Dr. Bühler in the results of his researches on the Jains of Western India.

2) See the edition in Hudson's "Geographi Græci Minores" Vol. i. p. 33, where the passage is translated: "Literis enim memoriaeque proditum est deam olim singulis mensibus ibi lavari fuisse solitam". The latest and more critical editor (C. Müller) has on the other hand: "Dea aliquando ibi commorata et lavata esse perhibetur." ("Geographi Græci Minores," p. 300 of vol. i. of Didot's Edition). It is therefore uncertain.

3) I pass over the statement of Iambulus ("Diodorus Siculus," ed. Dindorf, ii. 59 in vol. i. p. 222) as it is impossibie to explain it by any Indian alphabet as yet known.

4) See No. ii. of my "Specimens of South Indian Dialects".

The ultimate origin of the Vaṭṭeḻuttu is again a difficult problem in Indian Palæography. In the eighth century it existed side by side and together with the Grantha[1]; it is, therefore, impossible to suppose that the Vaṭṭeḻuttu is derived from the S. Açoka character, even if the conclusive argument of the dissimilarity between the phonetic values of many of the corresponding letters be neglected[2]. Again the S. Açoka character would have furnished a more complete representation of the Tamiḻ phonetic system than either the Vaṭṭeḻuttu or the modern (Grantha) Tamiḻ alphabet does[3]; it must, therefore, follow that the alphabet was formed and settled before the Sanskrit Grammarians came to Southern India, or we should find as accurate a representation as they effected for Telugu and Canarese. The Tamiḻ grammarians, however, evidently found the language already written when they began their labours, and thus this part of their grammars is comparatively imperfect[4]. Again as the Vaṭṭeḻuttu is an imperfect, alphabet it cannot be the origin of the S. Açoka character; for, if it were, the evidence of the extension and adaptation must be far greater than it is. It is plain that many of the aspirated letters in the S. Açoka character are formed from the corresponding unaspirated letters, but if that alphabet were formed from the Vaṭṭeḻuttu, it would have shown traces of a similar formation in the letters g, j, ḍ, d and h for which there are no forms in the Vaṭṭeḻuttu. But these letters appear to be primitive in the S. Açoka character. The only possible conclusion, therefore, is that the S. Açoka and Vaṭṭeḻuttu alphabets are independent adaptations of some foreign character, the first to a Sanskritic, the last to a Dravidian language. There are, however, resemblances between the two that point to a common Semitic origin; and these extend perhaps to two-thirds of the Vaṭṭeḻuttu letters; the others differ totally, yet several of these sounds (ḷ, ḻ, ṟ) exist in the other Dravidian languages, and distinct letters have been invented to express them. Thus the Tamiḻ Malayâḷam ḻ is expressed by ழ, the Canarese identical letter by ೞ. Again the Telugu-Canarese ṟ is expressed by ఱ, whereas the same letter in Tamiḻ is written ற, so the Telugu-Canarese and Tamiḻ ḷ which are identical in sound are written quite differently. There is also a peculiarity in the popular Tamiḻ way of naming the letters; in Sanskrit (excepting repha = r) names of letters are formed by adding -kâra to the letter in question; in Tamiḻ -na is affixed to short and -vêna to long syllables, every consonant being named with some vowel following it[5]. It is thus evident that the Vaṭṭeḻuttu differs greatly from the

1) Cfr. the grants to the Israelite and Christian communities in Travancore.

2) See Appendix A. 3) Do.

4) The Telugu and Canarese Grammars explain the respective phonetic systems by a steady reference to that of Sanskrit; the Tamiḻ Grammars do not refer to the Sanskrit at all in this way. I have already (p. 37) mentioned that the Grantha or Modern Tamiḻ alphabet has copied the Vaṭṭeḻuttu in some respects.

5) The order I have given to the Vaṭṭeḻuttu corresponds with that of the Tamiḻ alphabet, and is that of the Sanskritizing Grammarians. There is, however, a sûtra in the Nannûl which appears to me to indicate that this was not the case when the Grammarians began their labours. It runs: *S*iṟappiṇum iṇattiṇum šerinδ'îṇḍ' ammuδa ṇaḍattaṟâṇê muṟaiy âγum" (ii., 18). *i. e.* "The series of letters beginning with 'a' (and) arranged according to their priority and relationship, is *here* their order". îṇḍu=here (atra), *i. e.* in this Grammar. If this order were the usual one, this explanation would have been unnecessary: I am unable to find any trace of this other arrangement of the Tamiḻ alphabet. The Kuṟal (i., 1) mentions 'a' as the first letter. The Nannûl (ii., 71) directs -akaram for the names of consonants, -karam for short vowels, -kân for the foreign ai and au, and -kâram for the long vowels etc. This is clearly an imitation of the Sanskrit. Again the same work (ii., 43) mentions the tollai vaḍivu or 'old forms' of the letters.

Canarese and Telugu alphabets, but if one compares the forms of î, k, t, r, and even a and â, in both, it is hardly possible to avoid the conclusion that they are derived from the same source. That an alphabet should have been imported independently into Northern India (probably Gujarat) and also into the Tamiḻ country much about the same time seems strange, but it is nevertheless most likely, considering the circumstances of foreign trade with India as reported by the classical authors. The Periplus, for example, mentions a large trade with Ārikê *i. e.* Bombay and the country of the Prakrit-speaking peoples; there is then a gap, and again large trade with Dimurikê. Now this is simply the Western Tamiḻ country or Malabar [1], and between the two provinces there was the Pirate Coast which preserved its evil name till within recollection of many. There would be no trade there, and the Western and S. Western Coast would thus be in fact distinct countries. Again there could not have been any communication by land, for Fa-hian (400 A. D.) mentions the Deccan as uncivilized and inaccessible; it is, therefore, more likely that the S. Açoka character and the Vaṭṭeḻuttu are totally distinct importations, than derived the one from the other.

What was this source? There is quite as much reason for supposing a Semitic original in this case, as in that of the S. Açoka character, resemblances to some of the Phœnician and Aramaic letters being equally apparent in both [2]. Of all the probable primitive alphabets with which a comparison of the Vaṭṭeḻuttu is possible, it appears to me that the Sassanian of the inscriptions presents most points of resemblance [3]. The number of letters also in both, narrowly agree. At present the difficulty is to find certain and dated examples of the Aramaic character used in the early centuries B. C. and also similar specimens of the Vaṭṭeḻuttu; there is also the difficulty of deciding which of the many derivatives from the Phœnician alphabet but of which it is possible the Indian alphabets may have been formed, was actually used for this purpose.

Another remarkable feature in the Vaṭṭeḻuttu is the system of marking the secondary vowels. This is intermediate between the systems of the Northern and the Southern Açoka alphabets and thus connects both. I was led by this striking fact to suggest in an article on the

1) The Periplus and Ptolemy have Limurikê, but as the Peutingerian Table, the Ravenna Geographer and Guido have Dimirice, there can be no doubt that the copyists have mistaken *d* for *l*, an exceedingly easy error in Greek. Dimurikê is thus Tamiḻ + ikê; now Malayâḷam was called Tamiḻ formerly, and at the time of the classical writers the languages in no way differed. It is thus impossible to identify Dimurikê with Canara, (as was done by Vincent* following Rennell for quite illusive reasons), but it must be taken to mean S. Malabar, and the three great ports Tundis, Mouziris and Nelkunda (Nincylda) are Kaḍal(t)uṇḍi (near Beypore), Muyîrikkôḍu (Kishankoṭṭa part of Cranganore) and Kallaḍa (inland from Quilon up a large river). The Vaṭṭeḻuttu must, therefore, have been imported at one of these places. The reasons for this new identification would take too much space here, and must be given elsewhere.

2) I must, however, point out that Profr. Max Müller is not satisfied in respect of the S. Açoka character (Sanskrit Gr. p. 3). He quotes Prinsep's "Essays" by Thomas, ii., p. 42.

3) The development of the Pahlavî from the early Aramaic character is traced by M. F. Lenormant in the "Journal Asiatique" for August and September 1865 (pp. 180-226). The resemblance between some of the Vaṭṭeḻuttu letters and the corresponding Proto- and Persepolitan Pahlavî forms (as given by M. Lenormant) is very striking. cfr. a; Pahlavî d with t; î; l (r); m; n; p; k; s with *s* etc.

* "Commerce and Navigation of the Indian Ocean", ii. p. 456.

Vaṭṭeḻuttu [1] to suggest that the Northern alphabets had, in this respect, copied from it. At present it appears to me that it is best to consider the Açoka alphabets and the Vaṭṭeḻuttu as independent; the evidence afforded by the few facts that are satisfactorily known in respect of these characters is too imperfect to allow of more precise conclusions being drawn. Vaṭṭeḻuttu is the modern Malayâḷam name of this character, and means 'round hand' apparently to distinguish it from the Kôleḻuttu or 'sceptre hand'; it appears to be the best name for this alphabet as it prevents all confusion with the modern Tamiḻ.

§ 4. THE SOUTH-INDIAN NĀGARĪ ALPHABETS.

(*Plates* xvii., xviii., xxvii. *and* xxviii.)

The South-Indian form of the Devanâgarî character usually goes by the name of *Nandinâgarî*, a name it is quite as difficult to account for, as that of its source the Devanâgarî[2]. The Nandinâgarî is directly derived from the N. Indian Devanâgarî of about the eleventh century, but it is from the type that prevailed at Benares and in the West, and not from the Gauḍî or Bengâlî. This last is chiefly distinguished from the other types by the way of marking the secondary e and o, which is done by a perpendicular stroke before the consonant in the case of e, and by a similar stroke before and another after the consonant in the case of o, and this is, very nearly, the actual Bengâlî system. The other type marks these vowels in the same way as is done by the ordinary Nâgarî alphabet. Thus the S. Indian Nandinâgarî is derived from the *Siddhamâtraka* character used,

1) In the *Indian Antiquary* Vol. i., p. ffg. This article is, I believe, the first to call attention to this alphabet. Specimens of the character occur in the preface to Rheede's "Hortus Malabaricus" (1678), and in Fryer's "New Account" (1698) p. 33. The author gives it as Telugu, but the specimen on p. 52 is Telugu and not Malabar (Tamiḻ) as he states; he has made a mistake between them.

2) The word Nâga(rî') first occurs, it seems, as the name of an alphabet in the *Lalitavistara*, a life of Buddha that is in its original form perhaps two thousand years old; but as it exists in Sanskrit and Tibetan it would be very unsafe to put it at an earlier date than about the seventh century A. D. The Tibetan version (of which Profr. Foucaux has published a most excellent edition and translation) was made in the ninth century by three natives of India named Jinamitra, Dânaçîla and Munivarmâ with the assistance of a Tibetan Lotsava named Bande Ye-śes-sdes; this fact is stated in the Tibetan index to the great collection called Bkah-hgyur (Kandjur) in the description of the work in question (Rgya-tcher-rol-pa *i. e.* Lalitavistara), and is to be found on p. 16 (No. 95) of this index as reprinted at St. Petersburg. Nâga(rî) occurs as the name of an alphabet in ch. x. (v. p. 113 of vol. i. of Profr. Foucaux's edition) which describes how the young prince, afterwards known as Buddha, was taken to a school and completely posed the pædagogue. Sixty-four alphabets are mentioned some of which are, no doubt, mythical, but others are real (*e g.* Drâviḍa, Aṅga and Baṅga), though it is against all the evidence of the inscriptions that they existed as distinct alphabets before the ninth or tenth century A. D. If therefore the framework of the Lalitavistara be old, this passage is certainly an interpolation, though very valuable evidence regarding the ninth century A. D. But this Tibetan version by no means bears out the meaning usually assigned to the word Devanâgarî—"nâgarî of the Gods or Brahmans", nâgarî being usually referred to *nagara* and being supposed to mean 'writing used in cities'. The Tibetan text has here the ordinary name (in that language) of the Devanâgarî character—"klu-'i yi-ge" (as a translation of the Sanskrit 'nâga-lipi') and this is also literally "writing of the nâgas". It is evident, therefore, what the natives of India understood nâgalipi or nâgarî to mean in the ninth century A. D., and it only remains to be seen if this derivation is possible. I think this question must be answered in the affirmative, as not only Prakrit but also Sanskrit words exist which are formed in the same way. There is yet another possible explanation of 'nâgarî'—that it means the writing of the Nâgara or Gujarat Brahmans. (Cfr. 'nâgara' in Molesworth's Mahr. Dy.).

according to Albirûnî (1031 A.D.) in Benares, the Madhyadeça and Cashmere. It now differs greatly from that type or from the N. Indian Devanâgarî, and is remarkably illegible; but this deterioration took place very slowly, and is unquestionable owing to the practice of writing on palm-leaves. The Nâgarî inscriptions in S. India are all, with one exception, subsequent to the tenth century; this exception is at Seven Pagodas in the temple of Atiraṇacaṇḍeçvara near *S*alavâ*n*kappam, and is in nearly the same character as a dated inscription of the seventh century found near Nâgpur and published in the Bombay Journal[1]. As this inscription is given in two different characters, this must have been done for the benefit of pilgrims from the North. It has already been published[2].

In the Deccan, Devanâgarî inscriptions begin to appear during the temporary fall of the Kalyâṇa Câlukyas[3] and this character appears to have been almost exclusively used by the revolted feudatories[4]. On the revival of the original dynasty the use of this character continued, as the sovereigns betrayed a great partiality to N. Indian literary men. There is not, apparently, the least trace of any patronage bestowed by them or by their successors the Yâdavas of Devagiri[5] on vernacular culture.

The Muhammadan invasion of the Deccan in 1311, and the destruction of the old kingdoms, brought about the establishment of the Vijayanagara dynasty, under which not only the Sanskrit,

1) Vol. I. pp. 148 ffg.

2) "Transactions of the R. As. Society", II., pl. 15 (in Dr. Babington's Paper on Seven Pagodas). For the position of the place see the map in Madras Journal, xiii., and in Major Carr's reprint of papers on this subject. I had this little temple cleared of sand in 1867, and took copies of the inscriptions which I gave Major Carr.

3) For a specimen see the grant under Akâlavarsha d. ç, 867 (=945 A. D.) in the I. A. i. pp. 205 ffg.

4) The chief of these feudatories (often independent) are as follows:

i. Râshṭrakûṭa. General remarks on, and genealogy of this dynasty occur in *Bombay Journal*, i., p. 211 and iii., p. 98 "*Indian Antiquary*, i., pp. 207-9. For inscriptions see *As. J.* v., (*d.* 973 A. D.) *Bombay Journal*, i., pp. 209-224 (*d.* ç. 930 = 1008 A. D. in Devanâgarî); ii., p. 272, *n.* pp. 371-6 (*d.* ç. 675 = 753 A. D. also Dev. ! ?); iv., pp. 100-4 (*d.* ç. 855 = A. D. 933 also in Dev.) Râshṭra seems to be merely a brahmanical perversion of the Telugu "Reḍḍi".

ii. Kâlacurya or Kâlabhurya. It is uncertain which spelling is correct, and I have no means of attempting to decide it. Up to about 1000 A. D. č and bh much resembled each other.

Madras Journal ("Hindu Inscriptions" by Sir W. Elliot) vii., pp. 197, 211-21, and 224-225.

The most important of the three kings whose names occur is Vijjaladeva the first; he conquered Tailapa ii. (of Kalyâṇapura) and during his reign (1156-1165) the revolt of Basava and the Lin*g*âyats broke out which cost him eventually his throne and life.

iii. Kadamba (neighbourhood of Goa). Probably an old branch of the Câlukyas. "Notes on Sanskrit copper-plates found in the Belgaum collectorate" by J. F. Fleet (*Bombay Journal*, ix., pp. 231-246). "Some further inscriptions relating to the Kadamba kings of Goa" by the same (do. pp. 262-309). See also Sir W. Elliot's article in *Madras Journal*, vii., pp. 226-9.

The new dynasties which replaced the older Câlukyas in the Deccan from the 13th to the 14th centuries are:

i. Devagiri Yâdavas. See Lassen (I. A—K. IV. pp. 945-6).

ii. Dvârasamudra Yâdavas. (do. IV. pp. 972-3).

iii. Orukkal (Warangal). From the thirteenth century to 1311.

I have not been able to find any inscriptions of this dynasty.

iv. Vijayanagara; from about 1320 to 1564. In Tanjore up to 1674-5.

For the earlier kings see my Va*m*çabrâhmaṇa (pref. p. xvi., *n.*), and for the later Lassen's I. A—K. IV. (pp. 975-8.)

5) The well known law-book the Mitâxarâ was composed in the reign of Vikramâditya V. (1076-1127), but it is not known of what country the author was a native (*Bombay Journal* ix., pp. 134-8). The Vidyâpati of this king was a Cashmere Brahman named Bilhaṇa. (See letter from Dr. Bühler in I. A. iii., p. 89.)

but also the Vernacular literatures were much cultivated. The early inscriptions of this dynasty are either in the Haḷa-kannaḍa or Nandi-nâgarî character; the latest (of the 15th and 16th centuries) are almost exclusively in the last. They constitute by far the largest class of S. Indian inscriptions, for the sovereigns of this dynasty at the end of the 15th and beginning of the 16th century repaired or endowed most of the large temples in the South [1].

The S. Indian Nandinâgarî alphabet calls for very little remark as from the earliest examples of the fourteenth century up to 1600 A. D. there is scarcely any development. It is certainly one of the most illegible characters in use in all India.

MSS. in this character are not uncommon, as it is the favorite alphabet of the Mâdhva sect, which counts an immense number of adherents in S. India especially in Mysore, the neighbourhood of Conjeveram, and Tanjore. All members of this sect are Brahmans, and all learn more or less of the books on their dogmas written by Ānandatîrtha (Madhvâcârya) and his successors. The Nandinâgarî is used exclusively for writing on palm-leaves; for writing on paper, the ordinary Mahraṭha hand of Devanâgarî is used, and the writing is often exceedingly minute. All the inscriptions on copper-plates, and MSS. on palm-leaves that I have seen are numbered with the ordinary Telugu-Canarese numerals.

The modern Nâgarî (or Bâlbodh) character was introduced into S. India by the Mahraṭha conquest of Tanjore in the latter part of the seventeenth century [2], and was chiefly used in Tanjore, where it is still current among the numerous descendants of the Deccan Brahmans attracted there by the liberality of the Mahraṭha princes.

NOTE.

S. India had long been frequented by foreigners before the Europeans effected settlement there in the sixteenth and seventeenth centuries. Some of those early colonies still subsist, but the people while retaining more or less of their nationality have, however, lost the colloquial use of their own original tongues, and adopted S. Indian vernaculars which now are generally written with foreign characters. The most important of these foreign colonists are:—

A. *Arabs.*

The descendants of the early Arab colonists though very numerous in S. India are perhaps not in any case of pure descent. In Malabar and the south-west they are called 'Mâppiḷa'; in the east (or Tamiḻ country) their name is 'Labbai' or 'Lebbai'. There does not appear to be any

1) Many examples are already published. Bengal As. S. Transactions, iii., pp. 39 ffg.; also in vol. xx. Colebrooke's "Essays" ii., pp. 254-267. "*Indian Antiquary*", ii., p. 371.

2) The date of the conquest of Tanjore by Ekoji, and the end of the Nâyak (Telugu) princes is far from certain. Orme in the last century could not be sure about the date, though he had all the Madras Government records at his disposal. Anquetil Du Perron ("Recherches sur l' Inde", I. pp. 1-64) has gone into the question very elaborately, and puts the date at 1674-5, which appears to be as near as can be expected.

trace in the Telugu country of a similar race. True Muhammadans they are[1], but few have any knowledge of Arabic; their books and letters are now written in Malayâḷam or Tamiḻ with a modified Arabic character. This has, however, been introduced only in recent times. I have given an account of the system already elsewhere[2].

B. *Persians and Syrians.*

The earliest Christian settlements in S. India were Persian, and a few inscriptions in Pahlavî still remain which belong to that period[3]. They were, however, supplanted by the so-called Syrians who are now in appearance exactly like all the other inhabitants of Malabar, and use Malayâḷam as their language; this they often write with Syriac (Karshuni) letters to which they have added from the Malayâḷam 'Ārya' character the letters deficient in the former. Syriac is merely used in the churches, though apparently it is pretty generally understood by the more intelligent members of the community. A few tombstones and similar relics in Travancore show that the Syriac-Malayâḷam alphabet is of recent introduction, and that the Syrians originally used only the Vaṭṭeḻuttu character. Buchanan[4] mentions bells with inscriptions in Syriac and Malayâḷam, but I have not seen or heard of any.

As both these alphabets belong (as far as my information extends), to recent times, it is useless to do more than mention them here.

1) They all affect the S. Arabian costume especially the 'Qalansuwah' (a stiff cap of variegated silk or cotton. See Dozy's "Dictionnaire des noms des vêtements chez les Arabes". pp. 365-371) if they can afford it. The *Muhammadan* Arabs appear to have settled first in Malabar about the beginning of the ninth century; there were heathen Arabs there long before that in consequence of the immense trade conducted by the Sabeans with India according to Agatharchides.

2) "Specimens of Indian Dialects", No. ii.

3) Cfr. my paper "On some Pahlavî Inscriptions in S. India" (4° Mangalore 1873). The most important of these inscriptions is the miracle-working cross (or tombstone) of St. Thomas, at the Mount near Madras.

3) Z. d. D. M. G. xxii., p. 548 (from Land's "Anecdota") copied in Lenormant's "Essai sur la propagation de l' alphabet Phénicien" ii. pp. 24-5 (pl. vi.)

4) "Christian Researsches" p. 112.

CHAPTER III.

THE SOUTH INDIAN NUMERALS.

(*Plate* xix.)

THE history of the numerals used in India is of the last importance, as on it, probably, depends the solution of a very important question—the origin of the decimal system of notation by which the value of the numbers depends on position and which also involves the use of the cipher. The facts furnished by the S. Indian inscriptions unfortunately are of little more value than to throw doubts on the speculative conclusions arrived at by Woepcke originally[1], but which are now commonly asserted in popular manuals[2]. These are: the early Indian numeral signs and cipher are derived from the initial letters of the words denoting the same; that these numeral-figures were brought to Europe by two distinct courses—firstly, about the early centuries of our era by Neo-Pythagoreans through the intercourse between Alexandria and India; and secondly, by the Arabs, who adopted them about the ninth century[3]. The last proposition is the only one of the three which rests on historical evidence; the rest are inferences drawn by Woepcke with strong probability, and have been so far accepted by the most eminent Indianists[4]. Whether the inscriptions that have been discovered since these conclusions were arrived at, as well as some facts as yet unnoticed, do or do not support them, is now a matter for serious enquiry.

The earliest known example of an Indian numeral-figure occurs in the Kapur-di-giri inscription which has already been mentioned, and which belongs to the middle of the third century B. C.

---

1) Woepcke, "Mémoire sur la propagation des chiffres Indiens" (separate impression, 1863) pp. 2-3. The author mentions the imperfect evidence, and then asks if all attempt to draw conclusions must be abandoned. His own opinion he states as follows: "Je ne le pense pas, pourvu qu'en tâchant de construire un ensemble, on fasse consciencieusement connaître les parties conjecturales pour les distinguer d'avec les parties certaines, et pourvu que l'on ne présente les explications hypothétiques auxquelles on est obligé de recourir que comme la résultante la plus probable des faits connus dans le moment; pourvu en fin que l'on soit toujours prêt à modifier ses conclusions dans le cas où le découverte de documents nouveaux en rendrait la nécessité évidente." It appears to me that the explanation of the cave numerals, and the ascertainment of the complete series of units, as well (as I shall show) that these numerals were used over greater part of S. India, now warrant a different conclusion to that of Woepcke as regards the origin of the current figures.

2) A. Braun (Die Ergebnisse der Sprachwissenschaft p. 26.) says: Dass einige dieser Ziffern eine grosse Aehnlichkeit mit den unsrigen haben, sieht man sofort. In der That verdienen unsere Zahlzeichen es eigentlich auch nicht, arabische genannt zu werden, denn sie stammen ursprünglich aus Indien; die Araber waren nur die Ueberbringer, nicht die Erfinder derselben".

3) For the first proposition see pp. 44-52 of Woepcke's "Mémoire"; for the second, pp. 123-6; as regards the third, the Indian Embassy to Al-Mançur was in 773 A. D.

4) Max Müller, "Sanskrit Gr." p. 9 (2nd ed.); "Chips from a German Workshop," ii., p. 295. Also by Profr. Benfey in his "Geschichte d. sprachwissenschaft" p. 802.

In it the number 'four' is expressed by four upright lines, thus IIII.[1] Later inscriptions in the same character furnish other examples; the most important is one from Taxila, which is of the first century B. C. and in which the number 78 is expressed by $3 \times 20 + 1 \times 10 + 2 \times 4$; the figures for 20, 10 and 4 being distinct signs. The figures for four in these two inscriptions (IIII & +) show a considerable development between the third and first centuries B. C. It is therefore, certain that the method of denoting numerals which prevailed in the early centuries B. C. in the Panjab and Ariana began with the use of strokes equal to the number to be expressed, and that this primitive system had, by no means, become perfect in the first century B. C.

The Southern Açoka inscriptions which, as I have already said, are alone of importance for South-Indian palæography, do not contain any numeral signs, but there are inscriptions from Mathura, which are in nearly the same character, belonging to the first or second century A. D. *probably*, which show a well-developed system entirely distinct from that which is found in the Arianic inscription of Taxila of about the same date. In this the first three numerals are expressed by one, two and three horizontal strokes, the rest (four, etc.) have distinct figures, and there is a distinct figure for each of the orders of numbers (ten, twenty, etc.) up to one hundred which has, as well as one thousand, a sign to itself. The intermediate units are expressed by simply adding their signs; for example, twenty-five is expressed by the sign for twenty, followed by that for five. There is not the least trace of the use of the cipher in this system. It is obviously an independant and ingenious development of much the same elements as were used in the Arianic system, but far more perfect. It is quite impossible to derive these signs from the initial letters of the words for the numbers, as they bear no resemblance at all to the Southern-Açoka letters which begin the corresponding words, nor excepting the signs for eight and nine do they bear any resemblance to the same letters in the Kapur-di-giri character; and the likeness in both these cases is very superficial. This system of numerals was used in the cave inscriptions of Western India, and in many other parts of India during several centuries. The latest inscription in N. India appears to be dated 385 A. D.[2], but nearly the same numerals occur in inscriptions of the early Ve*n*gi dynasty of Kali*n*ga which must be referred to the fourth and fifth century, and the sign for 'ten' occurs in a Cêra inscription *d.* 466 A. D. The system of numeral figures still used by the Tamil̤ people forms a step in advance, the distinct signs for ten, hundred and thousand only being preserved, and those for twenty up to ninety being discarded. Apart from this still existing system, there is no evidence as to the use of these 'Cave numerals', as they are usually termed, after the fifth century, for inscriptions with dates in figures appear to be wanting from that time till about the tenth century in Northern India, and till about the year 1300 A. D. in S. India. At these dates we find, in the respective countries, the exclusive use of numeral figures with a value according to position and the cipher; and the figures have much the same forms as are now current,

1) The late illustrious scholar who deciphered this inscription (Mr. E. Norris) told me that this gave him the clue by which he recognized it as an Açoka edict, and was thus able to decipher it.

2) The Kaira plates. See Prinsep's "Essays" by Thomas, I. p. 257.

and which so closely resemble the Gobar numerals, also in use and with the same value according to position in Europe also about the eleventh century. Though it has often been asserted that the modern or Devanâgarî numerals are mere abbreviations of the initial letters of the words denoting the corresponding numbers[1], I think that a comparison of the later forms of the Cave numerals with them, will render it perfectly clear, that, this is not the case, but that, all the indigenous numerals used in the various parts of India are simply derived from the Cave numerals which are not, as I have already shown, of an alphabetic origin at all. This derivation is also the only one which satisfactorily explains the forms of the numerals used in the North as well as in the South of India[2].

It therefore appears that, neglecting all possibilities, in favour of which evidence does not exist, (such as the simultaneous existence of the more modern system of notation with the older in the fifth century A. D. or even earlier), the only possible conclusion is that, the great improvement of using numerals with a value according to position, and consequently the use of the cipher first occurred in Northern India between 500 and 900 A. D. Now though the inscriptions fail us as yet for this period, the almost unrivalled sagacity of Woepcke has detected some evidence in the works of the astronomers who lived in India during those centuries. These are: Âryabhaṭa who himself tells us that he was born in 476 A. D.; Varâha Mihira who died in 587 A. D.[3]; Brahmagupta who lived about 600, and Bhaṭṭotpala who lived about 1000 also of our era. All these writers composed their treatises in metre, and to suit the exigencies of the strict limits thus imposed on them, the three last were obliged to express the terms of their calculations by words, and these not the usual ones, but by symbolical words denoting natural objects, and in a conventional way, (as here used) also numerals. This peculiar system (which will be fully explained further on in this chapter) implies value by position, and also has words which express indirectly the cipher[4]. This same system is also used in the Sûryasiddhânta which is of very uncertain date in its actual form. It is thus perfectly clear that the Indians knew of numerals with a value according to position in the sixth century A. D., but the system of Âryabhaṭa which is totally different to the one described, *appears* to render impossible the assumption that he also about 500 A. D. knew of the cipher. He uses the successive vowels of the Sanskrit alphabet to express place, and thus his system agrees in principle with the Tamiḻ notation; a, â and i corresponding in value with the Tamiḻ signs for ten, hundred and thousand. Woepcke, however, considers that Âryabhaṭa invented this notation to suit his style of composition in verse, and that the system of notation by words

---

1) Woepcke, "Mémoire" pp. 44-53.

2) See pl. xix.

3) Bo. J. viii., p. 241.

4) It must be remarked that these words all mean *'blank'*, *'vacancy'* or *'sky'*, and that there is nothing to show that there was a distinct *mark* or *figure* for the cipher; thus the Indian notation by words exactly corresponds with the system of the abacus. Woepcke wrongly translates two of these words (Çûnya and kha) by *'le point'* (p. 103), and there is therefore nothing in the astronomical treatises to show that the cipher was used in India even in the sixth century A. D.

with value according to position was 'probably anterior to Āryabhaṭa'[1]. Would Āryabhaṭa have omitted all mention of real value by position had he been acquainted with it? Beyond the sixth century there is nothing to indicate the use of the cipher; for the high orders of numerals (equivalent to billions, trillions, etc.) first noticed by Profr. Weber[2] do not necessarily imply anything of the kind. An illustrious French Mathematician, and an equally eminent French Philosopher have shown that this invention may have occurred in the middle ages of Europe spontaneously[3]; it may also have occurred independently in India, but as the facts stand at present, it is difficult to connect India and Europe in the transmission of this particular invention from the first country to the other. As it is not proved to have been known in India before 500 A. D. it is almost impossible to see how it can have been transmitted from thence to Europe before the rise of the Arabs, for direct communication ceased about the fourth century A. D.[4], and in Europe, at all events, the very little intellectual activity that was displayed ran in entirely different courses during the sixth, seventh and eighth centuries. The Arabic numerals now in use certainly came from India, but numerals with value according to position and the cipher were already in use in Europe (by the Neo-Pythagoreans) before they were adopted[5]. If the derivation of the numeral figures from the initial letters of the Sanskrit words denoting the respective numbers be given up, there is nothing left to show where the figures were first used; by the Pythagoreans in Europe or the astronomers in India. The assumption that the last was the case, but which (as I have already said) an examination of the earliest forms of the numerals preserved in inscriptions will prove to be impossible, is the foundation of the theory that Europe is indebted to India in this respect; in fact Woepcke chiefly relies on it[6]. The theory in question was started by J. Prinsep about 1838, or long before the Cave numerals were explained. The resemblance between the Neo-Pythagorean numerals and their cursive form the Gobar on the one hand, and the India cave numerals and the forms derived from them on the other, is too striking not to be noticed, but this

1) u. s. p. 117. *n.* "Il ne faudrait pas conclure de l' existence d' une notation alphabetique inventée par Āryabhaṭa, que cette invention est nécessairement antérieure à celle des chiffres. Āryabhaṭa, qui écrivait aussi en vers, avait besoin d' une notation qui se laissait mettre en çlôkas, et trouvait peut-être que la méthode des mots symboliques, trés probablement antérieure à Āryabhaṭa, manquait de briéveté et de précision." Āryabhaṭa (so the MSS. have his name) wrote in Ārya metre, and words would suit him better than letters; the fact remains that he did not use value by position.

2) Z. d. D. M. G. xv. pp. 132 ffg.

3) Chasles who is supported by Comte. The last says ("Cours de Philosophie Positive", V. p. 326 *note*): "Personne n' ignore ni l' heureuse innovation réalisée au moyen âge, dans les notations numériques ni la part incontestable de l'influence catholique à cet important progrés de l' arithmétique (! ?). Un géomètre distingué, qui s' occupe, avec autant de succes que de modestie de la véritable histoire mathématique (M. Chasles), a tres-utilement confirmé, dans ces derniers temps par une sage discussion spéciale, au sujet de ce mémorable perfectionnement, l'aperçu rationnel que devait naturellement inspirer la saine théorie, du développement humain, en prouvant qu'on y doit voir surtout, non une importation de l'Inde par les Arabes, mais un simple résultat spontané du mouvement scientifique antérieur, dont on peut suivre aisément la tendance graduelle vers une telle issue par des modifications successives, en partant des notations primitives d' Archimède et des astronomes grecs".

The *abacus* of the ancients was so near the modern system of numeration, that they would have but little felt the want of it.

4) Reinaud "Relations politiques et commerciales de l' empire Romain", p. 265-9. Woepcke ("Mémoire" p. 67) allows that if the invention came from India, it must have been transported thence: "dans les premiers siécles de notre ère."

5) "Mémoire", p. 194.

6) Do. p. 53.

fact does not warrant a presumption that one is borrowed from the other; more probably, both are from a common source. The question of what might have been the common original of the Neo-Pythagorean and Cave numerals is one for the decision of which information must yet be discovered. Can it have been invented in Chaldæa (Babylonia) as one mediæval writer asserts of the abacus?[1] Egypt seems, however, a much more probable source. That country was, almost beyond doubt, the source from which the Phœnicians got their alphabet; as the late V*cte* de Rougé showed, the primitive Phœnician letters are selected from among the cursive or Hieratic characters[2], and the Egyptians were in the habit of using numerals long before any other nation on the earth, as the tombs of the early dynasties display them in common use. If the 'Cave' numerals be compared with the Egyptian Hieratic and Demotic numerals, a similarity between many of the forms and also in the systems will be at once observed. Thus of the Demotic forms given by M. de Rougé[3] the figures for 1, 2, 3, 4, 5, 6, 8 and 9 have a considerable likeness to the Cave numerals of the same value. Again the Hieratic and Demotic systems have separate figures for 10, 20, etc. like the 'Cave' system, and of these several show more or less likeness to the Indian figures. An Egyptian origin of the 'Cave' numerals would solve the difficulty that the likeness between the Indian and Pythagorean (Gobar) numerals now presents; it is much more probable that the cipher was introduced from Alexandria in the fourth century A. D. together with Greek astrology, than that it was invented in India previously, considering the very rudimentary state of Indian mathematics before that period. The Chinese numerals (which are apparently much older than the Indian) present also some similar forms. Considering the great resemblance to the Himyaritic character that the original Indian alphabet presents, it would appear that S. W. Arabia is the most probable source for the Indian numeral system, but since the explanation of the Himyaritic numerals by M. Halévy[4] it is of little use to look there.

It thus appears that all the figures now in use in India are derived from the 'Cave' character; there is no trace of an independent introduction as in the case of the Vaṭṭeḻuttu alphabet. Whatever may be the origin of value by position and the cipher, there can be no doubt that this important invention was first used in N. India.

---

1) Do. p. 22. The author in question is Radulphus of Laon who lived in the 12th century. († 1131).

2) Lenormant, "Essai sur la propagation de l' Alphabet Phénicien". I. pp. 88-94; 151-2.

3) "Chrestomathie Egyptienne" fasc. ii. plates i. ii., and iii. (pp. 113-7.)

4) "Etudes Sabéennes" in the Journal Asiatique. cfr. No. 4 N. S. (May-June, 1873) pp. 511-3. The numbers one to four are expressed by perpendicular strokes (I, II, III, and IIII) for five there is a separate figure, and six to nine are expressed by the addition of units on the left side of this figure. Ten is expressed by ɔ, and twenty etc. by a corresponding number of ɔ. Thus IIɔɔ is 22. For hundred and thousand the initial letters of the corresponding words are used.

The Persian numerals as known are also different from the Indian. From one to ten, they are expressed by a corresponding number of angular marks: the mark for ten is combined in the same manner for the tens up to a hundred. Cfr. Spiegel, "Altp. Keilinschriften" p. 160, and Kossowicz "Lit. Palæopersicarum enunciatio" (in his work on the inscriptions) p. 9.

§ 1. THE MODIFICATION OF THE 'CAVE NUMERALS' FOUND IN THE VEṆGI AND CĒRA INSCRIPTIONS.

The 'Cave numerals' given in Pl. xix. are taken from those which occur in the inscriptions of the Western Caves as far as the upper line is concerned; the lower are from the Mathura inscriptions[1]. The two inscriptions of the Ve*n*gi dynasty (as I have termed it already) which preceded the Câlukyas, and therefore must be earlier than the seventh century A. D., have the plates numbered. In one, numerals occur up to three, and in the other (which is given in Plates xx. and xxi.) up to four; these are collected in Pl. xix.

The horizontal strokes of the Cave numerals are here semi-circular, and the figure for four is also of a more cursive form.

Much the same numeral figures appear to have been in use in the Cêra kingdom at the end of the fifth century A. D. In the Mercara plates (ii. line 9)  sahasranâḍu occurs[2]. This is left unexplained by those who have attempted this inscription, but the figure is evidently a slight variation of the Cave numeral 10, and the words thus should be read "daçasahasranâḍu"; the 'Ten-thousand' being a division of the country, and probably referring to the tribute paid by it.

I have not met with any other examples of this system of numerals in Southern India.

§ 2. THE TAMIḺ NUMERALS.

The figures used in this system are given in Pl. xix. from a MS. at Tanjore which belongs probably to the end of the sixteenth or beginning of the seventeenth century; as Tamiḻ MSS. (except the very recent ones) are all undated, and these figures do not occur in inscriptions earlier than the sixteenth century, it is difficult to procure a complete series of an ascertained date. This is, however, of little importance; for the earliest examples are precisely of the same form as those still in use.

These figures are remarkable as forming the stage of development between the Cave numerals and the modern systems, and are, therefore, relics of a system that became more or less obsolete in the sixth century A. D.[3] we find here separate figures for ten, hundred and thousand nearly identical with the Cave forms; but the figures for twenty etc. are rejected, and tens, hundreds or thousands are expressed by prefixing the sign for the units to the left side of the figure represent-

1) *Bo. J.* viii. pp. 225-232; and J. R. A. S. New Series V. pp. 182 ffg. For the figures believed to represent 50 and 70, see I. A. i., pp. 60-1.

2) A good facsimile of these very important plates is given in the first volume of the I. A. The explanation, however, needs much amendment.

3) The Kuṟal mentions acquaintance with *numbers* (eṇṇa) and *letters* as being like eyes to men. This is probably older than the ninth century A. D.

ing the order. The use of the cipher and value by position are *Grantha* (or Brahmanical), and till lately have been but little used, though Sanskrit MSS. are almost invariably numbered in this way.

The figures to express fractions are peculiar to the Tamil̤ people, and there are many others in use besides those which I have given, and which I have chiefly taken from the first edition of Beschi's Koḍun-Tamil̤ Grammar (p. 149). They are derived, no doubt, from initials of corresponding words, which abbreviations are also combined in some cases; the invention must be attributed to the Tamil̤ traders of no very remote period[1].

The Tamil̤ numeral figures are obviously cursive forms of the 'Cave numerals' modified by the prevailing practice of writing on palm-leaves with a style, a practice which renders necessary curved rather than straight lines, as the last, when with the grain or course of the fibres of the leaf, are nearly invisible.

I have not been able to find any traces of distinct Vaṭṭel̤uttu numerals.

The Malayâḷam numerals (which I have given in Pl. xix.) are those in actual use. Their history is quite uncertain, as there are very few, if any, examples of them older than the middle of the last century, MSS. being numbered most generally with letters. They are evidently derived from the same source as the rest, and are nearest to the Tamil̤ figures, but include the cipher. The Malayâḷam way of expressing fractions is the same as we find in the Telugu and Canarese countries, and is, therefore, North-Indian.

§ 3. THE TELUGU-CANARESE NUMERALS.

These suddenly appear in full use about 1300 A. D.[2] with value by position and also the cipher, which is always represented in S. Indian documents by a small circle. In Northern India a dot also appears with this signification, but the necessity of writing on palm-leaves has, in S. India, led to the adoption of the circular form as alone perfectly distinct.

The Telugu-Canarese numerals (as given in Pl. xix. from a Halakannaḍa MS. of 1428 A. D.) are almost identical in all the inscriptions across the peninsula, and remained the same till quite recently. In the Telugu inscriptions I have, however, observed, in some cases, a slight difference in the form of the figure 5, which sometimes wants the middle connecting stroke. The figure 3 is generally perpendicular in the Telugu inscriptions.

The Telugu-Canarese system of fractions is, like the Tamil̤, based on a division of the unit into sixteen parts; they are marked by the N. Indian system, and this appears to be of recent introduction.

1) In the inscriptions (at Tanjore *e. g.*) all numbers and fractions which occur frequently, are written at full length.

2) If Sir W. Elliot's collection of transcripts of inscriptions in the neighbourhood of the Krishṇâ and Godâvarî can be trusted, the notation of dates by these numerals was not uncommon in the eleventh century; but I am inclined to think that this is not the case, and that the copyist has simply put the figures for words written at full length in the original. The oldest inscription with a date in figures in Java appears to be ç. 1220 = A. D. 1298. (v. Humboldt's "Kawi-sprache" I., p. 15.)

A comparison of the numeral figures in Pl. xix. will conclusively show that they are all more or less cursive modifications, of the Cave numerals. In the case of 5, 6, 8 and 9 it is evident that their originals must have been varieties of the latter which have not yet been met with; but as the Cave numerals are from Western and Northern India, and present already a number of distinct types, this is no real difficulty, for the perfectly evident origin of 1, 2, 3, 4 and 7 quite justifies the conclusion that the smaller number, of which the origin is less obvious, do in fact come from the same source[1].

NOTE:

The different Methods of marking dates used in South India.

The numeral figures are only used in comparatively modern inscriptions, in the older ones and also in many modern ones the numbers are commonly expressed by words or letters. The eras and cycles to which the dates are referred also present considerable difficulty.

§ 1. THE ERAS.

A. *The Kaliyuga.*

The commencement of the Kaliyuga is put at 3,101 B. C.

It was used in the fifth century A. D.[2], but has never become very general in inscriptions, and is now, in S. India, chiefly used in Malabar for the fanciful way of marking dates by a sentence. In most cases I have seen, the number of *days*, and not of *years* is mentioned[3].

B. *The Çaka Era.*

This era is now usually supposed to date from the birth of a mythical Hindu sovereign called Çâlivâhana, who defeated the Çakas, and began Monday, 14th March 78 A. D. (Julian style). The account of the origin of this era has apparently been repeatedly modified to suit current ideas. In the earlier inscriptions it is usually called Çakavarsha, 'Çakasa*m*vatsara' or 'Çaka-n*r*ipakâla'; about the tenth century it is termed the year of the Çakarâja, Çakâdhipa or Çaka-deva, and still later it is termed 'Çâlivâhanaçaka' or 'Çâlivâhanaçakâbda.'

---

1) The Gobar (or old Western and Pythagorean type) is from Woepcke's "Mémoire" p. 49; the Devanâgarî is from Prinsep's "Essays" as collected by Mr. Thomas.

2) By Āryabhaṭa.

3) Warren's "Kala Sankalita" (p. 18) states that in S. India it is usual to date documents in both the Kali and Çaka year. This is contrary to my experience.

Albirûnî (A. D. 1031) speaks of this era as one in use by the astrologers[1], and as they had a great deal to do with royal grants by determining the auspicious time for making them, it is easy to see how this became the most usual way of marking the dates of inscriptions. But it is certain that this era was quite unsettled and comparatively little used before the tenth century. The earliest authentic inscriptions in which it occurs belong to the end of the fifth century A. D., but it is first mentioned by Varâha Mihira, an astronomer who lived in the sixth century A. D.; and he makes the commencement of it coincide with Kali-year 3,179. The great popularity in all parts of India of this author's works is probably the reason why this is now the recognized computation, but it has been adopted since the tenth century. Up to that date and even later, there are inscriptions with dates by the Çaka as well as other methods, (*e. g.* the B*ri*haspati cycle) which show a variation of two or three years, more or less, from the usual computation. Albirûnî (A. D. 1031) mentions that the Çaka year then commenced 135 years after Vikramâditya; this is the received opinion, and from that century Çaka dates may be computed with certainty in the ordinary way. Before that period they must be considered as more or less uncertain.

The Çaka year seems to have been originally introduced by the Jains, but though the inscriptions prove that their computation of it was the same as the brahmanical, the account they give of it differs from the ordinary one. The Trilokasâra says: Paṇachassayavassa*m* paṇamâsajuda*m* gamiya Vîranibbuïdo | Sagarâjo; to Kakki caduṇavatiyamahiyasagamâsa*m* || 848 || C. Çrî-Vîranâthaniv*r*itte*h* sakâçât pa*n*cottarashaṭchatavarshâṇi pa*n*camâsayutâni gatvâ paçcât Vikramâ*n*kaçakarâjo 'jâyata | tata upari caturṇavatyuttaratriçatavarshâṇi saptamâsâdhikāni gatvâ paçcât Kalky ajâyata || Now the death of Vîranâtha (or Mahâvîra) the last of the Tîrtha*n*karas is put at 388 B. C.[2]; then, according to the above, the Çaka era would begin in 239 A. D., but this is impossible, so the era of Mahâvîra must be put at 527 B. C. and this again differs from the era mentioned by Prinsep as current in the North of India—512 before Vikramâditya or 569 B. C.[3] The Javanese Çaka era is 74 A. D., that of Bali 80 A. D. From these details some notion may be formed of the excessive uncertainty of Indian chronological data before the early centuries A. D. The more exact they appear to be the more suspicious they are. It is not too much to say that a tolerably exact chronology is only possible after the tenth century, and then by the aid of inscriptions only[4].

---

1) "L'ère de Saca, nommée pas les Indians Sacakâla, est posterieure à celle de Vikramaditya de 135 ans. Saca est le nom d'un prince qui a régné sur les contrées situées entre l' Indus et la mer. Sa résidence était placee au centre de l' empire, dans la contrée nommée Aryavartha. Les Indiens le font naître dans une classe autre que celle des Sakya; quelques-uns prétendent qu' il était Soudra et originaire de la ville de Mansoura. Il y en a même qui disent qu' il n'etait pas de la race indienne, et qu' il tirait son origine de régions occidentales. Les peuples eurent beaucoup à souffrir de son despotisme, jusqu' à ce qu'il leur vînt du secours de l' Orient. Vikramaditya marcha contre lui, mit son armée en déroute et le tua sur le territoire de Korour, situé entre Moultan et le château de Louny. Cette époque devint célèbre à cause de la joie que les peuples ressentirent de la mort de Saca, et on la choisit pour ère, principalement chez les astronomes". Tr. by Abbé Reinaud.

2) According to the Çatru*n*jaya-Mâhâtmya.

3) "Useful Tables" p. 166 in Prinsep's "Essays" by Thomas, Vol. II.

4) The equation for converting this era into the Christian date is: $+ 78\frac{1}{4}$.

C. *The Vikramâditya Era.*

The passion for systematizing and thus falsifying even history in accordance with the popular astrological and religious notions of the day, has, it is evident from the above, led to repeated alterations in the dates assigned to real or fictitious events in Indian history. The era of Vikramâditya is apparently one result of this folly. It is all but unknown in S. India (except in the Deccan), though under the name of 'Samvat' is the one most commonly used in the North. It is said to begin 57 years B. C.[1]

D. *The Koḷambam (or Quilon) Era.*

This is usually called a cycle[2], but it is in reality an era; it began in September 824 A. D. It is supposed to commemorate the founding of Kollam (Quilon), and is only used in the S. Tamil country and Travancore[3].

E. *Cycle of Bṛihaspati.*

Each year in this cycle has a name, and in the inscriptions this is coupled with the Çaka year or year of the king's reign. The earliest examples to be met with in S. India in which the cyclic years occur are of about the tenth century. The names are as follows:

1. Prabhava.
Vibhava.
Çukla.
Pramoda, Pramodûta.
5. Prajâpati.
Ā*n*girasa.
Çrîmukha.
Bhâva.
Yuva.
10. Dhâtu.
Īçvara.
Bahudhânya.
Pramâdi.
Vikrama.
15. Vishu, V*r*ishabha (?).
Citrabhânu.
Svabhânu.
Târaṇa.
Pârthiva.
20. Vyaya.
Sarvajit.
Sarvadhâri.
Virodhi.
Vik*r*ita.
25. Khara.
Nandana.
Vijaya.
Jaya[4].
Manmatha.
30. Durmukhi.

1) The equation is: + 56¾.
2) "Cycle of Paraçurâma" — Prinsep.
3) The equation is: + 824¾.
4) According to Mr. C. P. Brown the order is sometimes: Jaya, Vijaya.

Hevilamba.
Vilambi.
Vikâri.
Çarvari.
35. Plava.
Çubhakrit.
Çobhana, Çobhakrit.
Krodhi.
Viçvâvasu.
40. Parâbhava.
Plavanga.
Kîlaka.
Saumya.
Sâdhâraṇa.
45. Virodhikrit, Virodhakrit, Virodhyâdikrit.
Paridhâvi.
Pramâdîca.
Ānanda.
Râxasa.
50. Anala, Naḷa.
Pingala.
Kâlayukta.
Siddhârthi.
Raudra, Raudri.
55. Durmati.
Dundubhi.
Rudhirodgâri.
Raktâxi, Raktâxa.
Krodhana.
60. Xaya[1].

This cycle is originally founded on a practice of reckoning time by the revolutions of Jupiter (Brihaspati), but there is no record of its correct use; the present practice of erroneously reckoning sixty *solar* years as equal to five revolutions of the planet has always, it appears, prevailed as far back as reference to this method can be found. Though this cycle is in common use everywhere in the South, the names are often much varied, especially by the Jains[2]. It is not improbable that this system is an adaptation with Sanskrit names of an old way of reckoning time originally current in S. India; it is mentioned by Albirûnî in the eleventh century, but his reference to it is commonly understood to mean that it was of recent introduction in the North and West of India.

This cycle as used in North and South India differs not in the names or order of the names but in the period at which the first year comes. In S. India the present year (1874) is Bhâva or the eighth of the cycle. This difference is owing to the practice which obtains in S. India and Tibet of considering the years of the cycle as identical in duration with the ordinary luni-solar year.

F. *Other Eras but little used.*

Some of the Câlukyas attempted to set up local eras, but these dates occur in comparatively few and unimportant inscriptions, and are too uncertain to be worth mentioning here.

The South-Indian Côḷa and Pâṇḍya kings appear to mention the year of their reign most generally, and the second also, but rarely, the Quilon era. The task of establishing the succession of these dynasties and the dates is thus likely to prove very formidable; there is, however,

1) This list is compiled from Col. Warren's "Kala Sankalita", Mr. C. P. Brown's "Cyclic Tables", inscriptions, and the practice of the people of S. India.

2) The Tamiḻ names are merely corrupt forms of the Sanskrit. For them see Beschi's Koḍun-Tamiḻ Grammar.

some foundation in Marco Polo's mention of Sundara Pâṇḍya as the king of the South in his time (13th century), and also in the synchronism between the Côḷa king Kulottuṅga and the Câlukya Ahavamalla as established by Sir W. Elliot[1].

The explanation of the date in the grant to the Cochin Israelites is not as yet certain. The term is: "Yâṇḍu iraṇḍâm âṇḍaikk' eδir muppattâṟâm âṇḍu"—(*i.e.* literally) "the year opposite the second year, the thirty-sixth year." Ellis explained it[2] by the thirty-sixth year of the third (? second) cycle, but it is impossible to reconcile it with the Quilon era, and it appears to me to mean the thirty-sixth year (of the king's life) opposite to (or corresponding with) the second year (of his reign). Similar dates occur in the Tamiḻ inscriptions.

The above information is sufficient to decide *approximately* the dates of most S. Indian inscriptions; to do more it is necessary to know the complicated details of the luni-solar year as used in S. India, but this would need a large volume alone[3]. Eventually, no doubt, it will be necessary to take these details into account, as well as the references to eclipses which are so frequent in Indian grants, and by which it must often be possible to calculate the date with the utmost exactness; at present it is rather to be desired that existing inscriptions should be preserved, than that much time should be spent on any single one.

The expunged and intercalated months and days are a chief feature in the luni-solar calendar, and now-a-days great attention is paid to them in consequence of disputes on ceremonial matters; I have not seen these intercalated days or months marked in any old inscription, but in modern documents this is always done, and the absence of *nija* or *adhika* in such a case would discredit any modern deed.

§ 2. THE METHOD OF EXPRESSING NUMERALS.

A. *By words.*

The earliest inscriptions found in S. India in which the date is referred to an era have it written at full length in words. After the seventh century the dates are *mostly* expressed by significant words, and after the tenth century this is *always* done. These significant words appear to be a device of the Indian astrologers as the earliest examples occur in their treatises. The first com-

1) *Madras J.* xiii., pt. 2, p. 40. See above p. 20. *n.*

2) Do. pp. 3 and 10. Dr. Gundert (do. pt. i. p. 137) doubts the meaning of eδir. Dr. Caldwell (*Comp. Gr.* p. 60 *n.*) takes it to mean the year of the cycle of sixty to which the year of the kings' reign answers.

3) Warren's "Kala Sankalita" (4° Madras, 1825) is still the only work on this subject. The information in Prinsep's "Useful Tables" is mostly from it.

It has often been asserted and denied that traces are to be found of a primitive (Dravidian) S. Indian calendar anterior to the present one which is entirely of Sanskrit origin, but nothing has as yet been adduced to prove the position. I find, however, that there is a Tuḷu calendar which has names for the months different from the Sanskrit, and which are most derived from the Tuḷu names of crops reaped at those seasons. These months now agree practically with the luni-solar months, and the names are: Paggu̥; Beçâ; Kârtelu̥; Āṭi; Soṇa; Nirnâla; Bontelu̥; Jârde; Perârde; Pûntelu̥; Mâyi; Suggi. Of these the second, fourth, and perhaps the ninth are of Sanskrit origin; the rest are pure Tuḷu and have no connection with the Sanskrit names for divisions of time.

plete list is that given by Albirûnî (A.D. 1031); the following is from his list as translated by Woepcke[1] supplemented from Brown's "Cyclic Tables" and inscriptions. As no limits can be placed to a fanciful practice like this, I cannot give this list as complete; it is merely an attempt to make a complete list[2].

Cipher. ...... Çûnya; kha; gagaṇa; viyat; âkâça; ambara; abhra; ananta*; vyoma*.

1. .... Âdi; çaçin; indu; xiti; urvarâ; dharâ; pitâmaha; candra; çîtâmçu; rûpa; raçmi; prithivî*; bhû*; tanu*; soma†; nâyaka†; vasudhâ†; çaçânka†; xmâ†; dharaṇî†.

2. .... Yama; Açvin; ravicandrau; locana; axi; Dasra; yamala; paxa; netra; bahu*; karṇa*; kuṭumba*; kara†; drishṭi†.

3. .... Trikâla; trijagat; tri; triguṇa; loka; trigata; pâvaka; vaiçvânara; dahana; tapana; hutâçana; jvalana; agni; vahni*; trilocana*; triṇetra*; Râma*; sahodara*; çikhin†; guṇa†.

4. .... Veda; samudra; sâgara; abdhi; dadhi (?); diç; jalâçaya; krita; jalanidhi*; yuga*; koshṭha*; bandhu*; udadhi†.

5. .... Çara; artha; indriya; sâyaka; vâṇa; bhûta; ishu; Pâṇḍava; tata; ratna*; prâṇa*; suta*; putra*; viçikha†; kalamba†; mârgaṇa†.

6. .... Rasa; anga; ritu; mâsârddha; râga*; ari*; darçana*; tarka*; mata†; çâstra†.

7. .... Aga; naga; parvata; mahîdhara; adri; muni; rishi*; Atri*; svara*; chandas*; açva*; dhâtu*; kalatra*; çaila†.

8. .... Vasu; ahi; gaja; dantin; mangala; nâga; bhûti*; ibha†; sarpa†(?).

9. .... Go; nanda; randhra; chidra; pavana; antara; graha*; anka*; nidhi†; dvâra†.

10. .... Diç; âçâ; kendu; râvaṇaçara; avatâra*; karma*.

11. .... Rudra; Îçvara; Mahâdeva; axauhiṇî; lâbha*.

12. .... Sûrya; arka; âditya; bhânu; mâsa; sahasrâmça; vyaya*.

13. .... Viçva; Manmatha*; Kâmadeva*.

14. .... Manu; loka*; Indra*.

15. .... Tithi; paxa*; ahan*.

16. .... Ashṭi; nripa; bhûpa; kalâ*.

17. .... Atyashṭi.

18. .... Dhriti.

19. .... Atidhriti.

20. .... Nakha; kriti.

21. .... Utkriti; svarga*.

22. .... Jâti*.

24. .. .. Jina*.

1) "Mémoire" pp. 103-9.

2) This system was first explained by v. Schlegel. In the above list I give firstly those words given by Albirûnî about which there can be no doubt; then others mentioned by Mr. C. P. Brown which I mark *. Lastly I add terms not already mentioned which I have found in inscriptions, and which I mark †. This system is also used in the Javanese inscriptions. See V. Humboldt's "Kawi-Sprache" i., pp. 19-42.

25. .... Tattva.

Albirûnî says that numbers beyond twenty-five were not noted in this way.

27. .... Naxatra*.

32. .... Danta*.

33. .... Deva*.

49. .... Tâna*.

This list might be made much more extensive, as it is obvious that any synonyms of any word that can be used to signify a number can be used; *e.g.* any word signifying 'moon' besides those mentioned as equivalent to 1, may be used for the same purpose, and so with the others. The ordinary numeral words are commonly mixed with the words given above.

In marking numbers by this system units are mentioned first and then the higher orders; *e.g.* *R*ishinâgakhendusa*m*vatsara is year 1087; guṇaçâstrakhenduganitasa*m*va° = 1063; dahanâdrikhendu-ganitasa*m*va° = 1073. It appears, however, that occasionally in recent inscriptions the words are put in the same order as the figures are written.

From 600 A.D. up to 1300 nine out of ten inscriptions that bear dates, have them expressed in this style, which is, therefore, of the greatest importance.

B. *Expression of numbers by letters.*

Three systems of this kind are known in India: that of Āryabhaṭa, which he used in his treatises on astronomy, and which does not appear to have ever been used by any one else or in inscriptions; that used in S. India (but almost exclusively in Malabar, Travancore and the S. Tamiḻ country), in which the date is given by a chronogram; and a third system in which the letters of the alphabet are used to mark the leaves of MSS.

It is unnecessary to describe the first as it is never used in inscriptions, and the text of Āryabhaṭa's work (as yet almost inaccessible) is now being edited by Profr. Kern.

The second system gives values to the consonants of the Sanskrit alphabet as follows:[1]

k	kh	g	gh	ṅ
1	2	3	4	5
č	čh	j	jh	ń
6	7	8	9	0
ṭ	ṭh	ḍ	ḍh	ṇ
1	2	3	4	5
t	th	d	dh	n
6	7	8	9	0
p	ph	b	bh	m
1	2	3	4	5

y	r	l	v	ç	sh	s	h	ḻ
1	2	3	4	5	6	7	8	9

1) It was first explained by the late C. M. Whish (in pt. i. of the *Transactions* of the Madras Society). Mr. Whish was one of the first to pay attention to Sanskrit astronomy. He died at Cuddapah, April 13th, 1833. On this method of marking dates see also Z. d. D. M. G. xvii., pp. 773 ffg. (by Profr. Weber.)

The order of the letters is from right to left, in double letters the last pronounced consonant *only* counts, and vowels have no value. Thus Vishṇu = 54; badhnâti anna*m* sasarpi = 17750603.
4 5 3 0 6 0 5 7 7 1

The peculiarity of this system is that it allows dates to be expressed by words with a connected meaning. This system was in use in the fifteenth century[1], but, apparently, not long before then. It is now much used for remembering rules to calculate horoscopes, and for astronomical tables. Its resemblance to the Semitic chronograms is complete. This method is also used in a kind of anukramaṇî which exists for the *R*ig-, Yajur- and Sâmavedas, but apparently in S. India only These lists of contents (for they are no more) must be modern[2].

The third system is only applied to numbering the pages of MSS.; it was used a good deal in Malabar, and also occasionally in the Telugu country, but not to any extent in MSS. written in this century. It is also known in Ceylon and Burmah. By this system the consonants (with short a, and in their usual order) stand for 1, 2, etc. up to 34, and then they are repeated with lóng â, *e.g.* kâ = 35, khâ 36 and so on. By the addition of the other vowels the series may be continued to a considerable length. This is probably the use to which the Çabdamaṇidarpaṇa (p. 22) alludes when the author says that in Canarese the aspirates are only used as numerals. This grammar is of about the twelfth century.

CHAPTER IV.

ACCENTS AND SIGNS OF PUNCTUATION.

THERE is very little to be said about the method of accentuating Vedic MSS. in S. India, as this is but seldom done at all, and the accented MSS. hardly deserve mention here as they are rarely above a century old.

§ 1. RIG AND YAJUR VEDAS.

In the oldest MSS. only the *udâtta* is marked. In the Telugu MSS. this is generally done by a circle ○; in the Grantha MSS. the letter u or a circle is written above the syllable, thus: ഉ, ○.

1) I. A. ii., pp. 361-2.
2) "Catalogue" p. 49. "Index to Tanjore MSS." p. 4.

In this respect MSS. of the Sa*m*hitâ and Padapâṭha agree[1]. In the last the words are separated by a perpendicular stroke: | The *avagraha* is seldom marked, but when it is done a zigzag line is used: ⦚

§ 2. THE SĀMA VEDA.

The accentuation of the Sâma Veda as used in south India is a subject beset with difficulties, and of which it is impossible here to give more than a very brief notice, for not only do the MSS. of different *Çâkhâs* present different systems, but the MSS. of the text followed by one and the same Çâkhâ often present essential variations[2]. MSS. of the Ārcika parts of this Veda are seldom accented, as being of little importance, for the *gânas* really constitute the Veda. Occasionally one finds the *udâtta* marked by a circle. The musical notation of the gânas as practised in S. India is very complicated, and is explained in a separate *paribhâshâ*[3]. It appears to be on much the same principle as the musical notation of the ancient Greeks, and consists in using combinations of a consonant with a vowel to express a group of notes. This old system (as it is termed) has been nearly superseded by the N. Indian notation by numbers, which was introduced from Gujarat into Tanjore during the last century at the earliest. Even now, it is excessively hard to find a *Sâma-Vedî* who can give any explanation at all of these notes, and in a few years the only guides will be the treatises on the formation of the *gânas*, which indeed are probably the only safe ones at present.

Palæographically the notation of the Vedic accents is a subject almost devoid of interest. The different methods used for the different Vedas are all of very recent origin, comparatively; and have arisen in different parts of India much about the same time, and in consequence of the decay of the old way of learning the Vedas by heart. In S. India there is no pretence of a complete or even uniform system, and MSS. with accents do not appear to occur before the middle of the sixteenth century. The multitude of treatises on Vedic phonetics still existing in S. India must always have made the want of accented MSS. but little felt, and all the old Vedic Brahmans that I have met with, never attached the least value to them.

As the S. Indian alphabets have no system of accents at all agreeing with those in use in the North of India, it follows that in the early centuries A. D. the accents were not marked at all.

§ 3. PUNCTUATION.

The edicts of Açoka cannot be said to have any marks to indicate the close of a sentence, and the perpendicular stroke | is not much used in the inscriptions of the early centuries after the Christian era. In them the single | and double || stroke both occur with precisely the same signi-

1) As I have repeatedly stated elsewhere, the *Atharva Veda* is unknown to the S. Indian Brahmans. In Weber's "Indische Studien" (xiii., 118) there is an account of the accentuation of a Nandinâgarî MS. of the *Ṛig* Veda.

2) See my "Catalogue of a Collection of Sanskrit MSS." pt. i., pp. 38, 49.

3) I have already given specimens, with an account of the "*Paribhâshâ*" in my "Catalogue" pp. 44-5.

fications either to mark the division in a verse, or to indicate the end of a sentence or paragraph, and so far they have the same meaning as in the northern documents.

§ 4. ORNAMENTS TO MSS.

The oldest MSS. on palm-leaves contain merely the text, and that continuous from the beginning to the end; even the end of a section being marked by a | only. After the 15th century this awkward custom is generally given up, and the divisions of a text are plainly marked by ornamental flourishes which are various forms of the word 'Çrî'. About the same period were written the earliest examples of MSS. with diagrams or illustrative pictures[1]. The later inscriptions have commonly at the commencement very rude representations of sacred emblems, *e.g.* the trident and drum of Çiva[2].

§ 5. CORRECTIONS ETC.

Erasures are generally made by a line above or below the erroneous letter or word.

Omissions are marked by a small cross over the place, and the letter or words that are wanting are then written underneath the line[3], or in the margin. If there are several such corrections on the same leaf it is often difficult to make out the place to which each belongs, and this is a frequent cause of error in the transcripts of MSS. Copyists in India will always insert any marginal note they may see in the text[4], but are quite indifferent where they insert it.

In S. Indian MSS. of Commentaries on texts, the words of the original are very seldom given in full, but the first two or three syllables are quoted, a cross is then put, and then the last word or syllable of the sentence which is to be explained is then given. Thus: "athâto darça + vyâkhyâsyâma*h*.

The use of the *bindu* (○) in S. Indian Prakrit MSS. is very peculiar; it is put before a consonant to show that it is doubled (*e. g.* Sa°go = saggo), and this is done even if the consonant it precedes is aspirated (*e. g.* cho°thi = choththi for chotthi). This practice has probably arisen out of the inability of the Dravidians to pronounce aspirates, and which they, in consequence, often neglect.

1) See an example in Hunter's "Orissa" i., p. 168.
2) Cfr. Ellis "On Mirasi Right", p. 67.
3) There is an example in the Mercara plates of this.
4) See Bühler's Āpastamba-Dharmasûtra i., p. 7.

CHAPTER V.

THE DIFFERENT KINDS OF SOUTH-INDIAN INSCRIPTIONS.

THE South-Indian inscriptions present but very little variety, and are easily reduced to the following classes:

I. DOCUMENTS CONVEYING A RIGHT TO PROPERTY.

It is necessary to carefully distinguish (as is done in the Dharmaçâstra), between documents of this description by reigning sovereigns and by private persons. The first are of immense importance for history, the last are seldom (as I shall show), of any value in this respect.

A. *Royal grants.*

The pedantry of the brahmanical lawyers is not content with directing kings to be liberal to the priests, but also prescribes the exact forms in which this virtue is to be practised. According to the Nîtimayûkha (16th cent.) these are as follows: The king on rising is to perform his usual ablutions and, if the day for it, have his head shaved. He is then to hear the Almanac read, and thus know what luck is promised, and what should be done or not. Then he must give a cow with its calf to a Brahman, and having beheld the reflection of his face in ghee placed in a flat dish, he should give that ghee also with some gold to a Brahman. After this on occasion of the moon's quarters and eclipses, he should make a gift of land or a grant payable in kind, to Brahmans of course. The secondary Dharmaçâstras first mention grants of this description, and (*e.g.* Yâj*n*avalkya Dh. ç.) give the form of the wording, the same as appears in the oldest grants now existing. They were, therefore, drawn up according to rule, and the gradual extension of the original formula appears to correspond exactly with the rise of new dynasties.

The passage in Yâj*n*avalkya is as follows (i., 317-9):[1)]

datvâ bhûmi*m* nibandha*m* vâ kr̥itvâ lekhya*m* tu kârayet |
âgâmibhadranr̥ipatiparij*n*ânâya pârthiva*h* ||
paṭe vâ tâmrapaṭe vâ svamudroparicihnitam |
abhilekhyâ 'tmano va*m*çyân âtmâna*m* ca mahîpati*h* ||
pratigrahaparimâṇa*m* dânacchedopavarṇanam |
svahastakâlasampanna*m* çâsana*m* kârayet sthiram ||

1) Ed. Stenzler, p. 38.

As they stand, these lines may be ascribed to the earlier centuries of the Christian era. The Mitâxarâ on this runs: "Yathoktavidhinâ bhûmi*m* datvâ svatvaniv*r*itti*m* k*r*itvâ 'nibandha*m* vâ' ekasya bhâṇḍabharakasye 'yanto rûpakâ ekasya parṇabharakasye 'yanti parṇâni 'ti vâ nibandha*m* k*r*itvâ 'lekhyam kârayet' kimartham 'âgâmina' eshyanto ye 'bhadrâ*h*' sâdhavo bhûpatayas teshâm anena dattam anena parig*r*ihîtam iti 'parij*n*ânâya pârthivo' bhûpatir anena bhûpater eva bhûmidâne nibandhadâne vâ 'dhikâro na bhogapater iti darçitam | 'lekhyam kârayed' ity ukta*m* katha*m* kârayed ity âha 'paṭe' iti dvâbhyâm kârpâsike paṭe 'tâmrapaṭe' tâmraphalake 'vâ 'tmano va*m*çyân' prapitâmahapitâmahapit*r*în bahuvacanasyâ 'rthavatvât svava*m*çavîryaçrutâdiguṇopavarṇanapûrvakam abhilekhyâ 'tmâna*m* ca çabdât pratig*r*ihîtâram pratigrahaparimâṇa*m* dânacchedopavarṇana*m* câ 'bhilekhya pratig*r*ihyata iti pratigraho nibandhas tasya rûpakâdiparimâṇa*m* dîyata iti dâna*m* xetrâdi tasya ccheda*h* chidyate vicchidyate 'nene 'ti cchedo nadyâdau parimâṇa*m* tasyo 'pavarṇana*m* amukanadyâ daxiṇato 'ya*m* grâma*h* xetra*m* vâ pûrvato 'mukagrâmasyai 'tâvannivartanaparimâṇa*m* ca lekhyam evâ 'ghâṭasya nadînagaravartmâda*h* sa*n*câritvena bhûmer nyûnâdhikabhâvasa*m*bhavân niv*r*ittyartha*m* 'svahastena' svahastalikhitena mata*m* ma amukanâmno 'mukaputrasya yad atro 'pari likhitam ity anena sa*m*panna*m* sa*m*yukta*m* kâlena ca dvividhena çâkan*r*ipâtîtasa*m*vatsararûpeṇa ca dânakâle candrasûryoparâgâdinâ sa*m*panna*m* svamudrayâ garuḍavarâhâdirûpayo 'pari bahiç cihnitam a*n*kita*m* sthira*m* d*r*iḍha*m* çâsana*m* çishyante bhavishyanto n*r*ipatayo 'nena dânâc chreyo 'nupâlana*m* iti çâsana*m* 'kârayen' mahîpatir na bhogapati*h* sandhivigrahâdikâriṇa na yena kenacit "sandhivigrahakârî tu bhaved yas tasya lekhaka*h* svaya*m* râj*n*â 'dishṭa*h* sa likhed râjaçâsanam" iti smaraṇât dânamâtreṇai 'va dânaphale siddhe çâsanakaraṇa*m* tatrai 'va bhogâdiv*r*iddhyâ phalâtiçayârtham ||

The Mitâxarâ was (as has been shown by Dr. Bühler) written in the reign of the Câlukya Vikramâditya V., or at the end of the eleventh and beginning of the twelfth century A. D.[1]

About a century or so later than the Mitâxarâ the Smṛiticandrikâ was compiled by Devaṇṇa; this also belongs to Southern India, and the section on documents is, therefore, of interest. It runs:

Atha lekhyanirûpaṇam | tatra Vasishṭha*h* |

"Laukika*m* râjakîya*m* ča lekhya*m* vidyâd dvilaxaṇam" |

C. 'Laukikam' jânapadam || tathâ ca Sa*n*grahakâra*h* |

"Râjakîya*m* jânapada*m* likhita*m* dvividha*m* smṛitam" iti |

Tatra 'râjakîya*m*' çâsanâdibhedena caturvidham ity âha Vasishṭha*h* |

"Çâsana*m* prathamam j*n*eya*m* jayapatra*m* tathâ param |
âj*n*âpraj*n*âpanâpatre râjakîya*m* caturvidham" ||

Tatra çâsana*m* nirûpayitum âha Yâj*n*avalkyah | (See v. 317 above.)

C. 'Nibandha*h*' bânijyâdikâribhi*h* prativarsha*m* pratimâsa*m* vâ ki*m*cid dhanam asmai brâhmaṇâyâ 'syai devatâyai vâ deyam ityâdi prabhusamayalabhyo 'rtha*h* | atra yady api dhanadât*r*itva*m* bânijyâdikartus tathâ 'pi nibandhakartur eva puṇya*m* taduddeçenai 've 'tarasya prav*r*itte*h* | 'bhûmim' iti grâmârâmâdînâm upalaxaṇârtham | ata eva B*r*ihaspati*h* |

[1] *Bombay Journal*, ix., pp. 134-8.

"Dattvâ bhûmyâdika*m* râjâ tâmrapaṭṭe tathâ paṭe | [1]
çâsana*m* kârayed dharmya*m* sthânava*m*çâdisa*m*yutam" ||

C. 'Kârayet' sandhivigrahâdyadhikâriṇam iti çesha*h* | tasyai 'vâ 'tra lekhane kart*r*itvaniyamât | tathâ ca Vyâsa*h* |

Râjâ tu svayam âdishṭa*h* sandhivigrahalekhaka*h* |
tâmrapaṭṭe paṭe vâ 'pi vilikhed[2] râjaçâsanam |
kriyâkârakasambandha*m* samâsârthakriyânvita*m* || iti

C. Kriyâkârakayo*h* sambandho yasmin çâsane tat tatho 'ktam | samâsârthakriyânvita*m* sa*m*xiptârthopanyâsakriyayâ samanvitam ity artha*h* | tâmrapaṭṭâdau lekhanîyam artham âha Yâj*n*avalkya*h* |

Abhilekhyâ 'tmano va*m*çyân âtmâna*m* ca mahîpati*h* |
pratigrahaparimâṇa*m* dânacchedopavarṇanam || iti |

C. Uddh*r*itamahîmaṇḍalasya Çrîpate*h* varâhavapusho varadânapratipâdakam âçîrvâdam[3] âdâv âcâraprâptam 'abhilekhyâ' 'nantaram 'âtmano va*m*çyân' prapitâmahapitâmahapitrâkhyâ*m*s trîn uktakrameṇa çauryâdiguṇavarṇanadvârâ 'âtmânam' caturtham 'abhilekhya' 'pratigrahaparimâṇâdikam' lekhayed[4] ity artha*h* | pratig*r*ihyata iti pratigraha*h* | bhûmyâdir nibandhaç ca | tasya parimâṇam iyattâ | 'dânacchedo' dîyamânabhûmyâder maryâdâ |

Vyâso 'pi |

Samâmâsatadardhâharn*r*ipanâmopalaxitam |
pratigrahît*r*ijâtyâdisagotrabrahmacârikam || iti ||

C. Sampradânasyâ 'sâdhâraṇatvâvabodhaka*m* jâtikulaçâkhâdikam api lekhanîyam ity uttarârdhasyâ 'rtha*h* | tathâ 'nyad api[5] lekhanîya*m* sa evâ 'ha |

Sthâna*m* va*m*çânupûrvya*m* ca deça*m* grâmam upâgatam |
brâhmaṇâ*m*s tu tathâ câ 'nyân mânyân adhik*r*itân likhet ||
kuṭumbino 'tha kâyasthadûtavaidyamahattarân |
mlecchacaṇḍâlaparyantân sarvân sambodhayan ||
mâtâpitror âtmanaç ca puṇyâyâ 'mukasûnave |
datta*m* mayâ 'mukâyâ 'tha dâna*m* sabrahmacâriṇe || iti ||

B*r*ihaspatir api |

Anâcchedyam anâhârya*m* sarvabhâvyavivarjitam |
candrârkasamakâlîna*m* putrapautrânvayânugam ||
dâtu*h* pâlayitu*h* svarga*m* hartur narakam eva ca |
shashṭivarshasahasrâṇi dânâcchedaphala*m* likhet || iti ||

C. Âgâmin*r*ipâdibodhanârtham iti çesha*h* | ata eva Vyâsa*h* |

Shashṭivarshasahasrâṇi dânâcchedaphala*m* tathâ |
âgâmin*r*ipasâmantabodhanârtha*m* n*r*ipo likhet ||

Tathâ 'pi çlokântaram api lekhanîya*m*[6] tenai 'va paṭhitam |

---

[1] *v. l.* °paṭṭe 'thavâ paṭe.
[2] *v. l.* prali°
[3] *v. l.* âçîrvacanam.
[4] *v. l.* lekhyam.
[5] *v. l.* tad anyad api.
[6] *v. l.* çlokântaralekhanam api.

Sâmânyo 'yam dharmasetur nripâṇâm
kâle kâle pâlanîyo bhavâdbhiḥ[1] |
sarvân etân[2] bhâvinaḥ pârthivendrân
bhûyo bhûyo yâcate râmabhadraḥ || iti ||

Tato râjâ svayam svahastam likhet | tathâ ca sa eva |

Sanniveçam pramâṇam ca svahastam ca likhet svayam | iti ||

C. Matam me 'mukaputrasyâ 'mukasya mahîpater yad atro 'pari likhitam iti svayam likhed ity arthaḥ | lekhakaç ca svanâma likhet | tathâ ca sa eva |

Sandhivigrahakârî ca bhaved yaç câ 'pi lekhakaḥ |
svayam râjnâ samâdishṭaḥ sa likhed râjaçâsanam ||
svanâma tu likhet paçcân mudritam râjamudrayâ |
grâmaxetragrihâdînâm îdrik syâd râjaçâsanam || iti ||

C. Etac ca pratigrahîtûr arpaṇîyam tasyo 'payogitvât | ata eva Vishṇuḥ |

Paṭe vâ tâmrapaṭṭe vâ likhitam svamudrânkam câ 'gâminripatiparijnânârtham dadyât | iti ||

Sangrahakâro 'pi |

Râjasvahastacihnena râjoddeçena samyutam |
yuktam râjâbhidhânena mudritam râjamudrayâ ||
svalipyanavaçabdoktisampûrṇâvayavâxaram |
çâsanam râjadattam syât sandhivigrahalekhakaiḥ || iti |

C. Sandhivigrahalekhakair likhitam uktavidham anyasmai râjadattam çâsanâkhyam lekhyam syâd ity arthaḥ | etac ca çâsanam[3] na dânasiddhyartham tasya pratigraheṇai 'va siddheḥ | kim tu dattasya sthairyakaraṇârtham sthiratve 'xayaphalaçruteḥ | tathâ hi |

Ruṇaddhi rodasi câ 'sya yâvat kîrtis tarasvinî |
tâvat kilâ 'yam adhyâste sukritî vaibudham padam ||

Anenai 'vâ 'bhiprâyeṇa Yâjnavalkyeno 'ktam[4] |

Svahastakâlasampannam çâsanam kârayet sthiram | iti

C. 'Kâlasampannam' samvatsarâdiviçeshitadânâdino 'petam | tathâ ca Vyâsaḥ |

Jnâtam maye 'ti likhitam dâtrâ 'dhyaxâxarair yutam |
abdamâsatadardhâhorâjamudrânkitam tathâ |
anena vidhinâ lekhyam râjaçâsanakam likhet || iti ||

Tathâ sa eva jayapatram nirûpayitum âha |

Vyavahârân svayam drishṭvâ çrutvâ vâ prâḍvivâkataḥ |
jayapatram tato dadyât parijnânâya pârthivaḥ ||

Kasmai dadyâd ity apexite sa evâ 'ha |

Jangamam sthâvaram yena pramâṇenâ 'tmasâtkritam |
bhâgâbhiçâpasandigdho yaḥ samyag vijayî bhavet |
tasya râjnâ pradâtavyam jayapatram suniçcitam ||

Brihaspatir api |

Pûrvottarakriyâyuktam nirṇayântam yadâ nripaḥ |
pradadyâj jayine lekhyam jayapatram tad ucyate ||

---

1) *v. l.* mahâdbhiḥ.
2) *v. l.* yâmç câ 'py anyân.
3) *v. l.* çâsanadânam.
4) *v. l.* °nâ 'py uktam.

C. Pûrvottarakriyâyuktam iti v*r*ittântopalaxaṇârtham | yata âha sa eva |

Yad v*r*itta*m* vyavahâre tu pûrvapaxottarâdikam |
kriyâvadhâraṇopeta*m* jayapatre 'khila*m* likhet ||

Vyâso 'pi |

Pûrvottarak*r*iyâpâda*m* pramâṇa*m* tatparîxaṇam |
nigada*m* sm*r*itivâkya*m* ca yathâsabhya*m* viniçcitam |
etat sarva*m* samâsena jayapatre 'bhilekhayet || iti |

C. 'Kriyâpâdam' kriyâbhimarçanapâda*m* pratyâkalitapâdam iti yâvat | 'nigada*h*' sâxivacanam | 'yathâsabhyam' sabhyânatikrameṇa | 'samâsena' sa*m*xepena | Kâtyâyano 'pi |

Arthipratyarthivâkyâni pratij*n*â sâxivâk tathâ |
nirṇayaç ca yathâ tasya yathâ câ 'vadhrita*m* svayam |
etad yathâxara*m* lekhye yathâpûrva*m* niveçayet || iti |

C. 'Yathâpûrvam' ity etat tena prapa*n*citam |

Abhiyoktrabhiyuktânâ*m* vacana*m* prâ*n* viveçayet |
sabhyânâ*m* prâḍvivâkasya kulânâ*m* vâ tata*h* param |
niçcaya*m* sm*r*itiçâstrasya mata*m* tatrai 'va lekhayet || iti |

C. 'Matam' n*r*ipâdînâm iti çesha*h* | tal lekhana*m* tu svahastena parahastato matalekhanasya yathâ câ 'vadh*r*ita*m* 'svayam' ity anena pûrvam eva vihitatvat | ata evo 'kta*m* tenai 'va |

Siddhenâ 'rthena sa*m*yojyo vâdî satkârapûrvakam |
lekhya*m* svahastasa*m*yukta*m* tasmai dadyât tu pârthiva*h* ||
sabhâsadaç ca ye tatra sm*r*itiçâstravida*h* sthitâ*h* |
yathâlekhya*m* vidhau tadvat svahasta*m* tatra dâpayet || iti |

C. Râjâ tân sabhyân jânapadalekhyavaj jayapatre svahasta*m* dâpayed ity artha*h* | V*r*iddhavasishṭho 'pi |

Prâḍvivâkâdihastâ*n*ka*m* mudrita*m* râjamudrayâ |
siddhe 'rthe vâdine dadyâj jayine jayapatrakam ||

C. Evam ukta*m* jayapatra*m* paççâtkâram[1] ity âha Kâtyâyana*h* |

Anena vidhinâ lekhya*m* paççâtkâra*m* vidur budhâ*h* | iti |

C. Aya*m* ca paççâtkâro nirṇayaviçesha eva na sarvatre 'ty âha.sa eva |

Nirastâ tu kriyâ yatra pramâṇenai va vâdinâ |
paççâtkâro bhavet tatra na sarvâsu vidhîyate ||

C. Kriyâsâdhya*m* pramâṇenai 've 'ti vada*m*ç catushpâd vyavahâra eva paççâtkâro na dvipâd vyavahâra iti kathayati |

Spashṭîk*r*ita*m* cai 'tad B*r*ihaspatinâ |

Sâdhayet[2] sâdhya*m* artha*m* tu catushpâdanvita*m* jaye |
râjamudrânvita*m* cai 'va jayapatrikam ishyate || iti |

C. Dvipâdvyavahâre tu bhâshottarânvita*m* jayapatram asyai 'va paççâtkârasyai 'va tatra pratishedhât[3] | anyad api jayapatra*m* tenai 'vo 'ktam |

Anyapâdâdihînebhya itareshâm pradîyate |
v*r*ittânuvâdasa*m*siddha*m* tac ca syâj jayapatrakam ||

---

[1]) *v. l.* eva*m* jayapatram paççâtkârâkhyam.
[2]) *v. l.* sâdhayan.
[3]) *v. l.* 'vâ 'sadanuvâdakatvena tatra prati°.

C. "Itareshâm" hînavâdinâm ity arthah | âjnâprajnâpanapatre dve Vasishṭhena darçite |

Sâmanteshv atha bhrityeshu râshṭrapâlâdikeshu vâ |
kâryam âdiçyate yena tad âjnâpatram ucyate ||
ritvikpurohitâcâryamânyeshv abhyarhiteshu ca |
kâryam nivedyate yena patram prajnâpanâya tat || iti ||

Brihaspatir anyad api râjakîyam prasâdalekhyâkhyam[1] âha |

Deçâdikam yatra râjâ likhitena prayacchati |
sevâçauryâdinâ tushṭah prasâdalikhitam hi tat || iti |

C. Ato râjakîyam pancavidham caturvidham iti anâsthayo 'ktam[2] iti mantavyam |
Jânapadam punar Vyâsena nirûpitam |

Likhej jânapadam lekhyam prasiddhasthânalekhakah |
râjavamçakramayutam varshamâsârdhavâsaraih ||

C. 'Yutam' ity anushajyate | 'vâsaram[3]' dinam | anyad api lekhayitavyam ity âha sa eva |

Pitripûrvanâmajâtidhanikarṇikayor likhet |
dravyabhedam pramâṇam ca vriddhim co 'bhayasammatâm ||

C. Ubhayasammatir dravyâder api viçeshaṇam | ata eva Yâjnavalkyah |

Yah kaçcid artho nishṇâtah svarucyâ tu parasparam |
lekhyam tu sâximat kâryam tasmin dhanikapûrvakam ||

C. 'Dhanikapûrvakam' dhanikanâmalekhanapûrvam | 'sâximat' nishṇâtârthajnâtribhûtamadhyasthajananâmânvitam | tathâ kâladhanikarṇikasâxyâdilekhanîyasya yâvatâ viçeshaṇena nishṭhatvasiddhis tâvadviçeshaṇânvitam lekhyam kâryam ity âha sa eva |

Samâmâsatadardhâharnâmajâtisvagotrakaih |
sabrahmacârikâtmîyapitrinâmâdicihnitam ||

C. 'Sabrahmacârikam' bahvricah kaṭhâ ityâdi çâkhâprayuktam guṇanâma | 'âtmîyapitrinâma' dhanikasâxiṇâm api pitrinâma | 'âdi'-çabdena deçâcârâvâptavarâdi grihyate | ata eva Vyâsah |

Deçasthityâ kriyâdhânapratigrahavicihnitam | iti ||

C. 'Deçasthityâ' kriyâdeçâcârânusâreṇa karaṇam | 'âdhânam' âdhih | Nârado 'pi |

Lekhyam ca sâximat kâryam aviluptakramâxaram[4] |
deçâcârasthitiyutam[5] samagram sarvavastushu ||

Vasishṭho 'pi |

Kâlam niveçya râjânâm sthânam nivasitam[6] tathâ |
dâyakam grâhakam cai 'va pitrinâmnâ ca samyutam ||
jâtim svagotram çâkhâm ca dravyam âdhim sasankhyakam |
vriddhim grâhakahastam ca viditârthau ca sâxiṇau || iti |

Grâhakahastaniveçanaprakâram[7] âha Yâjnavalkyah |

Samâpte 'rtha riṇî nâma svahastena niveçayet |
matam me 'mukaputrasya yad atro 'pari lekhitam ||

---

1) v. l. °âkhyam patram.
2) v. l. anâdaroktam.
3) v. l. vâsarah.
4) v. l. aviluptakriyânvitam.
5) v. l. kramâxaram deçâcâra.
6) v. l. nivasanam.
7) v. l. °nivecapra°.

C. 'Upari' iti vadan pûrvalikhitâxarasa*m*sthânâd adhastât svahastâxarasa*m*sthânam iti darçayati | '*r*iṇî' iti sâxiṇâm api pradarçanârtham | tathâ ca sa eva |

> Sâxiṇaç ca svahastena pit*r*inâmakapûrvakam |
> atrâ 'ham amuka*h* sâxî likheyur iti te samâ*h* ||

C. Ye 'tra[1] lekhye likhitâ*h* sâxiṇas te 'py amukaputro 'muko 'trâ 'rthe sâxî 'ti pratyeka*m* likheyu*h* | te ca[2] dvitvâdisamasa*n*khyayâ viçishṭâ bhaveyu*h* | na tritvâdivishamasa*n*khyaye 'ty artha*h* | 'sâxiṇa*h*' iti bahuvacana*m* gurutarakâryalekhyavishayam |

> Uttamarṇâdhamarṇau ca sâxiṇau lekhakas tathâ |
> samavâyena cai 'teshâ*m* lekhyam kurvîta nâ 'nyathâ || iti |

C. Hârîtena lekhyamâtre 'sâxiṇau' ity uktatvâd na tritvâdivishamasa*n*khyaye 'ty artha*h* | kenacid akârapraçleshakalpanayâ sâxisa*n*khyâniyamo vaiparîtyena varṇita*h* | sa yasmin deçe yathai 'vâ 'câras tatrai 'va grâhya*h* nâ 'nyatrâ 'svarasârthatvât | eva*m* câ 'nyak*r*italekhyasyo 'ttamarṇâdhamarṇasâxidvayalekhakarûpa[3] pa*n*capurushârûḍhatvât pa*n*cârûḍha*m* patram iti loke vyavahâra*h* | sâxisa*n*khyâdhikatve câ 'ya*m*[4] vyavahâro gauṇa iti mantavyam | lekhyamâtra*m* prak*r*itya Vyâsenâ 'py uktam |

> *R*iṇihasta*m* nâmayuta*m* sâxibhyâm pit*r*ipûrvakam | iti |

C. Ato dviprabh*r*itibhi*h* samair bhavitavyam iti niyamo deçâcârâvirodhânusandheya*h*[5] | yadâ tu lipyanabhij*n*a*h* sâxî *r*iṇî vâ[6] tadâ Nârada âha |

> Alipij*n*a *r*iṇî ya*h* syâl lekhayet svamata*m*[7] tu sa*h* |
> sâxî vâ sâxiṇâ 'nyena sarvasâxisamîpata*h* ||
> vijâtîyalipij*n*o 'pi svayam eva likhel lipim[8] |
> sarvajânapadân varṇân lekhye tu viniveçayet ||

Iti Kâtyâyanasmaraṇâc ca | sâxisvahastalekhanânantara*m* Yâj*n*avalkya*h* |

> Ubhayâbhyarthitenai 'va*m* mayâ hy amukasûnunâ |
> likhita*m* hy amukene 'ti lekhako 'nte tato likhet ||

Vyâso 'pi |

> Mayo 'bhayâbhyarthitenâ 'mukenâ[9] 'mukasûnunâ |
> svahastayukta*m* sva*m* nâma lekhakas tv antato likhet |
> eva*m*[10] jânapade lekhye vyâsenâ 'bhihito vidhi*h* || iti |

C. Antato lekhyasye 'ti çesha*h* | evam uktalekhyam ashṭavidham ity âha sa eva |

> Ciraka*m* ca svahasta*m* ca tatho 'pagatasa*n*j*n*itam |
> âdhipatra*m* caturtha*m* ca pa*n*cama*m* krayapatrakam ||
> shashṭha*m* tu sthitipatrâkhya*m* saptama*m* sandhipatrakam |
> viçuddhipatraka*m* cai 'va*m* ashṭadhâ laukika*m* sm*r*itam || iti |

---

1) *v. l.* tatra.
2) *v. l.* te 'pi
3) *v. l.* °m. rûpa.
4) *v. l.* °sa*n*khyâdhikye tv ayam.
5) *v. l.* °virodhenâ 'nusandheya*h*.
6) *v. l.* lipyanabhij*n*â*h* sâxiṇa *r*iṇî ca.
7) *v. l.* sa*m*matam.
8) *v. l.* lipij*n*atvât.
9) *v. l.* yuktenâ.
10) *v. l.* esha.

C. Nâ 'tra sankhyâ vivaxitâ vibhâgapatrâder api laukikatvât | tatra 'cirakasya' laxaṇam âha Sangrahakârah |

Cirakam nâma likhitam purâṇaih pauralekhakaih |
arthipratyarthinirdishṭair yathâsambhavasamskritaih[1] ||
svakîyaih pitrinâmâdyair arthipratyarthisâxiṇâm |
pratinâmabhir âkrântam arthisâxisvahastavat |
spashṭâvagatasamyuktam yathâsmrityuktalaxaṇam || iti ||

C. 'Samstutaih' praçastair ity arthah | Kâtyâyanas tu svahastam âha |

Grâhakena svahastena likhitam sâxivarjitam |
svahastalekhyam vijneyam pramâṇam tat smritam budhaih ||

C. Evam eva dâyakena likhitam grâhakenâ 'bhyupagatam lekhyam upagatâkhyam vijneyam || âdhipatram âha Nâradah |

Âdhim kritvâ tu yo dravyam prayunkte svadhanam dhanî |
yat tatra kriyate lekhyam âdhipatram tad ucyate ||

Anvâdhilekhye viçesham âha Prajâpatih |

Dhanî dhanena tenai 'va param âdhim nayed yadi |
smritvâ tad âdhilikhitam pûrvam câ 'sya samarpayet ||

Krayapatram Pitâmaheno 'ktam |

Krîte krayaprakâçârtham dravye yat kriyate kvacit |
vikretranumatam kretrâ jneyam tat krayapatrakam ||

Sthitipatrâdîni punah Kâtyâyaneno 'ktâni |

Câturvidyapuraçreṇigaṇapaurâdikasthitih |
tatsiddhyartham tu yal lekhyam tad bhavet sthitipatrakam || [2]
uttameshu samasteshv abhiçâpe samâgate |
vrittânuvâde lekhyam yat taj jneyam sandhipatrakam ||
abhiçâpe samuttîrṇe prâyaçcitte krite janaih |
viçuddhipatrakam jneyam tebhyah sâxisamanvitam || iti |

Brihaspatir api lekhyavibhâgam âha |

Bhâgadânakriyâdhânam samvidânam sthirâdibhih |
saptadhâ laukikam lekhyam trividham râjaçâsanam ||

C. Atrâ 'pi na sankhyâ vivaxitâ | adhikânâm api lekhyânâm etebhyo darçitatvât | ata evâ 'trâ 'digrahaṇam kritam | anyathâ gaṇitair eva saptavidhatvasiddher âdigrahaṇam apârtham[3] syât | tenai 'va taj jnâyate lekhyasankhyâ nâ 'vadhâraṇârthe 'ti | ato vividhasankhyâvadvacanânâm avirodhah[4] | bhâgalekhyâdikam svayam eva vyâcashṭe |

Bhrâtarah samvibhaktâ ye svarucyâ tu parasparam |
vibhâgapatram kurvanti bhâgalekhyam tad ucyate ||
bhûmim dattvâ tu yat patram kuryâc candrârkakâlikam |
anâcchedyam anâhâryam dânalekhyam tu tad viduh ||
grihaxetrâdikam krîtvâ tulyamûlyâxarânvitam |
patram kârayate yat tu krayalekhyam tad ucyate ||

---

1) *v. l.* samstutaih.
2) *v. l.* sthitipatram tad ucyate.
3) *v. l.* anartham.
4) *v. l.* ato na vividha°............virodhah.

jangamam sthâvaram bandham dattvâ lekhyam karoti yat[1] |
gopyabhogyakriyâyuktam âdhilekhyam tad ucyate ||
grâmo deçaç ca yat kuryân matam lekhyam[2] parasparam |
râjâvirodhi dharmârtham samvitpatram vadanti tat ||
vastrânnahînah kântâre likhitam kurute tu yat[3] |
karmâṇi te karishyâmi dâsapatram tad ucyate ||
dhanam vriddhyâ grihîtvâ svayam kuryâc ca kârayet |
uddhârapatram tat proktam riṇalekhyam manîshibhih ||

Anyad api laukikam lekhyam âha Kâtyâyanah |

Sîmâvivâde nirṇîte sîmâpatram vidhîyate | iti

Yâjnavalkyo 'pi |

Dattva 'rṇam pâṭayel lekhyam çuddhyai 'vâ 'nyat tu kârayet | iti

Lekhyaprayojanam âha Marîcih |

Sthâvare vikrayâdhâne vibhâge dâna eva ca |
likhitenâ 'pnuyât siddhim avisamvâdam eva ca[4] ||

C. 'Âdhânam' âdhih | âdyaç caçabda riṇâdinishṇâtârthasangrahârthah | avisamvâdah kâlântare 'pi nishṇâtârthasyâ 'nanyathâbhâvah | evam ca sthâvarâdâv avisamvâdena siddhim âlocya râjavamçavarshâdilekhanîyânâm[5] | avâpodvâpau kâryau teshâm drishṭârthatvât | ato na dânâdilekhye dhanikarṇikâdilekhanîyam | nâ 'pi riṇâdânâdilekhye pratigrahâdikam | evam anyatrâ 'pi lekhye lekhanîyasamûhanîyam drishṭaprayojanatvâl lekhyasya | ata evâ 'kritaprayojanasya lekhyasya kâryâxamatvena lekhyântaram utpâdyam | ata evâ 'ha Yâjnavalkyah |

Deçântarasthe durlekhyo nashṭonmrishṭe hrite tathâ |
bhinne dagdhe tathâ chinne lekhyam anyat tu kârayet ||

C. 'Deçântarasthe' sarvadhâ 'netum açakyasthânasthe | 'durlekhye' duravabodhâxare | 'bhinne' dvidhâ jâte | 'chinne' çîrṇe | Kâtyâyano 'pi |

Malair yad bheditam dagdham chidritam vîtam eva vâ |
tad anyat kârayel lekhyam svedeno 'llikhitam tathâ ||

C. 'Vîtam' vigatam | 'ullikhitam' unmrishṭam | yat punar Nâradeno 'ktam |

Lekhye deçântaranyaste çîrṇe durlikhite hrite[6] |
satas tatkâlakaraṇam asato drashṭridarçanam || iti

C. Tat tathai 'va dhanadânodyatarṇikavishayam | tatra lekhyântarakaraṇe prayojanâbhâvât | 'kâlakaraṇam' ânayanârtham tasya patrasyâ 'nayanayogyakâlakalpanam | 'drashṭridarçanam' alabhyapatrârthajnâtrijnâpanam dhanapratidâne kâryam ity arthah | etac ca patrapâṭanâsambhave 'pi sâxiṇâm sâxitvanivrittaye kâryam | pratipâdanaprakâçanârtham ca pratidattapatram grâhyam | kâlântare tu dhane deye lekhyântaram kâryam eva | ata evo 'ktam tenâ 'pi |

Chinnabhinnahritonmrishṭadagdhadurlikhiteshu ca |
kartavyam anyal lekhyam syâd esha lekhyavidhih smritah || iti ||

---

[1] v. l. yah.
[2] v. l. matalekhyam.
[3] v. l yah.
[4] v. l. sâ.
[5] v. l. ° lekhanîyatayâ.
[6] v. l. tathâ.

Iti lekhyanirûpaṇam[1]|||

These two passages give all the real information respecting royal grants and documents transferring property, that I have been able to find in Sanskrit treatises belonging to the Dharmaçâstra. The Mâdhavîya treatise on vyavahâra merely copies the Smriticandrikâ, and the Sarasvatîvilâsa contains nothing worth quoting here[2]. Of the numerous kinds of deed, described in the passage I have given from the Smriticandrikâ, we have apparently only royal grants, private transfers of land, and inscriptions recording endowments which are of any considerable antiquity and, therefore, of interest. Of all these the royal grants are the most important, but though they are very numerous I have never met with any but grants of land, and (except one) all that I have seen are on stone or on plates of copper[3]. The 'cloth' (paṭa) on which they were also written must have been much the same as Nearchus describes[4], and must have been far from durable; after the introduction of paper by the Muhammedans, so inconvenient a material would soon fall into disuse, and thus the absence of documents written on it is sufficiently explained.

The changes in the form of the plates of copper deserves notice.

The earliest grants are those of the Vengi dynasty and are long narrow slips with only 2-4 lines on a side, obviously cut in this shape to imitate the ōlais of a palm-leaf MS.[5] From the 6th to the 14th century the usual shape is an oblong about twice as long as the width; and this shape is universal, except in the grants of the Vijayanagara dynasty which are all upon much larger plates with the end, where they are secured by the ring, ornamented or rounded. In these last the lines of writing are across the shortest part of the plate; in the Vengi, Cêra and Câlukya documents the lines are always lengthwise.

Grants are always on three or more plates, the outer side of the first and last being always left unused; the object of this practice is evidently to preserve the writing from injury. The earliest grants are on 3 plates; the later on many more, as was required by the gradually increasing prolixity of these documents. To assist in preserving the parts covered with writing a practice of raising margins round the plate (by beating up and flattening the edges) was soon introduced. The earliest instances belong to the 9th or 10th century, but in the 11th century this was always done, and the practice continued till the 17th century when the preparation of such documents began to be very careless.

Grants on stone are, in the Telugu and Canarese country, nearly always on slabs of stone

1) This passage is from the Tanjore MSS. Nos. 77, 9.253 and 9.254. The last was scarcely of any use. I have not given *all* the *vv. ll.*, nor have I noticed the numerous errors of the MSS.

2) The corresponding section in the Vyavahâramayûkha (16th cent.) is given in Stokes' "Hindu Lawbooks" pp. 26-30.

3) The only exception is a grant on thin plates of silver, executed on the W. Coast (Cochin) in the last century. In the Mahâvanso a king who, being a fugitive, could get nothing better, is said to have written a grant on a Pandanus leaf. ("Mahavanso by Turnour, p. 204). The above-mentioned fact was early noticed by the Portuguese. de Barros (in 1553) says: "As escrituras que elles querem que dure pera muitos seculos . . . . como letreiros de templos, doações de juro, que dam os Reys, estas são abertas em pedra ou cobre." (Dec: i., Liv: ix. Cap: iii.)

4) See p. 4.

5) *See* Plates xx., xxi.

which are planted in the ground in temple enclosures, near temple gates or under trees. The earlier ones are very plain steles devoid of ornament, the later ones (beginning with those of the tenth century) have ornamental and rounded tops, and in this space there is generally a rude representation of the sun and moon, and sometimes of a cow *i. e.* the figure of the land which is given. In the later ones (after the great revival of the Çaiva sects in the 14th century) a figure of the liṅga is generally the principal object.

In the Tamiḻ country grants are generally engraved on the basement walls of the temples, on the pavement, or on rocks.

It is remarkable that the grants engraved on stone are far less prolix and diffuse than those on copper plates; both on copper and stone the letters are incised and not in relief.

As regards the style of royal grants there is much worthy of notice as affording sure tests of the age and authenticity of these documents. The different clauses and requisites have been very well described by the writers on the Dharmaçâstra; they are: i. the king's genealogy; ii. description of the grant, its date, conditions and the persons on whom conferred, or objects for which it is made; iii. imprecations on violators of the grant; iv. seal.

I. The genealogical part.

The earlier the date of the document, the more simple is the genealogical part. In the very early grant of Vijayanandivarmâ it nearly complies with the direction of the Sanskrit lawyers, in giving the names of three generations. The earliest Eastern Câlukya grant is also comparatively simple in this respect.[1] The earliest Western Câlukya grants are much more prolix, and towards the end of the seventh century A. D. the Eastern Câlukya grants assume in the genealogies a style that is apparently peculiar to them—a simple enumeration of the succession of the kings with the years they reigned, and recite a few historical facts.[2] Those of the Western Câlukyas are far more bombastic, and mention only the king's parentage.[3] The peculiarity of these E. Câlukya grants is their historical character. The style of the genealogies remains almost the same for a long series of years. Thus from 700 A. D. down to the grants of the earlier Côḷa kings or about 1100 A. D. there is little change introduced. In the grants of the Western Câlukyas the same remark holds good of the old kingdom; under the revival a new style prevails.

The grants of the Cêra dynasty that are in existence agree in the style of the genealogical part very nearly with those of the Câlukyas; there is an enumeration of the ancestors of the donor with comparatively little exaggeration.[4]

The Vijayanagara style is purely conventional bombast, and in bad verse for the most part. The succession of kings is carelessly given, and often sacrificed to the exigencies of metre. The genealogy is mythical; fictitious conquests are mentioned in detail, and the king's character and

1) Pl. xxiv.

2) For an example see pl. xxv.

3) See pl. xxii.

4) See the Mercara and Nâgamaṅgala grants in the *Indian Antiquary.*

actions are made to correspond exactly with the ideal of a Hindu sovereign according to the Alaṅkâraçâstra and Astrological imaginations. This style continues much the same from the 14th century down to the end of the Vijayanagara kingdom about 1600 A. D.; the latest grants are, however, far the worst. In all of them the king's panegyric is extravagant, and spun out with childish conceits[1].

The old South-Indian dynasties (Côḷa and Pâṇḍya) differ from these already mentioned in this part of the grants, though, as all the existing Tamiḻ grants are on stone, and therefore very brief, the omission of a genealogy is of not much significance. In most of these grants the king's name only is mentioned, very rarely that of his father or other ancestors, and the usual eulogies are generally confined to questionable statements of conquests and victories.

II. Description of the grant, its Conditions, Date, etc.

After the genealogical part, that of most importance is the description of the grant made and its conditions, as this part contains information as to tenures and local administration, and shows how persistently the tenures varied in the different portions of South-India[2]. This difference of tenures is often sufficient to show from what part of S. India a document of this kind comes, and also to detect forgeries; for, since the Muhammadan conquest of the South, many of the old terms have fallen into disuse, or even foreign words have taken their place. Thus the old Tamiḻ tenure kâṇiyâṭsi is now called mîrâsi (*i. e.* mîrâs an Arabic word), and the real name is little known; but this is since about 1600 A. D. only; hence many grants in the Madras, Arcot, and Cuddapah provinces that I have examined, which purport to be of the 12th and 13th centuries, are forgeries; as indeed the style of writing shows.

As these grants nearly always mention the Veda and Çâkhâ of the Brahmans in whose favour they were made, they will furnish much information as regards the brahmanical settlements in South-India.

The different methods of marking dates have been already noticed. The day of the week on which the grant is made often occurs in grants of after the 5th century A. D., and this will assist in identifying the eclipses of the moon (which are generally the occasion of such grants) as otherwise there is some uncertainty. The names of the days of the week are, however, derived from the modern Greek astrology, and thus cannot well occur before the end of the 4th century A. D.[3] The oldest grants have only the *tithi* mentioned.

The boundaries are generally ill-defined in the older grants, but are more exact in the later ones. Objects such as are described for this purpose in the Dharmaçâstra are usually mentioned[4].

---

1) See pl. xxvii. For a specimen of the latest Vijayanagara grants see the one published in the *Indian Antiquary* vol. ii. (p. 371).

2) Mr. F. W. Ellis was the first to indicate this.

3) Burgess, "Sûryasiddhânta" p. 34. This fact settles the date of the present redactions of many of the Dharmaçâstras or smritis.

4) Cfr. Mânava Dharma. Ç. viii. 245-251. Mitâxarâ p. 236 (Calcutta edition of 1829).

Pl A.

SEALS.

E. Čālukya 7th cent A.D.

Do:

Do: 945 A.D.

N. Čōḷa 1134 A.D.

Čera.

Vijayanagara, 16th c:

Do: 1601 A.D.

Where personal privileges or dignities of any kind are granted, it is always as attached to a grant of part of the royal rights over land; the two are inseparable.

It is remarkable that the description of the grant, conditions, etc. are very often in the vernacular language in Cêra grants, even though the rest is in Sanskrit. Cô*l*a and Pâ*n*d*y*a grants appear to be always in Tami*l*; grants in Telugu do not occur before the 11th century.

III. Imprecations and conclusion; attestations.

The last clause in grants consists of imprecations on those who resume or violate them, in the words already given above from the Vyâsasm*r*iti etc.[1] As these words are nearly always the same in all grants, they furnish a ready means of deciphering unusual characters.

Finally the names of the writer, and, in later times, of the engraver are sometimes added. As regards royal grants, there is little uniformity of practice in these respects; the names of witnesses are not required, but they are often to be found in early grants[2].

Very often grants are without any witnesses, and then they must be supposed to be holographs of the sovereign. In such cases 'svahasto mama' or 'svahastalikhitam' are occasionally added. The addition of witnesses to prove a royal grant seems chiefly confined to those of the Cêra dynasty. In *every* case the name of the writer comes last.

Signatures (or rather marks) came into use about 1400 A. D. and are intended to represent objects sacred to Hindus, *e. g.* a chank shell (much used by ascetics), a goad (a*n*kuça), a sword, a peacock, etc.

IV. The Seal.

The seals on Royal grants are of great importance, but unfortunately few seem to be in existence. Types of the most important that occur in South-Indian grants are given in the opposite plate (A).

a. **Cêra.** Two or three examples occur, and in all these is simply the figure of an elephant.

b. **Câlukya.** Of the Kalyâ*n*a branch I am not able to give an example. Of the Eastern (Kali*n*ga) branch I have found four: two of the seventh, one of the 10th and one of the Cô*l*a successors of the Câlukyas of the 12th century. These are remarkable in having a device like those of the Valabhî dynasty of Gujarat[3]. That of the earlier Kali*n*ga Câlukyas, Çrîvishamasiddhi [*h*] is very appropriate. Beginning with the 10th century, we find the characteristic mark of the Câlukyas, the boar; this seems to have been used by both dynasties, and is clearly referred to by the author of the Sm*r*iticandrikâ.[4] A branch of the Câlukyas that reigned near Goa appears to have used a seal with the figure of a Jain (?) ascetic.

---

1) pp. 65-6.

2) Grant in possession of the Cochin Jews; Nâgamangala grant.

3) *Indian Antiquary*, i. plates opposite p. 16.

4) See above p. 64, *line* 16. What king or kings used the Garu*d*a seal, I cannot say. The boar alludes to the Varâhâvatâra and its object.

c. **Vijayanagara.** The kings of this dynasty adopted the boar of the Câlukyas, but their seals are without a motto.

d. The **Nâyaks** that ruled the old Ve*n*gi country and the North of the Nellore district in the 15th century, used a seal with the figure of a recumbent bull.

Of the **Ve*n*gi** and other dynasties I have not been able to find seals.

These seals are cast on the ring by which the plates are held together, and which thus has the form of a huge signet ring; but owing to the way in which this is done, the metal is always spongy, and thus is very liable to decay.

As far as I have been able to observe, the seals of royal grants used in S. India have changed as follows:

a. From the earliest times up to the tenth century they were small and consisted of little beyond a motto.

b. From the tenth to the fourteenth century they were much larger, and in addition to a motto, have a number of emblems.

c. From the fourteenth to the beginning of the seventeenth century they are again smaller, but have no motto and fewer emblems.

d. From the middle of the seventeenth century down to the present, seals contain almost exclusively titles in writing, and very rarely, an emblem.

A. 2. **Grants written by the Minister (Sandhivigrahâdhikâra) for and by authority of the King.**

Examples of these grants are comparatively rare, and the only one I have as yet found in South-India is given in pl. xxiii.

Royal grants are by far the most important documents for historical purposes that exist in South-India, such as they are; but they must be interpreted in the genealogical part with the greatest caution, especially those of the later dynasties, even if their authenticity be beyond suspicion. Unfortunately there is reason to believe that forgeries were common; for in the comparatively brief lists of crimes preserved in the Dharmaçâstra, the penalty of death is assigned for forgeries of Royal grants[1]. The Hindu Law has also a special chapter (Lekhyaparîxâ) on the scrutiny of documents, the rules given are strict[2], but such as are rather used in Law Courts than by Palæographists; they are evidently the abstract standard of lawyers rather than rules always followed in such cases, for many unquestionably authentic inscriptions present instances of the fatal defects mentioned there.

---

1) Mânavadharmaçastra, ix.; 232. Yâj*n*avalkya, ii. 240.

2) *e. g.* (Kâtyâyana) Varṇavâkprakriyâyuktam asandigdha*m* sphuṭâxaram |
ahînakramacihna*m* ca lekhya*m* tat siddhim âpnuyât ||
and Sthânabhrashṭâs tv apa*n*ktisthâ*h* sandigdhâ laxaṇacyutâ*h* |
yadâ tu sa*m*sthitâ varṇâ*h* kûṭalekhya*m* tadâ bhavet ||
Hârîta: Yac ca kâkapadâkîrṇa*m* tal lekhya*m* kûṭatâm iyât | bindumâtravihîna*m* ca, etc.

B. *Private transfers of property.*

Documents recording endowments by private persons are perhaps the most common among South-Indian inscriptions. There is scarcely a temple in South-India on the walls of which numbers of such are not to be found; others are on steles or rocks. They convey all kinds of property, sometimes land, more often they record donations of gold, etc., and vary accordingly in form from elaborate deeds in the style already described[1] down to brief notes of the gift[2]. The endowments to the Conjeveram temples are mostly of saltpans; in the S. Arcot district (at Tiruṇâmalai) flocks of goats etc. are mentioned, and these records of endowments show a very primitive condition of society down to comparatively recent times. Inscriptions of this nature to which there are not witnesses must be taken to be holographs.

These documents have not the seal, but in other respects the form is much the same as that of the royal grants; it must be, however, clearly understood that their value for historical purposes is very small. Some king's name is mentioned in nearly all of them, and perhaps also, the year of his reign in which they are supposed to be written; but very often a purely mythological king is mentioned, and in some recent documents of this kind, after some purâṇa mythology, Kṛishṇarâya or some other well known king is eulogized, and then the Muhammadan Government or the "Honorable Company" is praised[3]. These details are, then, nearly always worthless, and of no value for history. The year of the king's reign, when a real sovereign is mentioned, is (as might be expected) several years wrong. In constructing genealogies of S. Indian royal families it will be most important to exclude all information derived from private documents, the value of which consists entirely in the details of tenures etc. which are very complete in them.

Private documents of this description are generally in the vernaculars; the usual Sanskrit imprecations are sometimes added at the end.

The earliest I have found are Tamiḻ documents of about the tenth or eleventh centuries.

Forgeries of private documents are excessively common, and are caused by the usual motives; the lawbooks (and especially Varadarâja's treatise) explicitly state the fact of their being common[4]. Detection of these forgeries is easy. In the first place if an attempt be made to imitate an older character (which is very seldom done) it is so bad as to betray the forger at once. Again as the dates of the rise of the chief religious sects in the South are well known, forms of names and usages which owe their origin to these sects infallibly point to the period in which a forgery has been committed. All documents of this kind which contain recitals of previous transactions are very doubtful.

1) See *Madras J.* xiii., part 2, pp. 36-47. do: part i., pp. 46-56.

2) do: part i., p. 47.

3) Ellis ("On Mirâsi Right" pp. 67-82) gives four specimens of private deeds; two in Canarese, one in Telugu and one in Tamiḻ.

4) The early enquirers into Indian tenures do not appear to have been aware that this is the case. Some such documents seem to have been used to mislead Sir T. Munro. See his life by Gleig (1861) p. 163. (Letter from him to Col. Read, *d.* 16th June 1801).

II. OTHER DOCUMENTS.

A. *Historical inscriptions.*

These come mostly under the following heads:—

1. *Memorials of satî.* The practice of widows burning themselves with their deceased husband's corpse has never been common in S. India. Memorials of this description are to be found only in the Canarese-Telugu country.

2. *Memorials of religious suicide.* This practice has been known to be common in India from the time of Alexander's expedition. It seems to have been practised in historical times chiefly by Buddhists and Jains[1].

Monuments to deceased Hindus are not uncommon in S. India, but the custom of erecting them is very modern, and I have never yet seen an inscription on one[2].

3. *Inscriptions recording the erection or repair of temples, etc.* Contrary to what is the case in Northern India, these are all very modern. The earliest recording the restoration of a temple that I have seen, is of the end of the 14th century[3]. The only inscription of this kind that I know of on a fort, is of the 17th century.

4. *Inscriptions recording the dedication of sacred images, ponds, etc.*

Inscriptions recording the dedication of Jain images are to be met with in Mysore, S. Canara and in the S. Tamiḻ country. Some are old, but dates are rare in them. The most common form is: "So and so of such a country caused this sacred image to be made[4]." Inscriptions recording the construction and dedication of tanks are rare except in the country ruled by the later Vijayanagara kings; examples occur at Cumbum and Nellore. The great irrigation works of the Kâvêrî delta were chiefly constructed by Côḷa princes in the 11th and 12th centuries, but I have never been able to hear of any inscription referring to them, and Major Mead R. E. who has visited every part of them, tells me that he has never seen anything of the kind.

5. *Inscriptions recording erection of resting places.* In Malabar charitable persons often erect two stones about five feet high, and place a flat slab on them; this is intended for the convenience of people who carry burdens, and who can thus rest on their way; as, if their loads were placed on the ground, they could not lift them again without help. The name of the persons who have had these erected is generally found inscribed.

6. *Inscriptions recording the dedication of temple utensils: vessels, bells, lamps, etc.*

These are to be found in all temples, but as there is hardly a single S. Indian temple that has not been pillaged more than once, very few of these inscriptions are of any remote period, and they are nearly always records of gifts by strangers, even from N. India[5].

---

1) For examples see the *Indian Antiquary*, vol. ii., pp. 266 and 323-4.

2) Cfr. Colebrooke's Life by his son, p. 152 *n.*

3) For example see *Indian Antiquary*, vol. ii., p. 361.

4) For another and longer inscription at Kârkal (in S. Canara) see the "*Indian Antiquary*" vol. ii., pp. 353-4.

5) For an inscription on a bell see *Indian Antiquary*, vol. ii., p. 360.

B. *Devotional and explanatory inscriptions.*

Devotional inscriptions are exceedingly common on the floors and in all parts of S. Indian temples; they simply record the adoration of perhaps wealthy and distinguished pilgrims, and are very short. The inscription at Seven Pagodas[1] is the most diffuse that I have observed of this nature.

Inscriptions explanatory of sculptures appear to occur only on the so-called r a t h a s at the same place.

Inscriptions in two characters occur very rarely; they are generally recent and intended for the benefit of pilgrims. The first character is that in use at the place, the second is nearly always some form of Nâgarî.

The above list will show what epigraphic documents are to be found in S. India of a date previous to 1600 A. D.; this branch of Indian literature is of evident value, though the facts it is likely to furnish are not such as to be of immediate application in restoring history.

It is not impossible that other kinds of documents may yet be found, as it is certain they once were in use. Of Hindu letters we have apparently no specimens of more than one hundred years old, except perhaps among the Mahraṭhas. Allusions to letters are frequent in the dramas and the earlier of the modern artificial poems, and some of such allusions go back at least 1200 years[2].

There is also a "Letter-writer" attributed to a Vararuci, one of a Vikramâditya's "nine jewels" of course[3]; it is a small treatise, but shows that some attention was paid to the subject, and that, therefore, letters were in common use: it, however, refers to letters on paper or the like, whereas in S. India (except among foreigners) palm-leaves have always been used for this purpose. For this purpose a strip of palm-leaf is cut in the usual form, and smeared with turmeric or some similar colour for ornament. The ends are split a little way to secure the whole which is folded in a ring, and then fastened by a thread. The earliest description of such a letter that I know of is of the beginning of the 16th century in De Barros' "Asia"; he says: "As outras cousas, que servem ao modo de nossas cartas mesmas, e escritura commum, basta ser a folha escrita, e enrolada em si, e por chancella ata-se com qualquer linha, on nervo da mesma palma[4]." The writing of letters is also often mentioned in the curious Tuḷu Sagas which refer to the Bhûta worship of Canara and the Concan. Thus in the Saga of Kôṭi and Cannayya after a clerk has been sent for on a certain occasion he is ordered to write a letter. "Another man was sent to . . . . . . to bring leaves of a young palm-tree. He had the leaves exposed to the morning sun, and taken up in the evening. By this time the clerk had come . . . . He asked the Ballâḷ (chief) why he had been sent for? The Ballâḷ said: I want you now to write a letter. The clerk sat down on

1) See above p. 30, *note*.

2) *e. g.* Vâsavadattâ (ed. by Dr. F. E. Hall) p. 163—Sâ ca kritapraṇâmâ Makarandâya patrikâm upânayat.

3) "Notices" i., pp. 196-7. There is much in this tract that appears to be derived from Muhammadan custom, and not to be of Hindu origin.

4) "Asia", Decada i.; Livro ix.; Cap. iii. (vol. i.; pt. ii.; p. 323 of the edition of Lisbon, 1777).

a three-legged stool. The Ballâḷ had the bundle of palm-leaves placed before him; he (the clerk) took out a leaf from the bundle, cut off both ends and laid aside the middle. He had oil and turmeric rubbed on it, and asked the chief what he should write?[1]"

Hiouen-Thsang mentions[2] the use of palm-leaves (tâla) for writing documents in the Mysore territory, and says that these leaves were in use in all India; this was undoubtedly the only writing material used for a long time in S. India.

In what is now the Mysore territory, however, slips of cloth covered with a black paste and dried, and which can then be written on (like a slate) with a steatite or metal pencil, are much used up to the present time for accounts and even for writing copies of literary productions. The earliest reference to this material, which is called in Canarese Kaḍatam, is of about 1250 A.D.[3]

Of the use of ink (masi or masî) in S. India there are no traces till quite recent times. The earliest in use in India was made of powdered charcoal, mucilage and water, but of late years a superior kind, made of lac (I am told), has been introduced from the Mahraṭha country into some parts of S. India. This last is almost indelible, and is not injured by the action of water or damp; it is probably an invention of the Muhammadans[4].

The oldest paper documents in S. India are on either Portuguese (Goa) or English foolscap; Venetian and North-Indian paper seem not to have been used.

I have already[5] discussed the best ways of copying Indian inscriptions, and as my suggestions have been reprinted in the *Indian Antiquary*[6], and partly circulated by the Madras Government, it would be useless to give details here. I can only recommend impressions made with moist paper ("estampages") as the most certain and best method; this method never fails, but in many cases photography cannot be well applied. In some cases where inscriptions on stone are much worn, it is possible to read them with ease when the sun's light falls slantingly, so as to throw depressions into the shade, as was practised by Rafn who thus succeeded in reading the Runic sentences at the Piraeus. *Accurate* copies of Indian inscriptions are now the most pressing want of those occupied in researches respecting India, and it is impossible to take too great care in making them.

1) From a MS. Collection in my possession. During a residence of two years and a half in Canara I was able to collect some 26 of these very singular Sagas. The worship to which they refer exists at present in Canara, Malabar ?, Tinnevelly and Ceylon. Some account of it as practised in Tinnevelly is to be found in Caldwell's pamphlet on the Tinnevelly Shanars, and that of Ceylon is well described in Callaway's "Yakkun Nattanawa" (1829).

2) "Pélerins Bouddhistes" iii., p. 148.

3) I owe this fact to the Rev. F. Kittel. Cfr. also my Vaṁçabrâhmaṇa, p. xxxvii.

4) In the Mahavanso (by Turnour; 4° p. 162) vermilion (hiṅgula) is spoken of as being used for ink. This seems to be a Chinese usage.

5) "A few Suggestions as to the best way of making and utilizing copies of Indian Inscriptions". 8° Madras, 1870.

6) Vol. ii., pp. 183-7.

APPENDIX A. (See p. 40.)

For the successful interpretation of the S. Indian inscriptions, as well as for extended researches into Dravidian Comparative Philology, it is now indispensable that a history of Dravidian phonetics should be drawn up. The materials that exist for this purpose are more extensive than might be supposed, and go back to perhaps nearly two thousand years. The earliest traces are a few words recorded by the Greek Geographers of the early centuries A. D.; secondly, some Tamiḻ words mentioned by Kumârilasvâmin (700 A. D.), and others in the Mahavanso and in the travels of Chinese pilgrims; thirdly, the earlier inscriptions recording the campaigns of the Câlukyas and Coḷas; fourthly, the native grammarians of about the tenth century A. D. for the most part. Much help will also be gained from the earlier metrical compositions[1]. The Cêra inscriptions show that the Canarese language had the peculiarities which now characterise it, already in the 5th century A. D.; and Tamiḻ inscriptions of a date a few centuries later prove the same of that language.

An investigation of this nature is important from a palæographical point of view, but, at present, I can do no more than show with reference to the propositions I have advanced above (on p. 40):

i. That the Tamiḻ alphabet has always been and is still a very imperfect system for expressing the Tamiḻ sounds.

ii. That the Canarese and Telugu alphabets are adaptations of the Sanskrit alphabet, and are tolerably perfect expressions of the sounds found in those languages.

The Dravidian languages naturally separate into two classes—the Telugu which stands by itself, and the Tamiḻic dialects which comprehend all the other languages of S. India. As far however, as the history of the expression by alphabetic signs of the sounds used in these languages is concerned, the Tamiḻ and old Malayâḷam stand apart; the Canarese and Telugu must be classed together.

§ 1. Tamiḻ phonetics.

As the Tamiḻ alphabet now stands it is a very imperfect representation of the sounds to be met with in Tamiḻ.

There are at present vowel-marks for a, â, i, î, u, û, ĕ, ê, ai, ŏ, ô and au; but of these in addition to the usual pronunciation of u and ai, these two letters have very commonly the value

---

1) Dravidian words adopted in Sanskrit, and they are many, are too much disfigured and of too uncertain source to deserve a place in this list of materials for the phonetic history of these languages.

of ụ, and this is noticed by the earliest grammarians[1]. Again a, i, î, and û have distinct secondary[2] values in some cases, viz, they become 'mixed'.

These values occur in certain definite circumstances, but they are so numerous as to render the Tamiḻ alphabet very defective as far as the vowels are concerned.

The expression of the consonants is also defective[3].

Thus the following letters have distinct values:—

Letter		1. *Initial*	2. *Medial*	3. *Medial* (*if doubled*)
k	=	k	γ	k
š	=	š	j	t_s
ṭ	=	ṭ	ḍ	ṭ
t	=	t	ð	t
p	=	p	b	p

According to the pronunciation of some places k following a nasal = g, and t following a nasal = d, but it is impossible to ascertain now if this was originally the case[4].

Now the earliest specimens of Tamiḻ words that are to be found in foreign works show that the language then possessed these sounds for which there are no separate alphabetic characters, and which seem to have puzzled the Tamiḻ grammarians who leave them unnoticed[5]. These words are as follows:

In the second Girnar tablet of Açoka's edict (ç. 250 B. C.) we find Pâ(ṇ)ḍâ as the name of a king; there can be no doubt that Pâṇḍiyan or the Madura king is here intended; and Pliny, Ptolemy and the Periplus also have Pandion.

The next traces we find are in Ptolemy and the Periplus of the Red Sea which may be put as representing Tamiḻ from the first to the third centuries A. D.; and Kumârila Bhaṭṭa who lived in the 7th century. As regards the various powers of some of the vowels there is not much satisfactory evidence to be found[6], but the evidence regarding the consonants is conclusive. It is as follows:

1) Tôlkâppiyam i., 2, 24. Nannûl ii., 6, etc.

2) The cause of this I have been able to discover by means of Mr. Melville Bell's admirable book "Visible Speech". These simple vowels are effected by the *following* consonant when it closes the syllable in certain cases. These consonants are ṭ, ḻ and ḷ, but at the end of a syllable they necessarily induce modification of the vowels. As Mr. Bell (p. 75) says: "The various positions of the tongue which produce 'centre-aperture' consonants, form vowels when the channel between the organs is sufficiently expanded and firm to allow the breath to pass without oral friction or sibilation. The vowel positions thus bear a definite relation to the consonant attitudes of the different parts of the tongue."

3) It is quite certain that the Tamiḻ alphabet was always limited in extent, for the Tôlkâppiyam (i., 1, 1) and Nannûl (ii., 4) expressly put the number of *letters* at thirty. The Nannûl (ii., 8) says also: "Beginning with a, twice six are vowels; beginning with k, (there) are thrice six consonants: thus say the learned."

4) In Canarese and Telugu as spoken in some places ಡ (d) has distinctly the value of ð; but not everywhere.

5) Except they intended to include them under vague statements of irregularities of pronunciation.—Nannûl, ii., 33, etc., copying Tôlk. i., 3, 6.

6) Except in the words which occur in Bhaṭṭa Kumârila, and as these neglect the final u (as it is now written), it is safe to assume that it was then pronounced u̥ as is the case at present, and was therefore neglected in the Nâgari transcriptions as being a sound unknown to the Sanskrit alphabet, and almost imperceptible.

k, γ. [1]Sangara (=šaṅγâḍam) in Periplus Maris Eryth. § 60 [2]Sangamarta = Tam. šaṅγa-maratta (*i. e.* the town or camp by the Monetia Barlerioides trees; a station of the Nomad Sorae. Ptolemy vii., 1, § 68). [3] Bêttigô (Ptolemy vii., 1, § 68) which Dr. Caldwell has rightly identified with the Pôδiγai mountain.

ṭ, ḍ. [1] Pandion = Pâṇḍiyan. (Periplus Maris Eryth. § 58. Ptolemy vii., 1, §§ 11 & 79. Pliny, vi., 105.) [2]Túndis, *i. e.* the Tam. tuṇḍi (Periplus Maris Eryth. § 54. Ptolemy, vii., 1, § 8). [3]Cottonara (Pliny vi., 104); the last part is here evidently nâḍu (country) and the expression of ḍ by r is also found in the 'sangara' of the Periplus. [4] Kumârila has naḍer = naḍai[1].

t, δ. [1] Kolandiophônta (Periplus Maris Eryth. § 60). The first part of this name for boats or ships (as compared with the sangara or raft) is most probably the Tam. kuḻinδa = hollowed; the last, ôḍam = boat. [2] Modoura = Maδurai. (Ptolemy vii., 1, § 89. Pliny vi., 105.)

p, b. [1] Kêprobotros = Keraputra (Periplus M. Er. § 54). The b here clearly shows the influence of the Tamiḻ pronunciation. Pliny (vi., 104) has Caelobothras. [2] Kumârila has pâmb or pâmp = pâmbu. The best MSS. I now find have pâmb.

It would be easy to add other words from the Greek geographers which point to this fact, but as their identification presents more or less difficulty, I shall omit them here.

The omission of the Tamiḻ grammarians to notice this fact that the consonants have double values (viz., as surds and sonants) is unaccountable except that they had to deal with a language already reduced to writing. Tamiḻ words, however, appear to have puzzled northern and Singalese authors, and they evidently were aware that the Tamiḻ and Sanskrit or Pâli t did not mark the same sounds. Thus the Pali has Damila; the Sanskrit Dramila, just as Ziegenbalg in his Tamil Grammar (1716) calls the language "Lingua Damulica," though Baldæus (1672) being a Dutchman has T[2]. To show how the Dravidian sounds differ from the Sanskrit sounds indicated by the same letters would take too much space to be admissible here, and would need the use of special type. Since Mr. Melville Bell's "Visible Speech" has been published, and the Prâtiçâkhyas have been edited by Prof. Whitney and others, an enquiry of this kind need not present any special difficulties. At the present stage of philological research in S. India it is indispensable.

The Tamiḻ alphabet differs from the other Dravidian alphabets in using ṉ which is simply a *final* n (*i. e.* of the syllable), and is therefore unnecessary according to the S. Indian system. It is here, however, a primitive letter from the Vaṭṭeḻuttu, in original form not unlike the Sassanian generally read *man*.

It follows, then, that the pronunciation of Tamiḻ cannot have changed materially since the third century B. C.; but, as it is impossible to put the introduction of writing into the Tamiḻ country at so early a date, it is evident that the Tamiḻ alphabet is an imperfect expression of the phonetic system of that language from its origin, and that it cannot have become so by progress of phonetic decay. As the alphabets used in the Açoka inscriptions prove, the Sanskrit

1) I have already discussed the passage where these words occur in the *Indian Antiquary*, vol. i., pp. 309-310.

2) So the Peutingerian Map and the Ravenna geographer (ed. Parthey, pp. 14, 40, etc.) have Dimirice (*i. e.* Tamiḻ + ikê) which is the proper reading for the name, and not Limurikê as printed in the Periplus and Ptolemy.

grammarians had already extended the alphabet to suit their marvellously accurate discrimination between the different sounds of that language in the 3rd century B. C.; it is impossible, therefore, to suppose that the Tamil̤ alphabet is to be attributed to them. Besides their treatment of the Canarese and Telugu phonetics is totally different, as I shall now show, though the Canarese grammar was formed on the same model as the Tamil̤.

§ 2. Canarese phonetics.

The Hindu civilization of the Canarese country is quite as old as that of the Tamil̤ people, but the earliest traces we find of writing are in a modified form of the Açoka character, and the orthography, with a few unimportant exceptions and allowing for the obsolete form of the letters, is just what we find now. About the tenth century A. D. Canarese grammar was treated on the principles of the Sanskrit grammarians of the Aindra school[1], and with steady reference to Sanskrit phonetics; the author of the Canarese Grammar "Çabdamaṇidarpaṇa" evidently considered the alphabet he used as a mere adaptation from the Sanskrit, and he was perfectly right in doing so. His account is as follows[2]:

There are fourteen Sanskrit-Canarese vowels (a, â, i, î, u, û, r̥i, r̥î, lr̥i, lr̥î, e, ai, o and au) and in Canarese e and o have both long and short forms. There are 34 Sanskrit-Canarese consonants classed (vargâxara) and unclassed (avargâxara) that is to say the ordinary Sanskrit alphabet with xa, but of these aspirates are not used in Canarese except in some peculiar cases. To these are added the peculiarly Canarese letters r̥, l̤ and ḷ. The author then states (p. 44) that there are only 47 letters in pure Canarese— a, â, i, î, u, û, ĕ, ê, ai, ŏ, ô, au, k, kh, g, gh, ṅ, c, ch, j, jh, ń, ṭ, ṭh, ḍ, ḍh, ṇ, t, th, d, dh, n, p, ph, b, bh, m, y, r, l, v, s, h, x, r̥, l̤, ḷ. The Sanskrit prepossessions of the author have induced him to include erroneously the aspirates and x; h is the modern representative of p. Rejecting these letters, therefore, the remainder represent very nearly the sounds we find really exist in Tamil̤.

This Canarese Grammar is, like the Tamil̤ Tôlkâppiyam and Nannûl, a very complete work, and is really what it professes to be.

§ 3. Telugu phonetics.

Here again the grammar has been formed on Sanskrit models, but the pattern is either Pâṇini's or Hemacandra's treatise, and the terminology that of Pâṇini[3].

1) What is to be understood by the Aindra grammar will be explained in a paper on it and its history which will shortly be published by me.

2) Kittel's "Çabdamaṇidarpaṇa" pp. 13-45.

3) The dates of Nannaya Bhaṭṭa and Âtharvaṇâcârya can easily be fixed. Nannaya Bhaṭṭa translated the first part of the Mahâbhârata into Telugu for Vishṇuvardhana who was Râmânujâcârya's chief convert, and therefore lived in the middle of the 11th century. ["Cyclic Table" by C. P. Brown; Madras J. x., p. 52; Brown's "Telugu Grammar" (2nd ed.), p. i.]. Âtharvaṇâcârya is generally supposed to have preceded Nannaya; but this cannot be the case, as he twice cites Hemacandra by name ("Triliṅgaçabdânuçâsana" i., 5; iii., 13 of the Madras MS.). Hemacandra was probably born in 1088 A. D. and died in 1172 A. D. (Bombay J. x., p. 224); Âtharvaṇâcârya must, therefore, have written about fifty years later than Nannaya, and was probably a Jain rival of the Brahman Nannaya.

The earliest of the two grammars is by Nannaya; he begins by saying that Sanskrit has fifty letters, Prakrit ten less, but that Telugu has thirty-six as the other letters only occur in Sanskrit words which have been adopted in that language. These letters he says are: a, â, i. î, u, û, ĕ, ê, ai, ŏ, ô, au, two anusvâras (o and c), k, g, two č (č and t), two j (j and d), ṭ, ḍ, ṇ, t, d, n, p, b, m, y, r, l, v, s, ṛ, ḷ[1].

Âtharvaṇâcârya is by no means so precise, but as he is later than Nannaya what he says is of little importance. He mentions seven or (excluding ai and au) five vowels (*i.e.* a, i, u, e, o) which might be short, long or *pluta*[2]. He does not specifically enumerate the consonants.

Thus two Telugu grammarians not of the Aindra school have treated the Telugu alphabet far more completely than was done by Aindra grammarians in respect of the Tamiḻ, though the Telugu grammarians hold the strange theory that the Telugu language is a "Vik*r*iti" of Sanskrit[3], and treat the Grammar as a mere appendix to Sanskrit and Prakrit Grammar.

This theory is an important one in considering references to foreign words in Sanskrit grammatical works, and has been, as yet, quite misunderstood. The meaning of the term vik*r*iti, as thus used, is as follows: The grammarians (as is required by the Hindu cosmogony[4]) considered all languages to be eventually derived from the Sanskrit, much as in Europe, in the Middle Ages, Hebrew was supposed to be the source of all the languages then known; they also considered merely the *external* forms of words and not the *meaning*[5]. It was thus easy to find a plausible explanation of any foreign word by means of Sanskrit. The Mîmâmsists contended against this doctrine, as they attached more importance to the *meaning* than to the *form*[6]. In considering foreign words mentioned by Sanskrit grammarians it is necessary to keep the nature of this theory in view.

Comparing the Telugu-Canarese alphabets with the Tamiḻ it is impossible to suppose that the last is the work of Sanskrit grammarians; for had they been the authors of it, it would have been far more perfect[7], and would have shown signs of adaptation which are wanting in it. Add

---

1) "Ândhraçabdacintâmaṇi" i., 14-18 and 23.

2) "Triliṅgaçabdânuçâsanâ" i., 8-11. "Prâṇâ*h* sapta svarûpeṇa" (8) "vaca*m* (*read* auca*m*) vinâ svarâ*h* pañca hrasvadîrghaplutais tridhâ" (9).

3) "Ândhraçabdacintâmaṇi" i., 12. iii., 8. 43. 59. 83. iv., 2. 11. 23. 28. 42. 46. The first of these sûtras is: "Âdyaprak*r*iti*h* prak*r*itiç câ 'dye, eshâ tayor bhaved vik*r*iti*h*". Ahobala says on thus: " 'âdyaprak*r*iti*h*' iti sarvabhâshâmûlakatvena Ândhrabhâshâhetutvena câ 'dye Sa*m*sk*r*itabhâshâ."—"'eshâ' Ândhrabhâshâ."

4) *See* Muir's "Sanskrit Texts" i. pp. 480 flg. where several passages are to be found in which it is asserted that peoples of quite different races, *e. g.* Oḍras, Draviḍas. Kâmbojas, Yavanas and Cînas (Manu, x., 43-4); Yavanas, Cînas, Pahlavas, Ândhras and Kâmbojas (Çântiparvan); Çakas, Yavanas, Kâmbojas, Colas, and Keralas (Harivamça) were originally Xattriyas.

5) Thus Durgâcârya (on Yâska, Naig. ii., 2) says: Ekeshu deçeshu prak*r*itaya eva dhâtuçabdânâm bhâshyante vik*r*itya ekeshu | dhâtor âkhyâtapadabhâvena ya*h* prayoga*h* sâ prak*r*iti*h* | nâmîbhûtasya tasyai 'va ya*h* prayoga*h* sâ vik*r*iti*h* || There is no question of meaning here, but of form merely.

6) See the article by me (on a passage in Kumârilasvâmin's "Tantravârttika") in the *Indian Antiquary*, vol. i.

7) The Sanskrit-Malayâḷam alphabet as adapted to Malayâḷam uses g, j, ḍ, d, b to express γ, ǰ, ḍ, ð, and b.

to this that the Tamil letters ḷ, ḻ[1] and ṟ are totally distinct from the Telugu-Canarese corresponding letters and ṉ superfluous, and the amount of proof that the Vaṭṭeḻuttu is of independent origin, and not derived from the S. Açoka character, appears to be conclusive[2].

APPENDIX B.

As alphabets of the hands and styles of writing current at different periods give but a faint impression of the character of the documents from which they are derived, I shall now give specimens of the most important inscriptions from which I have derived the alphabets discussed already.

Without inordinately extending the size of this work it would be impossible to give complete copies of all these inscriptions, as most of them are, at least, five or six times as long as the specimens given. Nor do I give a translation of the passages as it would be irrelevant to my purpose. I give however a transliteration of the specimens that are likely to prove not easy to read at first. Where I have found it necessary to add a syllable that has been omitted, I have done so in ( ) . My object being purely palæographical, I have been obliged to choose these specimens accordingly.

Plates xx. *and* xxi.[3]

1*b. line* 1. svasti. vijayaVeṅgîpurâd bhagavacCitrarathasvâmipâdânuddhyâno Bappabha-
2. ṭṭâraka[4]pâdabhaktaḫ paramabhâgavataç Çâlaṅkâyano[5] mahârâjâ Ca-

1) In Telugu ḻ is always expressed by ḍ; *e.g.* Côḍa=śôḷa.

2) It may perhaps be as well to remark that the Tamil people (as Mr. F. W. Ellis first noticed) have always put their language and literature on a level with the Sanskrit, calling their own tongue Teṉmoḻi (Southern speech) and the Sanskrit Vaḍamoḻi or northern speech. The Tamil literature, as it now exists, shows nothing that is not of Sanskritic origin. (This was long ago remarked by Mr. Curzon in J. R. As. Soc.)

3) This document was first described by Sir W. Elliot (in Madras J. xiii., pp. 302-6) who then showed that it belongs to a dynasty that preceded the Eastern or Kaliṅga Câlukyas. According to that account the plates were "found in the *kol* or lake near Masulipatam, some years ago (*i. e.* prior to 1840) and had been laid aside as utterly unintelligible." A facsimile and transcript in Nâgarî are promised in this article, but I have not been able to find them in any copy of the Madras J. accessible to me. I have used an impression made on china paper, which I got from a man formerly in Sir W. Elliot's employ; of the original plates I can learn nothing.

4) ? Some local deity.

5) Cfr. gaṇa râjanyâdi (P. iv., 2, 53); it is included among the Bhṛigu gotras of Âçvalâyana, and was of course that of the family-priest.

2. 1. ṇḍavarmmaṇas sûnur jyeshṭho mahârâjaçrîVijayanandivarmmâ Kuḍuhâravishaye
2. Viḍenyurpallikâ[1]grâme Munyaḍasahitân grâmy(â)n samâjñâpayati: asti
2b. — 1. asmâbhir asmatkulagotradharmmayamkânti[2]kîrttipravarddhanâya eteshâ(*m*) Karava-
2. kaçrîvarâgrâhâre vâstavyânâm nânâgotracaraṇasvâddhyâyânâ*m*
3. — 1. saptapañcâçaduttaraçatânâm brâhmaṇânâm esha grâmaḫ pratta*h*. tad avetya
2. deçâdhipatyâyuktakavallabharâjapurushâdibhis sarvaparihârai*h*
3b. — 1. pariharttavyo raxitavyaç ca. pravarddhamânavijayarâjyasaptamasa(*m*)vatsara-
2. sya Paushyamâsak*r*ishṇapaxasyâ 'shṭamyâm paṭṭikâ[3] dattâ || tatrâ 'jñapti*h*
4. — 1. mûlakarabhojakâ[4] || "bahubhir vvasudhâ dattâ bahubiç câ 'nupâlitâ
2. yasya yasya yadâ bhûm(i)*h* tasya tasya tadâ phala*m* ||
3. shashṭivarshasahasrâṇi svargge k(r)îḍati bhûmida âxeptâ câ 'bhimantâ ca tâny eva na(ra)ke vase(t).

Plate xxii.

West (Kalyâṇa) Calukya 608 A. D.[5]

jayaty âvishk*r*ita*m* Vishṇor vvarâhaxobitârṇṇavan daxiṇonnatadra*m*shtrâgra*m* viçrânta*m* bhuvana*m* vapu*h*[6] çrîmatâ*m* sa(2)ka(labhu)vanastûyamânaMânavyasagotrâṇâ*m* Hârîtiputrâṇâ*m* saptalo-(ka)mât*r*ibhis saptamât*r*ibhir abhiva*m*(3)-di(tânâ*m* Kâr)ttikeyapariraxaṇaprâptakalyâṇapara*m*parâṇân Nârâyaṇaprasâdasamâsâditânâ*m* varâhalâ*m*ca(4)nexaṇaxaṇavaçavaçîk*r*itâçeshamahîbh*r*itâ*m* Câdukhyânâ*m*[7] kulam ala*m*karishṇor açvamedhâvanapade pade Ga*m*gâja(5)lasnânapavitrîk*r*itagâ(?)trasya çrîPŏlukeçivallabhamahârâjâdirâjaparameçvaraparamabhaṭṭârakapar(â)(6)kramâkrântaBediva*m*syâdiparan*r*ipatimaṇḍalapraṇibaddhaviçuddhaKî(r)ttivarmaçrîp*r*ithuvîvallabhamahârâja(7)râjaparameçvaraparamabhaṭṭârakaputra*h* samarasa*m*çaktasakalottarapatheçvaraçrîHarîshavarddhanaparâja(8)-yopalabdhaparameçvaraparamanâmadheyasya Satyâçrayaçrîp*r*ithuvîvallabhamahârâjâdirâjaparame-(9)çva(ra)sya p*r*iyatanaya*h* Citrakaṇṭhapravaratura*m*gameṇai 'kenai 'va pratîtânekasamaramukhe ripun*r*ipatiru-(10)dhi(ra)jalasvâdanarasanâyamânajvalananiçitanistri*m*çadhârâ yadavabh*r*itadharaṇîdharabhu-[pl. ii.]jaṅga—*etc.*

---

1) In modern Telugu pallikâ is palliya.

2) ? sa*m*krânti.

3) paṭṭikâ for patrikâ, and the construction asti . . . . pratta*h* point to prakrit influences.

4) The grant is therefore of the royal dues from the village. The village itself (or the proprietary right to the ground) could not be given by Hindu Law as it belongs to the occupants; all the king could give is his right to certain shares of the produce etc. (See the discussion which settles this point in Mîmâ*m*sâsûtra, vi. 7, 2.).

5) For putra*h* (7) read putrasya. The only explanation of the errors in this and similar documents is, that they were *dictated* to the engraver (*lipikara*). The irregular lengthening of accented vowels points to this fact.

6) This is a çloka.

7) Calukya, Callukya, Calkya and Câlukya also occur.

Plate xxiii.

This document is in Old Canarese, and presents many difficulties in parts of the second leaf. I give the transliteration, therefore, of the first leaf only, about which there cannot be any doubt, and leave the rest to Mr. Kittel who alone can deal with documents like this.

1. svasti. çakan*r*ipakâlâtîtasa*m*vatsara*m*gaḷ eḷnûṟippattârane-
2. yâ Subhânu e*m*bhâ va(r)shadâ Vaisâkhamâsak*r*ishṇapa-
3. xapañcame b*r*ihaspativâramâgi svastiprabhû-
4. tavarshaçrîp*r*ithuvîvallabhamahârâjâdhirâjapa(ra)me-
5. çvaraGoyindarabhaṭâraragâ Muṇḍajjamahâde-
6. viykagi râjyapra(va)rdhamânakâladôḷ *etc.*

The third leaf contains the usual Sanskrit imprecations.

Plate xxiv.

This document was found near Vizagapatam in 1867, and is now (?) in the Government Office at Madras.[1]

Pl. 1. *line* 1. svasti: çrîmatCalukyakulajalanidhisamudito n*r*ipatiniçâkara*h* sva-
2. bhrûlatâvajñanamitaripun*r*ipatimakuṭamaṇiprabhâvicchuritacaraṇâravinda-
3. dvaya*h* Satyâçrayaçrîvallabhamahârâja*h*; tasya priyânuja*h* sthalajala-
4. vanagirivishamadurggeshu labdhasiddhitvâd vishamasiddhi*h* dînânâthadvijavasuv*r*ishṭi-
5. pravarshaṇatayâ Kâmadhenu*h* yuvatishu madanâyamânacâruçarîratvân Makaradhvaja(*h*)

2. 1. svadânârṇṇaveshu parimagnakaliprabhâva*h* anekasamaravijayasamudita(*h*)
2. vimalayaçoviçeshavibhûshitasakaladiṅmaṇḍala*h* Manur iva vinayajña*h* P*r*ithu-
3. riva p*r*ithukîrtti*h* Gurur iva matimân Paramabrahmaṇya*h* çrîVishṇuvarddhanamahârâja*h*
4. Dimilavishaye Kâlvakoṇḍa(?)grâmâdhivâsina*h* kuṭumbinas samavetân imam arttham â-
5. jñâpayati yathâ: adhîtâvagatavedavedâṅgasya Brahmaçarmmaṇa*h* pautrâbhyâm adhi-

2*b*. 1. gatasvaçâkhâcoditasvakarmmânushṭhânatatparasyaDu(r)gaçarmmaṇa*h* putrâbhyâ(*m*)ve-
2. dâṅgetihâsapurâṇadharmmaçâstrâdyanekâgamatatvavidbhyâ*m* Gautam(a)gotrâbhyâ*m*
3. Taittirikacaraṇâbhyâ*m*[2] VishṇuçarmmaMâdhavaçarmmabhyâ*m* Pûki(?)vishaye Ceṟupura-
4. grâmam adhivasata*h* Çrâvaṇamâse candragrahaṇanimitte sarvvakaraparihâre-
5. ṇâ 'grahârîk*r*itya[3] svapuṇyâyurârogyayaçobhiv*r*iddhaye, grâmo 'ya*m* datta*h*; asya

---

1) For the lunar eclipse mentioned in pl. 2*b*., only that which occurred in 622 A. D. appears to satisfy all the necessary conditions.

2) Should be Taittirîya; it is here correctly called a Caraṇa. Max Müller's A. Sanskrit Literature, p. 371.

3) *i. e.* the inhabitants were constituted into an agrahâra and the village was then given to the 2 persons named, who had then a right to the dues formerly paid to the king.

3. 1. kaiçcid api na bâdhâ karaṇîyâ | atra Vyâsagîtau: bahubhir vvasudhâ dattâ bahu-
2. bhiç câ 'nupâlitâ; yasya yasya yadâ bhûmi*h* tasya tasya tadâ phala*m* shashṭivarsha-
3. sahasrâṇi svargge modati bhûmida*h* âxeptâ câ 'numantâ ca tâny eva narake
4. vaset. çrîMatîmatsya ? lîprasuta*h* svabhujabalapratâpâvanataripu-
5. r âjñaptiradavidurjjaya*h* sa ? â ? ? â ? ka ? igâru: [1]

Plate xxv.

This plate gives the first eighteen lines of an Inscription d. 945 A. D. and thus of the most flourishing period of the eastern or Kaliṅga Câlukyas. This text runs:

I. (1) svasti. çrîmatâ*m* sakalabhuvanasa*m*stûyamânaMânavyasagotrânâ*m* Hârî-(2)tiputrâṇâ*m* Kauçikîvaraprasâdalabdharâjyânâ*m* mât*r*igaṇaparipâlitânâ*m* (3) svâmiMahâsenapâdânudhyâtânâ*m* bhagavanNârâyaṇaprasâdasamâsâdi(4)tavaravarâhalâ[ñcha]nexaṇaxaṇavaçîk*r*itârâtimaṇḍalânâm aç-vamedhâ-(5)vabh*r*itasnânapavitrîk*r*itavapushâ Câlukyânâ*m* kulam ala*m*karishṇo*h* Sa-(6)tyâçraya vallabhendrasya bhrâtâ Kubjavishṇuvarddhano 'shṭâdaça varshâṇi Veṅgî-(7 de)çam apâlayat | tadât-majo Jayasi*m*has tri*m*çata*m* | tadanujendrarâjana-(8)ndano Vishṇuvarddhano nava | tatsûnur mMa-ṅgiyuvarâja*h* pañcavi*m*çati*m* | tatputro (9) Jayasi*m*has trayodaça | tadavaraja*h* Kaukikilish shaṇ mâsân | tasya jyeshṭo bhrâ—

II. (1) tâ Vishṇuvarddha(nam) uccâṭya saptatri*m*çata*m* | tatputro Vijayâdityabhaṭṭârako (2) 'shṭâdaça | tatsuto Vishṇuvarddhanash shaṭtri*m*çata*m* | tatsuto Vijayâdityanarendra-(3)m*r*igarâjaç câ 'shṭâcatvâri*m*çata*m* | tatsuta*h* Kalivishṇuvarddhano dvyarddhava(r)shâṇi || (4) tatsuto Guṇagâ*m*ka-vijayâdityaç catu(çc)atvâri*m*çata*m* | ta-(5)danujayuvarâja*h* Vikramâdityabhûpate*h* sûnuç Câlukya-(6) bhîmabhûpâlas tri*m*çata*m* || tatputra*h* Kollabhigaṇḍavijayâ-(7)ditya*h* shaṇ mâsâ(n) | tatsû(nu)r Ammarâja*h* sapta varshâṇi || tatsutam Vijayâ(8)-ditya*m* bâlam uccâṭya Tâlapo mâsam ekam | ta(m) jitvâ yudhi Câlukya(9)-bhîmabhûmipates suta*h* Vikramâditya bhûpo 'pân mâsân ekâdaça xiti*m*. |

Plate xxvi.

It is unnecessary to give a transcript of this, as, coming after the earlier grants, the character presents no difficulty.

Plate xxvii.

1. (çri) ya*m* Bhukkabhûpati*m* yatkîrtilaxmâ*h* krîḍanty â(va)-
hamaṇḍa*m* ratnamaṇṭhapa*m* muktâcchatra*m* çaçâ(*m*)-

[1] Is this intended for a signature?

kasudîpa*h* çukradivâkarau | dharm(e)ṇa raxati
x(o)ṇ(î)*m* vîraçrîBhukkabhûpatau | nirâta*m*kâbha-
yât tasmin nityabhogotsavâ*h* prajâ*h* Gaurîsaha-
carât tasmât prâdurâsîn Maheçvarât | çaktyâ
pratîtaska*m*ça*m*ço (*sic?*) râjâ Harihareçvara*h* | sarva-
varṇasamâcârapratipâlanatatpare | tasmin
catu*h*samudrâ*m*tâ bhûmi*h* kâmadughâ 'bhavat si*m*-
hâsanajushas tasya kî(r)tyâ bhâ*m*ti diço daça | u-
dayâdrigatasye 'ndo(r) jyotsnâ yeva[1]) kalânidhe*h* |
tulâpurushadânâdimahâdânâni shoḍaça | k*r*i-
tavân pratirâjanyavajrapâtâtmavaibhava*h* ||
çrîmadrâjâdhirâjarâjaparameçvara*h* | pû(r)vada-
xiṇapaçcimottarasamudrâdhîçvara*h* | sa nishkâ-
ritadushṭarâjarâjanyabhuja*m*gavainateya*h* |
dâraṇâgatavajrapa*m*jara*h* | kalikâladharma*h* |
Karṇâṭakalaxmîkarṇâvata*m*sa*h* | catu(r)varṇâdara-
(ṇa) pâlaka*h* | kulagiritaṭalikhitaghoshaṇa*h*
raṇara*m*gabhishaṇa*h*·| pararâjarâjî 'va sudhâka-
ra*h* | paranârîsahodara*h* | puṇyaçl(o)kapraha(r)sha*h* |
çârdûlamadabha*m*jana*h* | CeraColaPâṇḍyasth(â)-
panâcârya*h* | Vedabhâshyaprakâçaka*h* | vaidîkamârga-
sthâpanâcârya*h* | karmopetâdhvary(u)*h* | râjakalyâṇaçekhara-
[sidhasârasvatetyâdivirudâvalibhûshita*h* sa khalu DravirapratâpaHariharamahârâya*h* *etc.*]

Plate xxviii. *b.*

The MS. from which this is taken is a Vratavallî which was written for the last of the Telugu Nâyaks of Tanjore—Vijayacokka. He was conquered by the Mahraṭhas soon after 1670. There is no distinction made between long and short i, otherwise every letter is perfectly distinct and legible.

Plate xxix. *a.*

In the want of Tamiḻ types, I cannot give a transcript of this, for which see Madras Journal, xiii., pt. i., p. 126.

[1]) Yeva, the common Telugu way of writing eva. cf. *pl.* viii. There are several errors in orthography in this document. Much is in çlokas

Plate xxix. *b.*

I give this document in full as transcribed by a Nâyar accustomed to read the character.

പുളിയപ്പറമ്പിൽ വായിക്കര-നമ്പുടിപ്പാട്ടിലെ എളമീന്ന-എഴുന്നെള്ളി തമ്പുരാനെ കണ്ടപ്രകാരവും, കൊടുത്തയച്ച പ്രകാരവും എഴുതിയ കണക്ക.

കൊല്ലം ൻ൦൦-ാമത-എടവഞായറ ൧൫ ൹- വ്യാഴാഴ്ച നാള-പൊന്നാനി വായ്ക്കൽ-പയിരനെല്ലൂരകോവിലകത്ത ഇരുന്നരുളെ.

മുൻമ്പ വ്വ ൹- ബൊധനാഴ്ച നാള അസ്തമിച്ച, എളയനമ്പുടി, തിരുമുൽപ്പാട്ടന്ന എഴുന്നെള്ളി, തമ്പുരാനെ കാണുകയും ചെയ്തു. രണ്ടെടത്തും ഇരുന്നരുളി കണ്ടതും ഇല്ലാ ൧൫ ൹- യാത്ര ഉണൎത്തിച്ച, പുറപ്പെടുകയിൽ, അന്ന യാത്ര ഉണൎത്തിക്കുമ്പോള മരിയാദ ആകും വലിമ തന്നെ വേണമെന്ന ഉണൎത്തിച്ചതിൻെറ ശേഷം, അന്ന വലിമ തന്നെ എന്ന അരുളിച്ചെയ്തു. നമ്പൃതിരി തിരുമുൽപ്പാട്ടിന്ന തിരുമുൻമ്പിൽ എഴുന്നെള്ളിയാറെ, ഇരിപ്പാൻ ഒരു കരിമ്പടം കൊടുത്തതിൽ, ഇരുന്ന യാത്ര ഉണൎത്തിച്ച പൊറപ്പെടുകയിൽ കൊടുത്ത—

ശകലാസ്സു കുപ്പായം	—൧	മെ-അപ്പുറ നമ്പൃതിരിക്ക വീരവാളി മുണ്ട	—൧
മെ-കൊടുത്ത കസവതൊപ്പി	—൧	മെ-പുതുക്കുടികൊക്കത്ത നമ്പൃതിരിക്ക വീരവാളി മുണ്ട	—൧
മെ-ഒക്കത്തക്ക വന്നതിൽ പുപ്പകുന്നന്മേൽ നമ്പൃ		തന്നിമങ്ങലത്ത കണക്കപ്പിള്ളക്ക വീരവാളി മുണ്ട	—൧
തിരിക്ക കൊടുത്ത വീരവാളി മുണ്ട	—൧	ആകെപേര വ്വ-ന്ന കൊടുത്ത വീരവാളി മുണ്ട	—വ്വ
മെ-എളേടത്ത കൊളേരി നമ്പൃതിരിക്ക കൊടു		മെ-കൂടിവന്ന-നമ്പ്യാര.ന്മാര-പേര ഫ-ന്നും—പൊതു	
ത്ത വീരവാളി മുണ്ട	—൧	വാന്മാര-പേര ൩-ന്നും—കണക്കപ്പിള്ളമാര-പേര ൬-ന്നും	
മെ-തെവർ-തല-മല്ലിശ്ശേരി നമ്പൃതിരിക്ക വീരവാളി മുണ്ട	—൧	ആകെ പേര ധ൧-ന്ന കൊടുത്ത കന്നിയൊല മുറിപട്ട	—ധ൧
മെ-കൊട്ടൊൽ നമ്പൃതിരിക്ക കൊടുത്ത വീരവാളി മുണ്ട	—൧	മെ-നായന്മാരപേര ൨൪-ക്ക കൊടുത്ത കവണി	
മെ-മുണ്ടൊട്ടുപുലിയപറമ്പിൽ നമ്പൃതിരിക്ക കൊടു		ഉറുമാല	—൧൩൪൪
ത്ത വീരവാളി മുണ്ട	—൧	മെ-വാലിയക്കാരപേര ധഫ-ന്ന കൊടുത്ത റുമാല	—ഗധന്ന

എഴുന്നെള്ളി പാൎത്തന്ന നാള ൻ ദിവസവും ഇരുന്ന കഴികയും ചെയ്തു.

മെ-നമ്പുടിപ്പാട്ടിലെക്ക ഒര ആനവേണമെന്ന പറഞ്ഞതിനെ ചീവളയനാട്ട അമ്മക്ക ഇരുത്തിയ ചെറിയ കൊമ്പനാന കിടാവിനെ കൊടുക്കയിൽ വിലവെച്ച ൱൫൰൨ — ൱ ൨൰൫൭൬-ന്ന കൊറവടികഴ്ച — വാങ്ങിയ വില്ലിട്ട-ത്തുമ്പ കറവിയും കൂടി ആമാട ൮൭൰൬.

മെ-വരവുപുതുപ്പണം ൩൭൰൯ ശേഷം പണം ൨൰൫-രത്തിന്ന ഉറുപ്പിക കൊടുത്ത വിടുകയും ചെയ്തു.

This is taken from a Granthavari (or book of counterparts of leases, etc.) belonging to the Zamorin.

Plate XXX. *a.*

This is a page of a Vṛitti on the Pûrvamîmâ*m*sâ sûtras of Jaimini, which is called Phalavatî

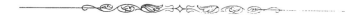

ADDENDA AND CORRIGENDA.

Page

4 *note* 2. Profr. Haug ("Ueber das Wesen und den Werth des wedischen Accents", p. 18) says: "Den ersten Anstoss zur schriftlichen Aufzeichnung wedischer Texte gab ohne Zweifel der Buddhismus, durch den die Schreibekunst eigentlich erst recht in Indien verbreitet wurde".

5 *line* 8. cfr. Chabas, "Études sur l'antiquité historique", 2nd ed. p. 94.

— 16. This identification is due to Mr. E. Thomas.

— *notes, line* 1. *For* toγai *read* tôγai (Can: sôgĕ). The long ô is a conclusive proof that this word is not an adaptation of the Sanskrit çikhin.

— — — 11. *For* capi *read* cepi.

6 *note* 3. *For* App. B. *read* App. A.

— 4. Lassen (in the second edition of his I. A.—K. ii. p. 477) puts Pâṇini at 330 B. C.

7 *note* 1. Profr. Max Müller (*Rigveda* iv. p. lxxiv. *n.*) points out that l i p i k a r a means a man who makes public inscriptions. He considers that Yavanânî lipi is most likely that variety of the Semitic alphabet which previous to Alexander and previous to Pâṇini became the type of the Indian alphabet. May it not mean the Bactrian or N. Açoka character as used by the Greeks in Bactria or even their Greek character, and be an interpolation in the text of Pâṇini perhaps by a pupil? If Pâṇini be put in the 3rd century B. C. or half a century later than is usually done, there could be no difficulty about the word.

9 *line* 23. Profr. J. Oppert ("Journal Asiatique" vii. *ème* série, iii. pp. 238 flg.) has shown that the cuneiform characters of the Achæmenidan inscriptions are probably the invention of Cyrus, and has given the principle of derivation from the Babylonian cuneiform.

last line. On the clay contract-tablets see also Sayce's "Principles of Comparative Philology" p. 196; according to which Aramaic was the commercial language of the Assyrian world from the time of Tiglath Pileser or B. C. 745.

10 — On Indian materials for writing cfr. Schlegel's "Râmâyaṇa" i., pp. xv., xvi. The oldest Sanskrit MS. yet discovered (of the 13th cent.) is written with ink upon Talipat leaves; it was found by Dr. Bühler.

11 *note* 3. Coḷa is the Sanskrit form of the name; Côḍa, the Telugu and šôḷa the original Tamiḻ form.

12 *note* 4. Mr. Kittel informs me that the Liṅgâit Canarese books have K a ṅ c i and not K â ṅ c i.

13 *line* 8. *For* (B) *read* (A).

— 16. *For* Haḷakannaḍa *read* Ha*l*a-Kanna*d*a.

14 *note* 2. Veṅgî or Veṅgi. The last is probably the correct form as shown (Mr. Kittel tells me) by Canarese books in which the metre requires a short i; it is also proved by the form Veṅγai of the Tanjore inscription, which represents Veṅgî. Veṅgî must be taken to be the Sanskritized form.

16 I have had this page reprinted, to include Profr. Eggeling's important discovery of the date of Maṅgalîça's accession; the other dates are not confirmed as yet.

19 *Genealogical table.* Kubja-Vishṇuvardhana I. appears to have been reigning in 622. (See remarks on transcript of pl. xxiv.)

21 *note.* In respect of the derivation of Telugu from $\sqrt{}$tel or $\sqrt{}$teḷ I should have added that the Telugu l = Tamiḻ ḷ. (Caldwell's Comp. Gr. p. 194.)

22 *line* 8. Vijayanagara. Both this form and Vidyânagara seem to have been in common use. Mr. Kittel tells me that the Canna-Basavapurâṇa (lxiii., 2-3) has Vidyânagara. This is a good authority, but a grant of 1399 A. D. has "Vijayâhvaye nagare"; so I give this form of the name. Cfr. Colebrooke's "Essays" ii., p. 263.

28 *note* 1, *line* 6. *Read*—was not used in S. India so early as the third century.

Page

30 *last line* of *note* 2. *For* "tamed" *read* "famed". The characters used in the Seven-Pagodas inscription are nearly identical with those of the Pagger Roeyong inscription in Sumatra. *See* Friederich's "Over inscriptien van Java en Sumatra" (Batavia 4°. *s. a*) pl. iii.

31 *line* 19. I should have remarked that Raffles ("Java" i., p. 370) had already noticed the almost complete identity of the Kawi and Square Pali characters.

— 24. The Chinese account of Cambodia translated by Remusat only goes back to the 7th century A. D. and modern French research in the country has not led to the discovery of any thing which contradicts these annals.

The only specimens of the old Cambodian inscriptions that are accessible to me are in Dr. Bastian's article "On some Siamese Inscriptions" in vol. xxxiv. of the Bengal As. Soc. Journal (pp. 27 flg.). what the short words there given are, I cannot say, as they are in some Indo-Chinese language, probably old Khmer; but the identity of the letters with the E. Cêra and E. Câlukya characters of about the 10th century is evident. In most respects they are nearest to the E. Câlukya forms. This resemblance was pointed out to me by Dr. Rost on seeing plates iv-vi.

The only possible objection that I can see to the evidence I have given to show that the Indo-Chinese Kamboja is intended and has therefore been interpolated in the gaṇas and Pata*n*jali[1], is the fact that Wilson found this word in the Açoka inscriptions of the third century B. C.; but on examining again the texts of these inscriptions, I find it is evident that he was hasty in doing so. The Kapur-di-giri text has clearly Kambayi; that of Girnar has Ka*m*b... (there is a fracture of the stone here) and that of Dhauli, Kambocha (?). The Ganjam copy being much broken, can give no help here. Except, therefore, the doubtful reading of the Dhauli text (which has never been properly copied) there is no reason to assume that the word was Kamboja, and against this supposition the Kapurdigiri text is decisive for the present.

The Sanskrit texts give most contradictory accounts of Kamboja. Varâha Mihira (B*r*ihat-sa*m*hitâ c. xiv.) puts it in the S. West of India. A breed of horses is called Kâ*m*boja according to Çâlihotra's treatise on Veterinary Medicine, compiled by Gaṇa[2]; the Bhela-Sa*m*hitâ has (*c.* 31, *çl.* 4):

Masûrayavagodhûmatilakoddâlasevina*h* |
bhûyishṭham arçasas tena Kâmbojâ dantajâh (*sic*) sm*r*itâ*h* ||

Other texts place them in different geographical situations and give different descriptions of them, but the epithet muṇḍa[3] clearly points to Buddhists. The name occurs in a Jâtaka (xxi., 1, 6)[4] which gives the following account of the people:

Kîtâ pataṅgâ uragâ ca bhekâ hatvâ kimi*m* sujjhati makkhikâ ca | ete hi dhammâ anriyarûpâ kambojakânâ*m* vitathâ bahunnan 'ti ||

C. ete kîtâdayo pâṇe hantvâ macco sujjhatîti etesa*m* 'pi kambojanaṭṭhavâsînam bahunnam anariyâna*m* dhammâ te pana vitathâ adhammâ 'va dhamma 'ti vuttâ.

There is nothing here to suggest a people of N. India or Afghanistan. If the Kambojas were a people of N. W. India or the Persian frontier, how is it that Ptolemy and the Chinese pilgrims do not mention them? It is certain that they were well known in India and probably Buddhists, the absence of all mention of them by these writers is, therefore, inexplicable if they belonged to the part of Asia which is usually supposed to have been their home. The Pali texts appear to identify Kambojâ with Cambodia in Indo-China[5].

In some Vijayanagara grants the kings of that dynasty are represented as conquering the Kâmbojas. The notion that the kingdom of Kamboja was in the north appears to be of Indian origin, but I have only found this indicated in one recent work, viz., Durgâcârya's "Niruktav*r*itti". In commenting on the

1) The allusions in the Mahâbhâshya are very meagre, *see* Profr. Weber's notice in I. S. xiii., p. 271.
2) ? The Pegu ponies, which are now imported into India in great numbers.
3) In gaṇa to P. ii. 1, 72. *See* Profr. Weber in I. S. xiii. p. 371.
4) I take this from Minayeffs Pali Grammar (translated into French by Guyard) p. xvii.
5) *v.* Childer's Dictionary of Pali, pt. i. § 77. *s. v.* Kamboja.

Page

words "Kambojâ*h* kambalabhojâ*h* kamanîyabhojâ vâ kambala*h* kamanîyo bhavati"[1] he says: "Kambojâ*h* kambalabhojâ*h*." te hi prâyeṇa kambalân upabhu*n*jate himaprâyatvât tasya deçasya | "Kamanîyabhojâ vâ" | "kamaniyâni" "prârthanîyâni ca te hi dravyâṇy ubhabhu*n*jate; pracuraratno hi sa deça iti | "kambala*h* kamanîyo bhavati | "prârthanîyo hi çîtârtair bhavati." The author, being a native of S. India in all probability, deserves little credit for the statements he makes here.

By the Hindu Cosmogony[2] the Kambojas (like all other people known to the Hindus) were considered to be degraded Xattriyas, and therefore their language (it necessarily follows) was supposed to be connected with Sanskrit. The single word which is quoted (Naig. ii., 2) viz. çu or çav (= to go) proves no connection between the Kambojans and the Aryan races, for the meanings in Sanskrit differ radically. The Sanskrit grammarians in treating of foreign languages were content to find an external resemblance between Sanskrit and foreign words, and troubled themselves (like those of the middle ages) but little with the meaning; an error which Kumârilasvâmin[3] exposed. Does çu or çav exist in the Khmer language with the meaning 'to go'?

32 *line* 27. This interesting passage has been correctly published by Dr. F. Kielhorn in the *Indian Antiquary* vol. iii., p. 286. For *nilâvita* it appears that *viplâvita* must be read.

— *note* 4. Friederich ("Over Inscriptien van Java en Sumatra" p. 78) says: "man vergelijke bij voorbeeld het oude Hala Canara alphabet in de inscriptie van Mr. Wathen . . . van het jaar van Çâka 411."

33 — 2. *For* "Pagger Roejong (in Java)" *read* "Pagger Roejong (in Sumatra)". Friederich *u. s.* p. 18.

37 *line* 24. The Javanese appear to have invented a character for ĕ very early, viz., about the 11th century. (Friederich, *u. s.* pp. 4 and 54.) As now used, this sign in the Javanese alphabet is evidently of independent, and not of Indian origin

38 — 19. The Tôlkâppiyam (i., 1, 14) distinguishes the forms of *p* and *m* in a manner that clearly points to the Vaṭṭeḻuttu and not to the Grantha-Tâmiḻ alphabet.

43 *note* 4. Mr. Kittel informs me that the Basava Purâṇa and the Canarese texts prove Kalabhurya (in Can. Kalaburigĕ) to be the correct form.

44 There is yet another kind of Nâgarî used in 3 inscriptions found in the Ganjam and Vizagapatam Districts and which appears to be the original type from which the Uriya character is derived. The grants in question are of about the 10th or 11th century and appear to belong to Jayapura in the former District.

50 *line* 6. Vcte. E. de Rougé's admirable Essay on this point has fortunately been quite recently discovered and printed by his son ("Mémoire sur l' origine Égyptienne de l' alphabet Phénicien" 8° Paris, 1874). The author has proved the Egyptian origin of the Phænician alphabet by being able to use the Egyptian transcription of Semitic words, and has thus been able to detect the original hieratic letters from which the Phænician letters were adapted. This is unfortunately the very clue which is wanting in India to enable one to trace back the Açoka character to a Semitic (Aramaic) prototype.

54 Friederich ("Over Inscriptien" p. 78) says that the Çaka era only is used in the Archipelago inscriptions.

— *line* 18. I print the last part of this Prakrit gâthâ as it occurs in 2 MSS., but I do not understand the last phrase which seems wrong.

55 — 12. For this list see also Burgess's "Sûryasiddhânta" p. 36 and As. Researches (Bengal) vol. iii.

— 17. Subhânu also occurs as a name of the 17th year. For the tenth one finds also dhât*r*i; for the 13th pramâthin; for the 15th Bh*r*içya; for the 31st and 32nd hemalamba and vilamba; for the 47th pramâdi.

It is scarcely necessary to remark that these are all neuter adjectives agreeing with sa*m*vatsara.

58 *note* 2. See Crawford "On the Hindu Religion in Bali" (As. Res. of Bengal, xiii. pp. 150-1) and Burgess's "Sûryasiddhânta" p. iii.

59 *line* 18. It should be noticed that there is yet another system of marking numbers by letters, and which (as pointed out by Goldstücker in his "Pâṇini's Place" p. 53) is attributed by Pata*n*jali and Kaiyaṭa to Pâṇini. This was used to indicate the extent of the a d h i k â r a of a s û t r a, where this did not exceed the number of the

1) "Nirukta" ed. Roth, p. 40.

2) See above p. 85.

3) See my article on this passage in the *Indian Antiquary*, i. pp. 309-311.

Page

letters of the alphabet; and as the example given—i = 2, the letters must have had their numerical value determined by their position in the alphabet. (Cfr. Mahâbhâshya on P. i., 3, 11. pp. 242 and fig. of the Benares edition.) There is no trace of this system in inscriptions, and it will be seen that it is precisely similar to the Greek and Semitic notation of numerals by letters of the alphabet. There is no trace of it also in our MS. of Pâṇini, a fact that should be considered by those who assert that we possess the text as Pâṇini composed it.

60 *lines* 13-15. *dele* "This is probably the use . . . . twelfth century". Mr. Kittel has kindly informed me that the Canarese will not bear this interpretation, and that the passage refers to the orthography of certain words.

62 *line* 13. This small cross is termed kâkapâda or ha*m*sapâda. Where words or letters have been written in wrong order this is corrected by writing numerals above corresponding to the required order.

63 — 23. *For* datvâ *read* dattvâ.

64 — 2. do. do.

— 34. bânijyâ° — bâṇigyâ°.

71 — 22. *Read* durlekhye.

76 — 19. Sandhivigrahâdhikârin.

I have not noticed ordinary mis-prints, and occasional irregularity of transcription in which I follow the system of Lepsius as near as possible. As an excuse I must plead that this book has taken a long time to print (owing to my official work), and that for the most part I have been at a great distance from the Press. As far as my experience goes, it is useless to ask readers in India to look at a list of Errata!

Corrections to be made in the Plates.

Pl. i. *Compounds. For* ggî *read* rgge. Correct rjye (which is defective in some impressions) by the original pl. xx., 2. line 1.

iii. pau (11 × 21) is doubtful.

iv. *Compounds.* for ṭç *read* cch.

vii. *dele* ṭî (4 × 11).

xiv. This is the complete alphabet as taught in schools; many of the letters do, however, not occur in reality.

CONTENTS.

List of Plates and direction to the binder.

Map, to face title.

The tinted parts indicate the extension of the earlier alphabets (Câlukya-Cêra and Vaṭṭeluttu), the lines enclose the country over which the modern or secondary alphabets extended before 1600 A. D.

A. Alphabets.

Plate:	i.	Veṅgi Alphabet,		4th century.
	ii.	Cêra do.		466 A. D.
	iii.	W. Câlukya Alphabet,		608 A. D.
	iv.	Do. do.		689 A. D.
	iv.*	Eastern Câlukya Alphabet,		about 680 A. D.
	v.	Do.	do.	945 A. D.
	vi.	Transitional	do.	1079 A. D.
	vii.	Do.	do.	1134 A. D.
	viii.	Old Telugu	do.	1356 A. D.
	ix.	Ḥaḷa-Kannaḍa	do.	1428 A. D.
	x.	Cêra	do.	11th century.
	xi.	Gaṇeça temple (at Seven Pagodas) Alphabet (E. Cêra).		
	xii.	Côḷa-Grantha Alphabet		1073 A. D.
	xiii.	Modern Grantha	do.	
	xiv.	Do. Tuḷu	do.	
	xv.	Vaṭṭeḷuttu	do.	774 A. D.
	xvi.	Old Tamiḻ	do.	1073 A. D.
	xvii.	Nandi-Nâgarî	do.	1399 A. D.
	xviii.	Do.	do.	1601 A. D.
	xix.	Numerals.		

B. Facsimiles.

xx. & xxi. Grant by Vijayanandi (4th century), Veṅgi.

xxii. One leaf of W. Câlukya Grant, d. 608 A. D.

xxiii. Cêra Grant in Canarese, d. 804 A. D.

xxiv. Grant by Vishṇuvardhana (Eastern Câlukya) of about 630 A. D. (? 622)

xxv. Two leaves of E. Câlukya Grant (by Ammarâja) d. 945 A. D.

xxvi. One leaf of Grant, d. 1079 A. D.

xxvii. Do. Nandi-Nâgarî Grant d. 1399 A. D.

xxviii. Specimen of Nandi-Nâgarî (about 1600 A. D.) and Telugu (about 1670 A. D.) from Palm-leaf MSS.

xxix. One leaf of the Grant to the Persian Christians (about 825 A. D.), and Specimen of Kôleḻuttu, d. 1724 A. D.

xxx. Specimens of Grantha and Tamiḻ MSS. on Palm-leaves of about 1600 A. D.

Plate A. Seals on Grants. To face p. 75.

Plates i.—xxx. *to come at the end.*

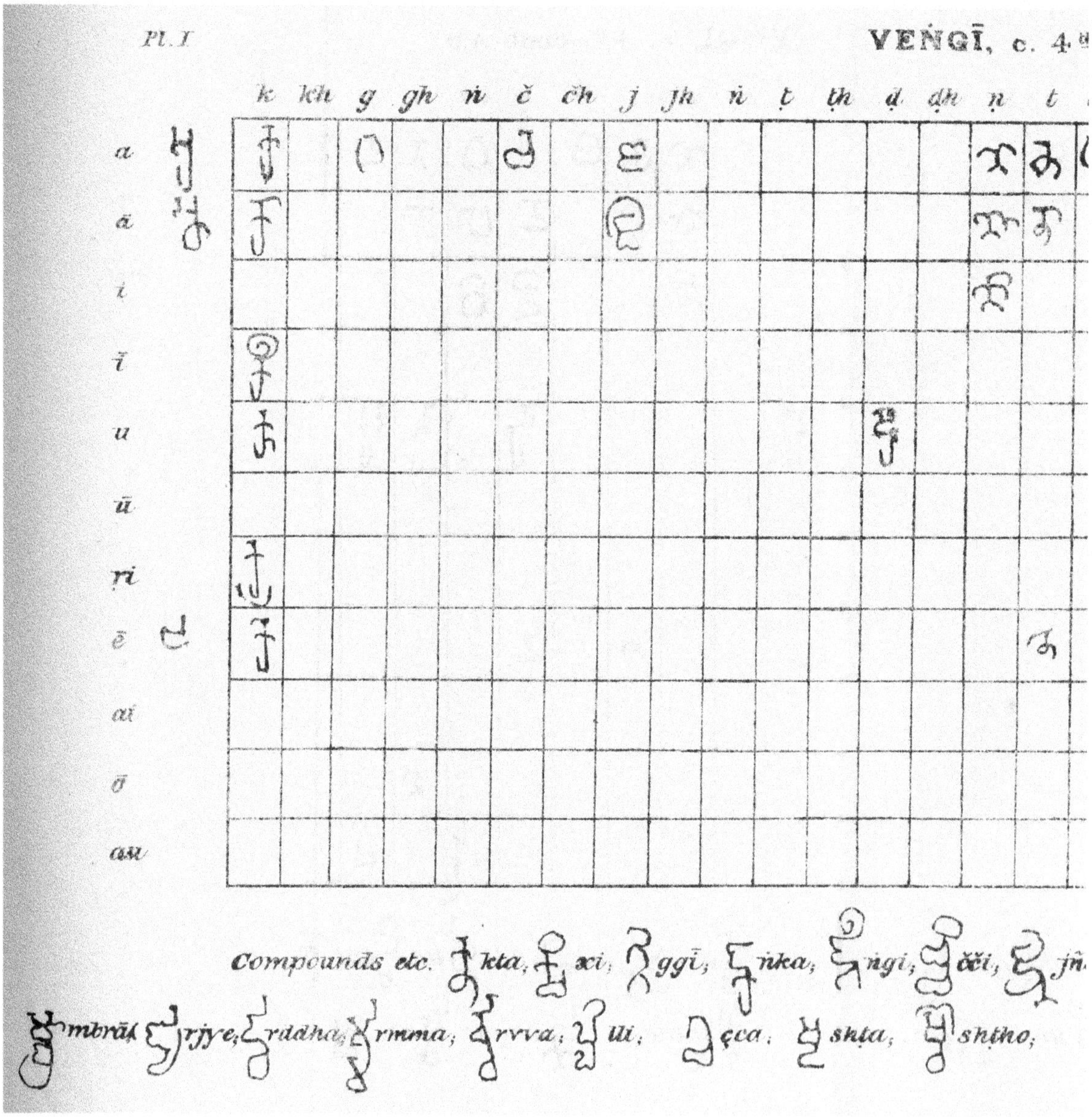
Pl. I
VEṄGĪ, c. 4th
k kh g gh ṅ č čh j jh ñ ṭ ṭh ḍ ḍh ṇ t
a
ā
i
ī
u
ū
ṛi
ē
ai
ō
au
Compounds etc. kta, xi, ggī, ṅka, ṅgi, čči, jñ
mbrā, rjye, rddha, rmma, rvva, lli, çca, shṭa, shṭho,

c. 4th cent - A.D.

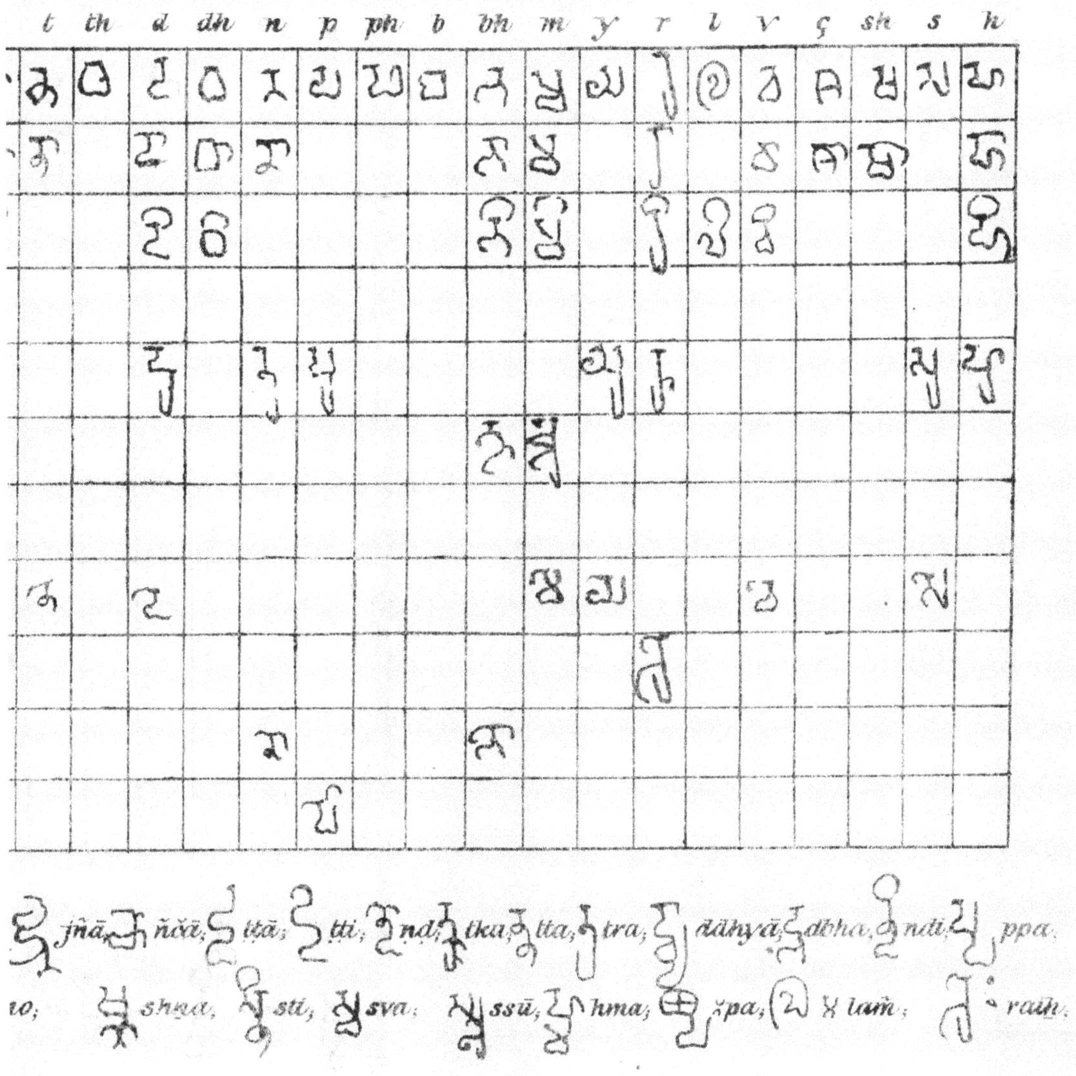

t th d dh n p ph b bh m y r l v ç sh s h
jñā, ñăā; ṭṭā; ṭṭi; ṇḍ; tka, tta, tra, dāhyā, dbha, nti, ppa,
io; shṇa, sti, sva; ssū, hma; ẋpa; ẋ lam; raṃ.

Pl. II.

ČĒRA-

(Mercara Inscr

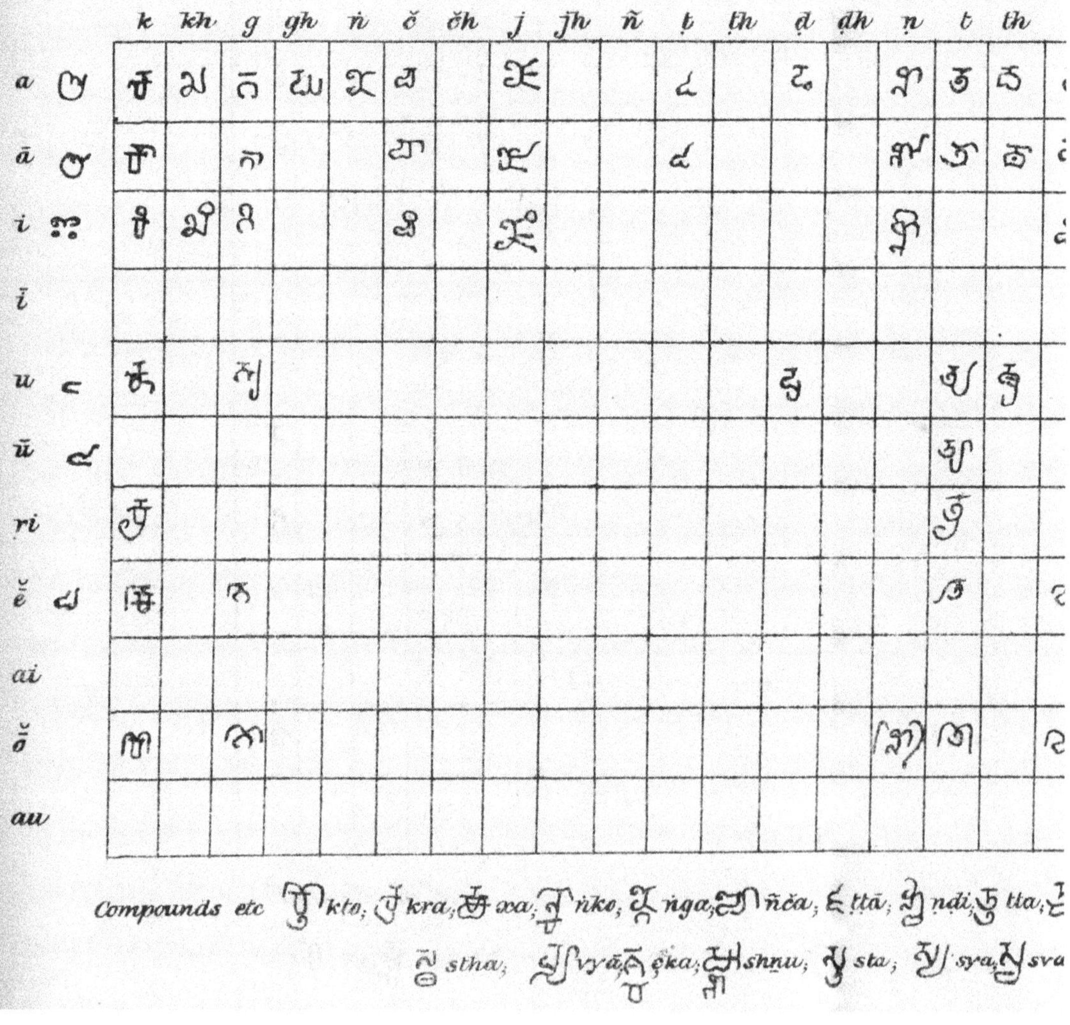

k kh g gh ṅ č čh j jh ñ ṭ ṭh ḍ ḍh ṇ t th
a
ā
i
ī
u
ū
ṛi
ĕ
ai
ŏ
au
Compounds etc
kta; kra; xa; ṅka; ṅga; ñča; ṭṭā; ṇḍi; tta;
stha; vyā; ṣka; shṇu; sta; sya; sva

4 6 6 A.D.

scription.)

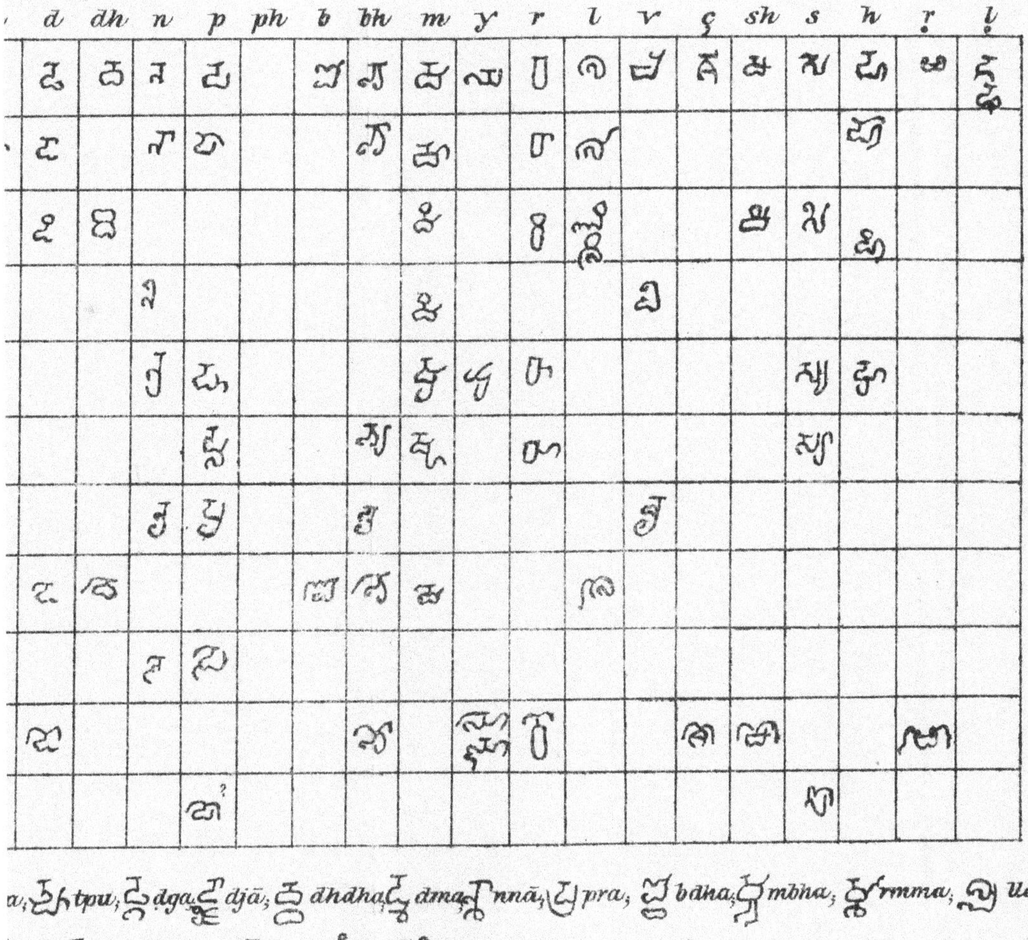
d dh n p ph b bh m y r l v ç sh s h ṛ ḷ
a; tpu; dga; djā; dhdha; dma; nnā; pra; bdha; mbha; rmma; lla;
sva; hna; rpra; ḷḷu; raṁ; raḥ; ḷa.

III.

WESTERN (KALYĀṆA) (

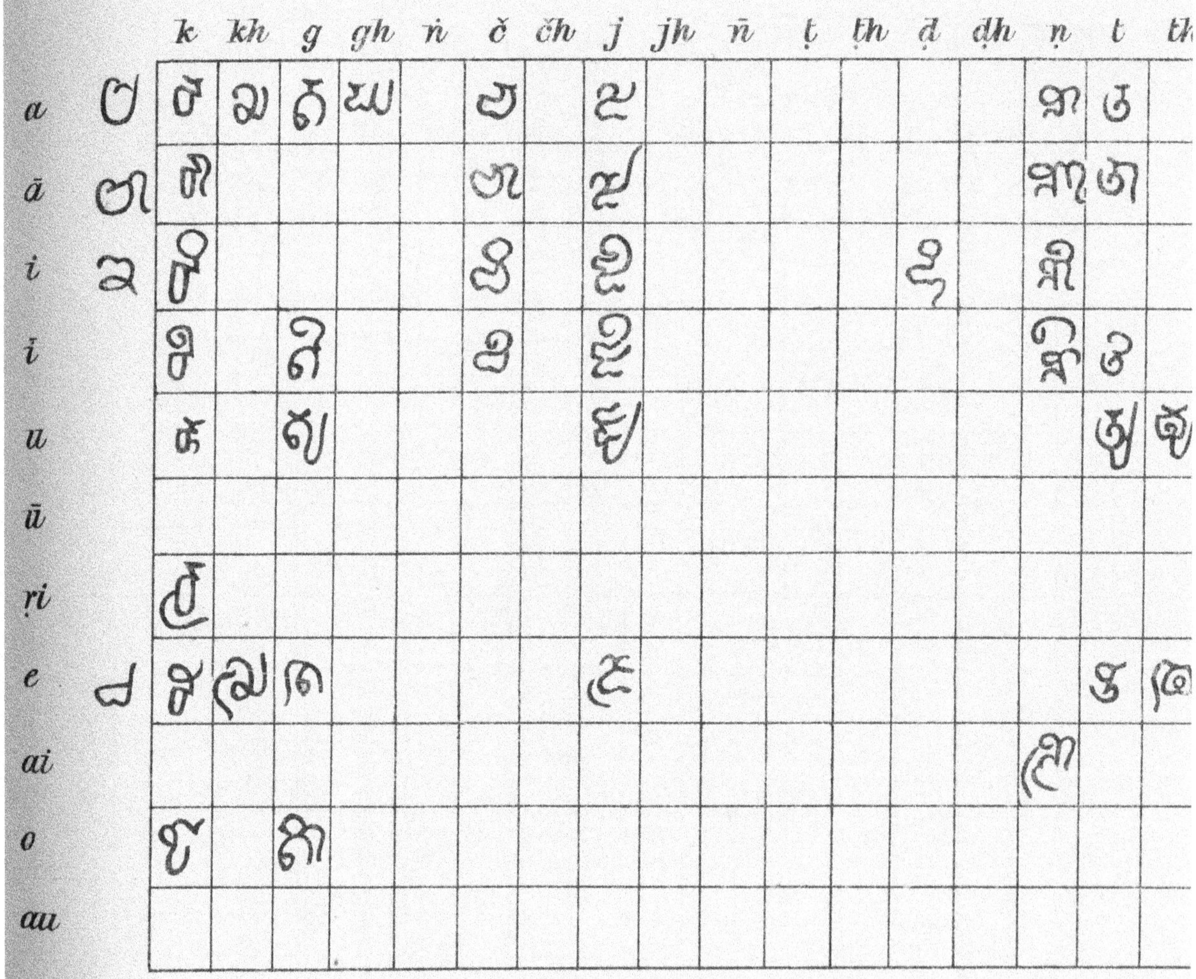
k kh g gh ṅ č čh j jh ñ ṭ ṭh ḍ ḍh ṇ t th
a
ā
i
ī
u
ū
ṛi
e
ai
o
au

Both forms of e (affixed as above) occur in

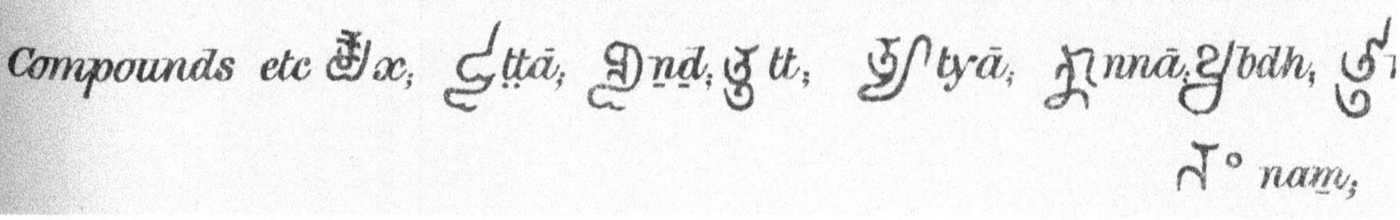
Compounds etc
x,
ṭṭā,
nḍ,
tt,
tyā,
nnā,
bdh,
nam,

) ÇALUKYA, d. 608 A.D.

th
d
dh
n
p
ph
b
bh
m
y
r
l
v
ç
sh
s
h
ṛ

indifferently: also is put for ku.

rtt, rmm, rvv; ll; çv; shkṛi; shṭrā, shṇo, snā, ss,

; ṇaḥ.

IV. WESTERN CĀ

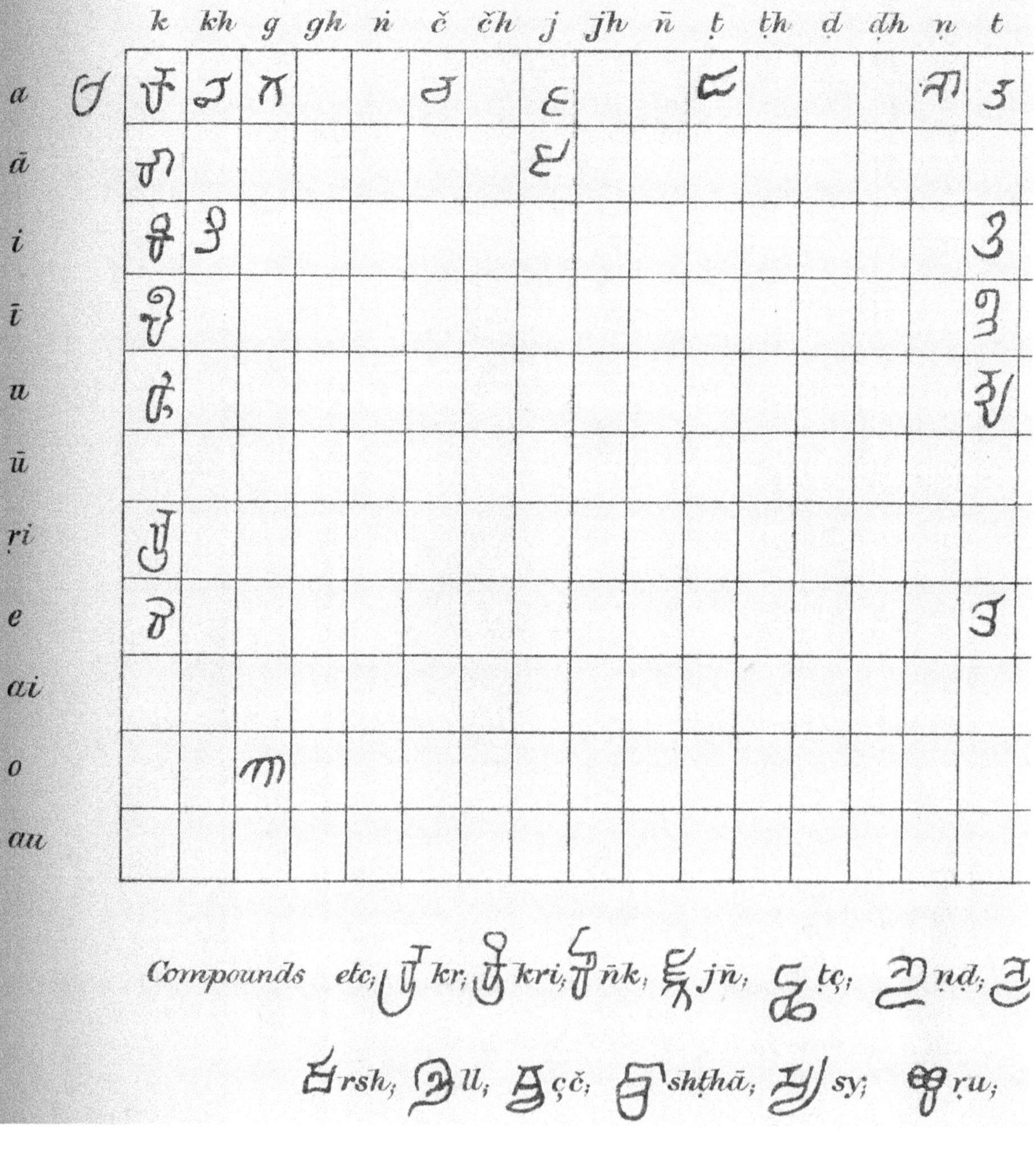

k kh g gh ṅ č čh j jh ñ ṭ ṭh ḍ ḍh ṇ t
a
ā
i
ī
u
ū
ṛi
e
ai
o
au
Compounds etc;
kr; kri; ñk; jñ; ṭç; ṇḍ;
rsh; ll; çč; shṭhā; sy; ṛu;

ĀLUKYA, D. 689 A.D.

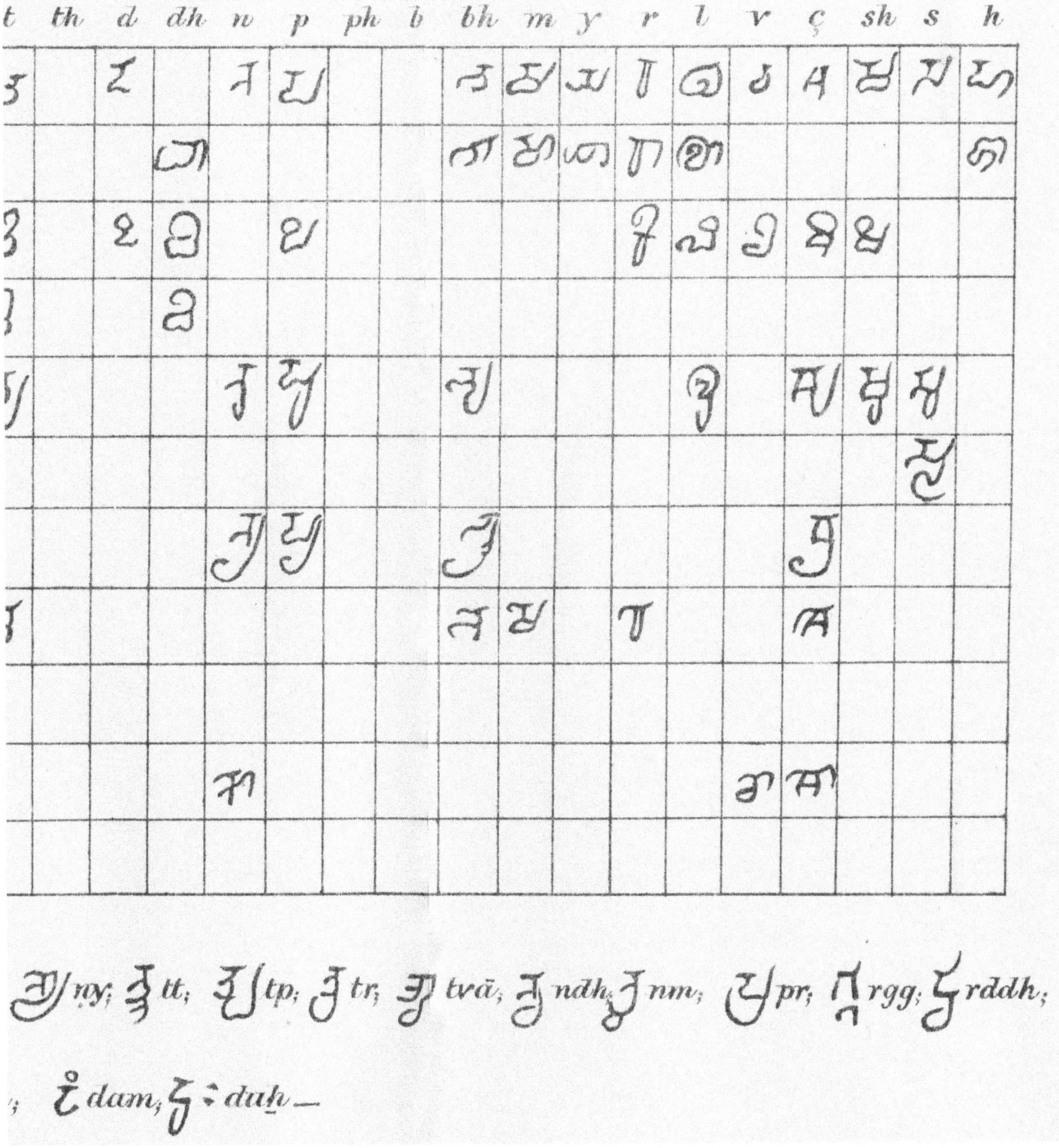
t th d dh n p ph b bh m y r l v ç sh s h
ṇy; tt; tp; tr; tvā; ndh; nm; pr; rgg; rddh;
; dam; duḥ—

Pl. IV.*

EAST (KALINGA) ČĀLUK

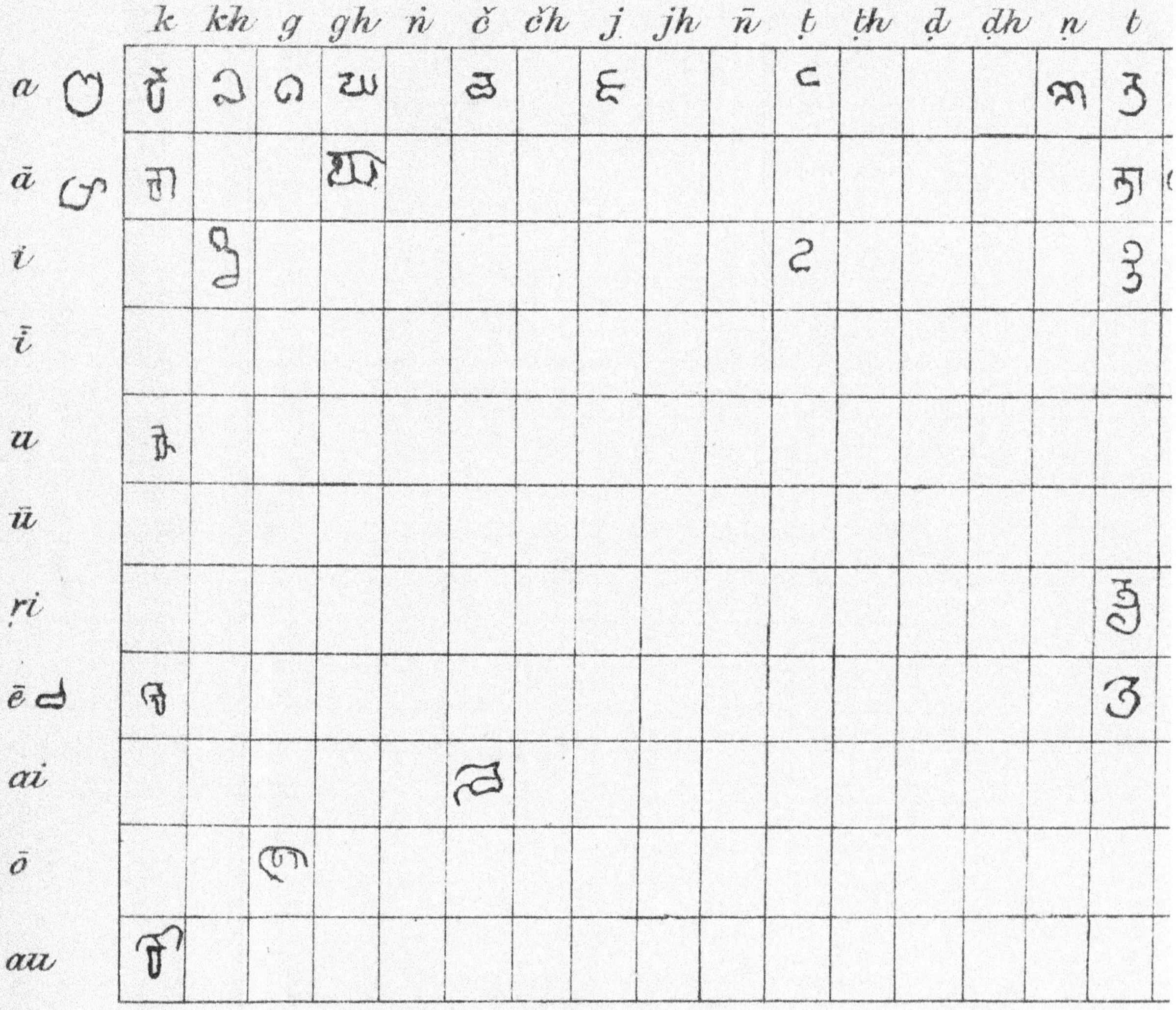

The Compound letters in this document do not present any peculiarities. Final

for it.

.UKYA (C. 680 A.D.)

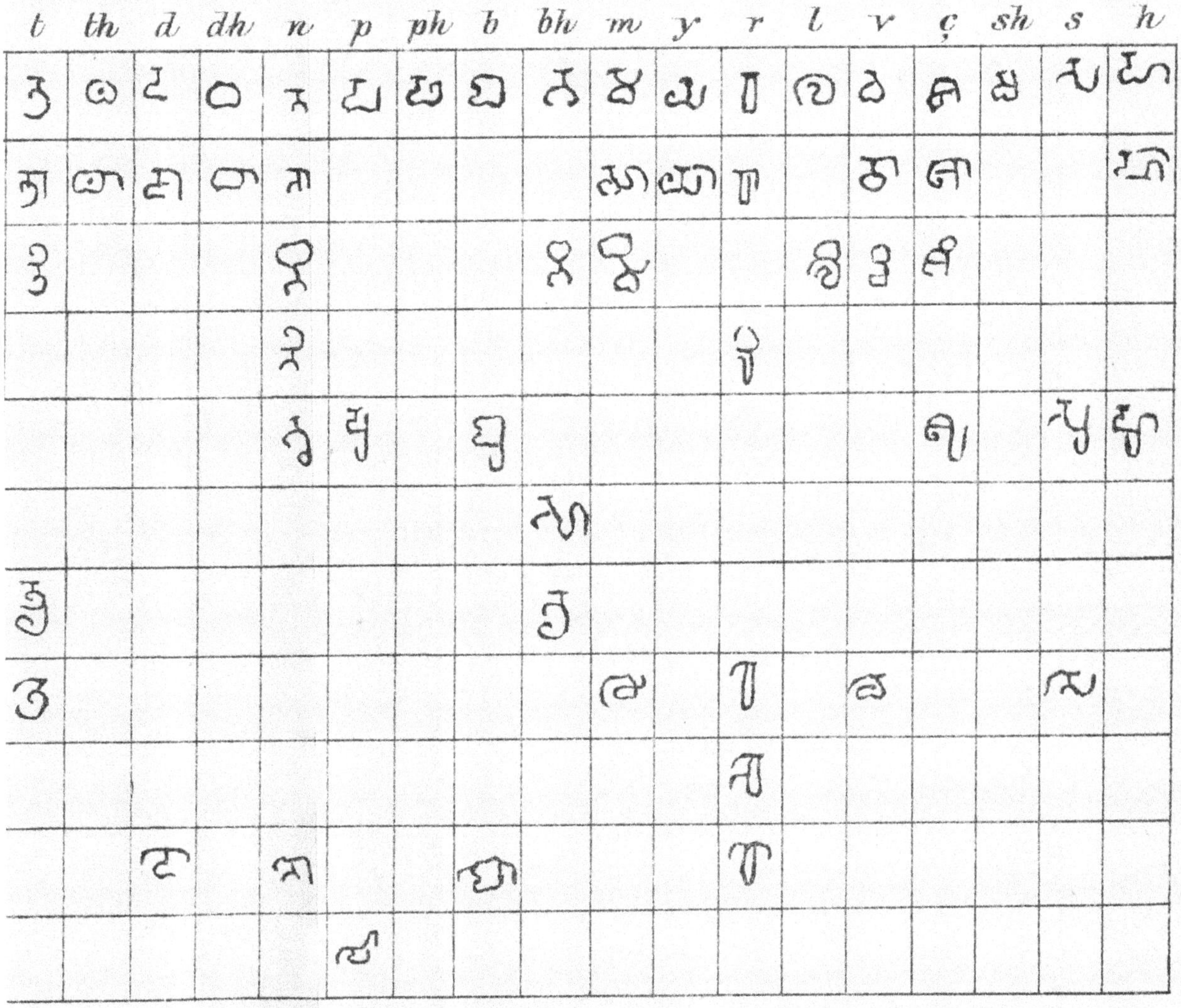

Final m is thus: °lam. The <u>*bindu*</u> *is above the line; but is sometimes written*

it.

V.

EAST (KALINGA) C

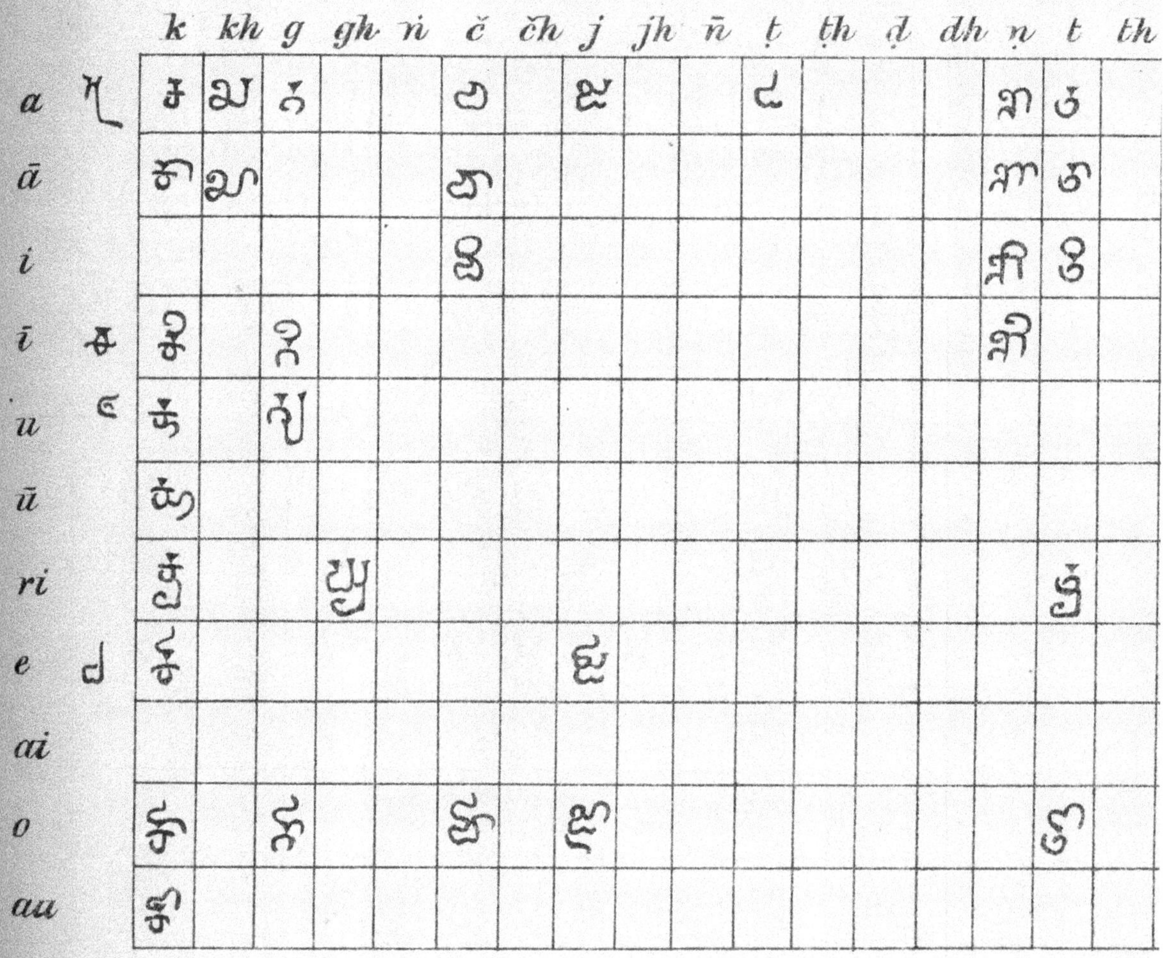

Compounds etc. *kt;* *ky;* *kr;* *jñ;* *ṭṭā;* *ṇḍ;* *tpu;*

sy; *sv;* *tam;* *tah. Final t with virāma do:*

) CĀLUKYA, A.D. 945.

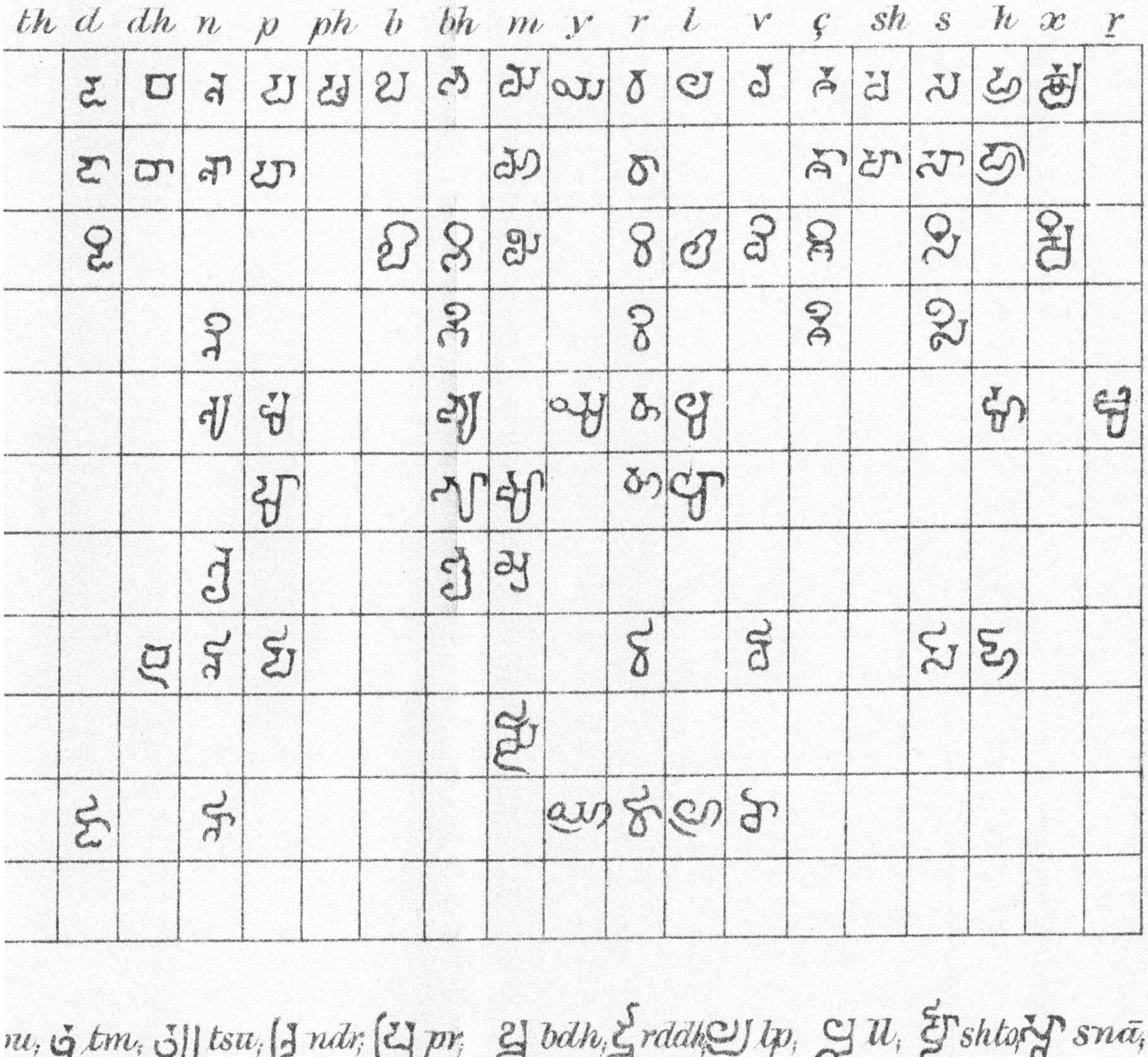

th d dh n p ph b bh m y r l v ç sh s h x r̤
nu, tm, tsu, ndr, pr, bdh, rddh, lp, ll, shṭo, snā,

do: n

VI.

EASTERN CĀLUK

(The letters marked *

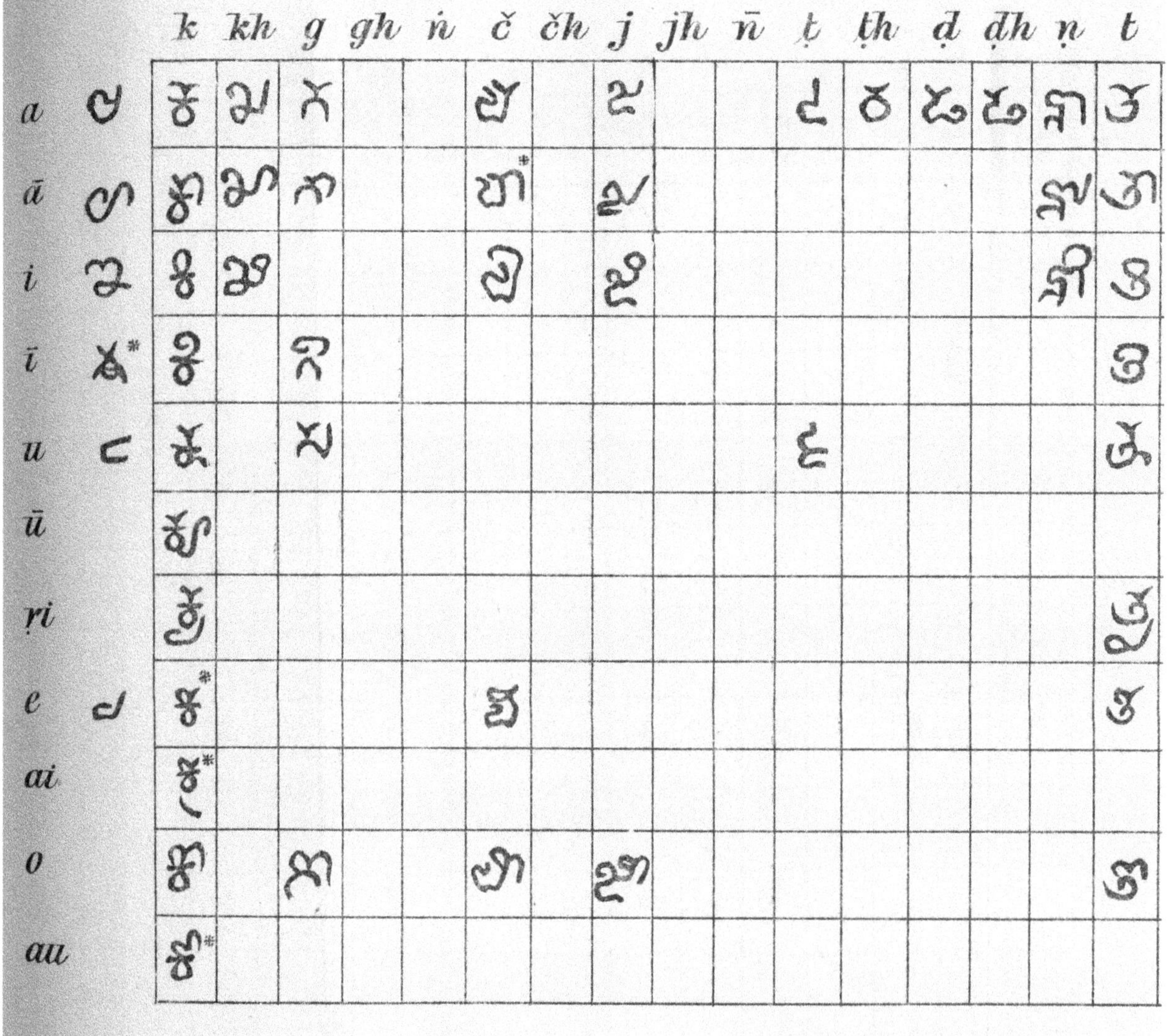

k kh g gh ṅ č čh j jh ñ ṭ ṭh ḍ ḍh ṇ t
a
ā
i
ī
u
ū
ṛi
e
ai
o
au

N.B. In the inscription d.

Compounds etc kr; ččhā; jñ; ṇḍ; tk; tpu; tsu;

sy; sv; ○nām; gaḥ; Final t with vir

KYA (TRANSITIONAL) d. A.D. 1079

are from an inscription d. 1134)

th d dh n p ph b bh m y r l v ç sh s h x

. 1079 we find etc, besides the forms given above.

ddh, dr, pt, bj, mnā, mmā, rsh, ll, shna,

irāma do: n

Pl.VII.

EASTERN ČĀLUKYA (

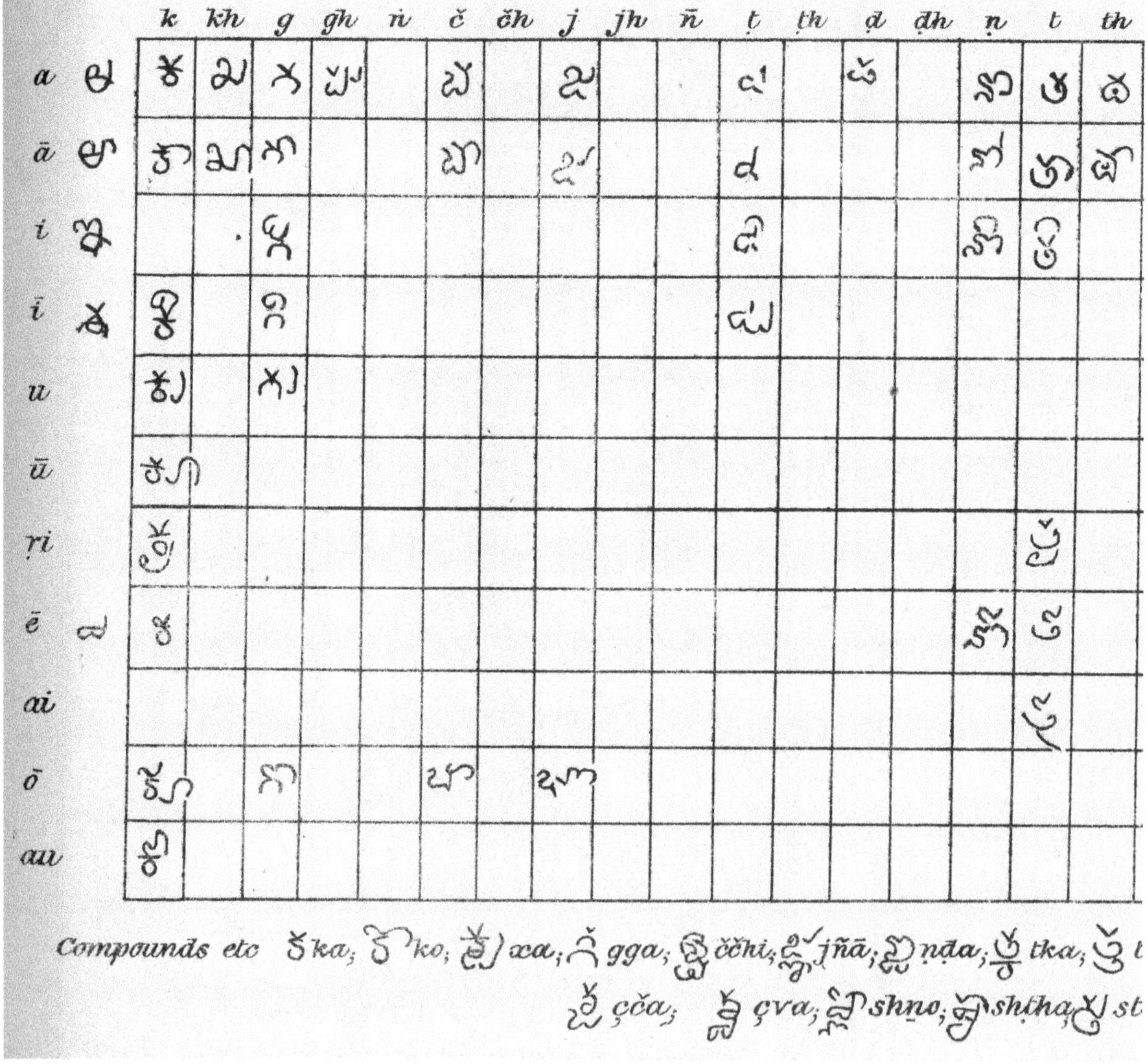
k kh g gh ṅ č čh j jh ñ ṭ ṭh ḍ ḍh ṇ t th
a
ā
i
ī
u
ū
ṛi
ē
ai
ō
au
Compounds etc ka; ko; xa; gga; čči; jñā; ṇḍa; tka;
ça; çva; shṇo; shṭha; st

(TRANSITIONAL) ḋ 1134 A.D.

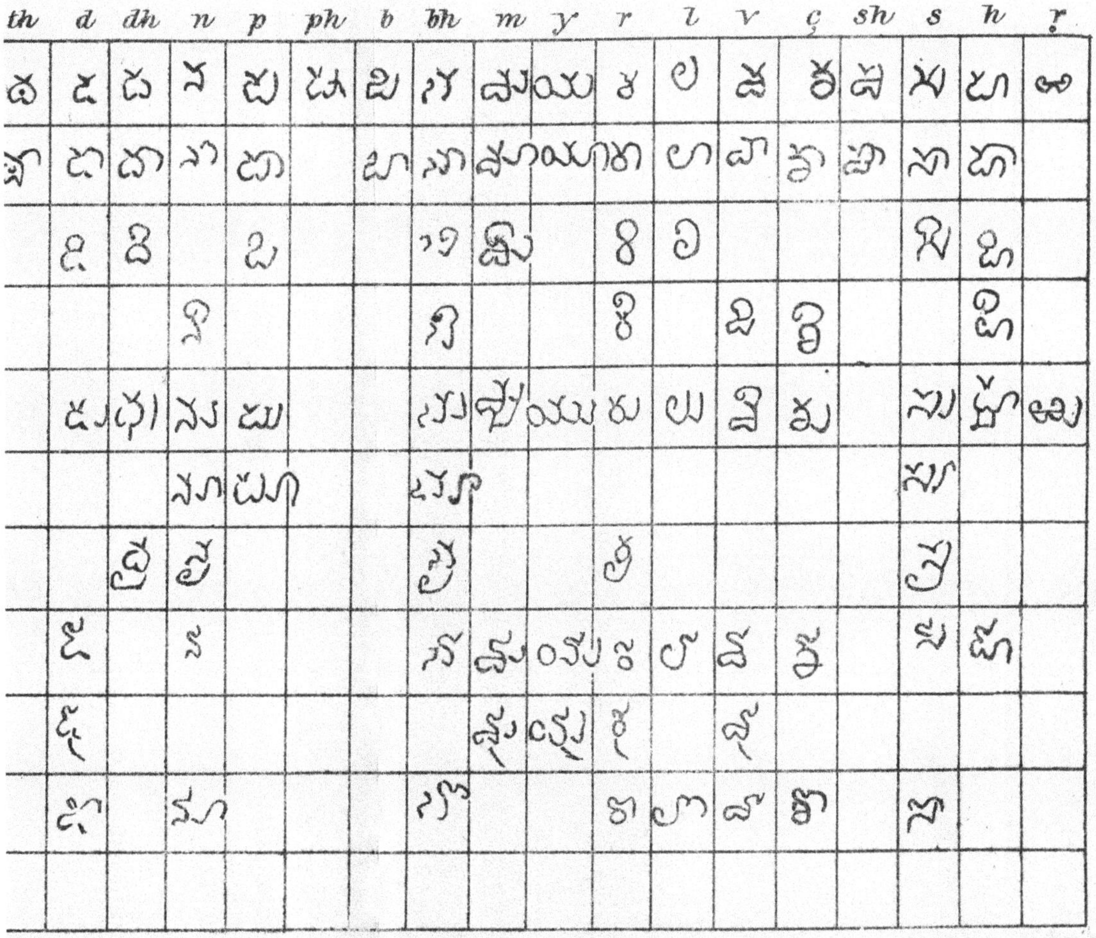

tta; tsa; nnā; pra; bja; bdha; yya; rvvā; lla; lvyā;
sta; yām; taḥ; t (with virāma).

		k	kh	g	gh	ṅ	č	čh	j	jh	ñ	ṭ
a	అ	క	ఖ	గ	ఘ		చ		జ			ట
ā	ఆ	కా	ఖా	గా					జా			
i	ఇ	కి	ఖి		ఘి				జి			
ī				గీ								
u	ఉ	కు		గు					జు			
ū		కూ										
ṛi												
e	ఎ	కె										టె
ai		కై										
o		కొ		గొ								
au		కౌ & కౌ										

Compounds etc ' జ్ఞ jñ; త్తా ttā; త్థి tthi; త్సా tsā; ద్బ

OLD TELUGU, d. 1356 A.D.

(From an inscription on Copper plates)

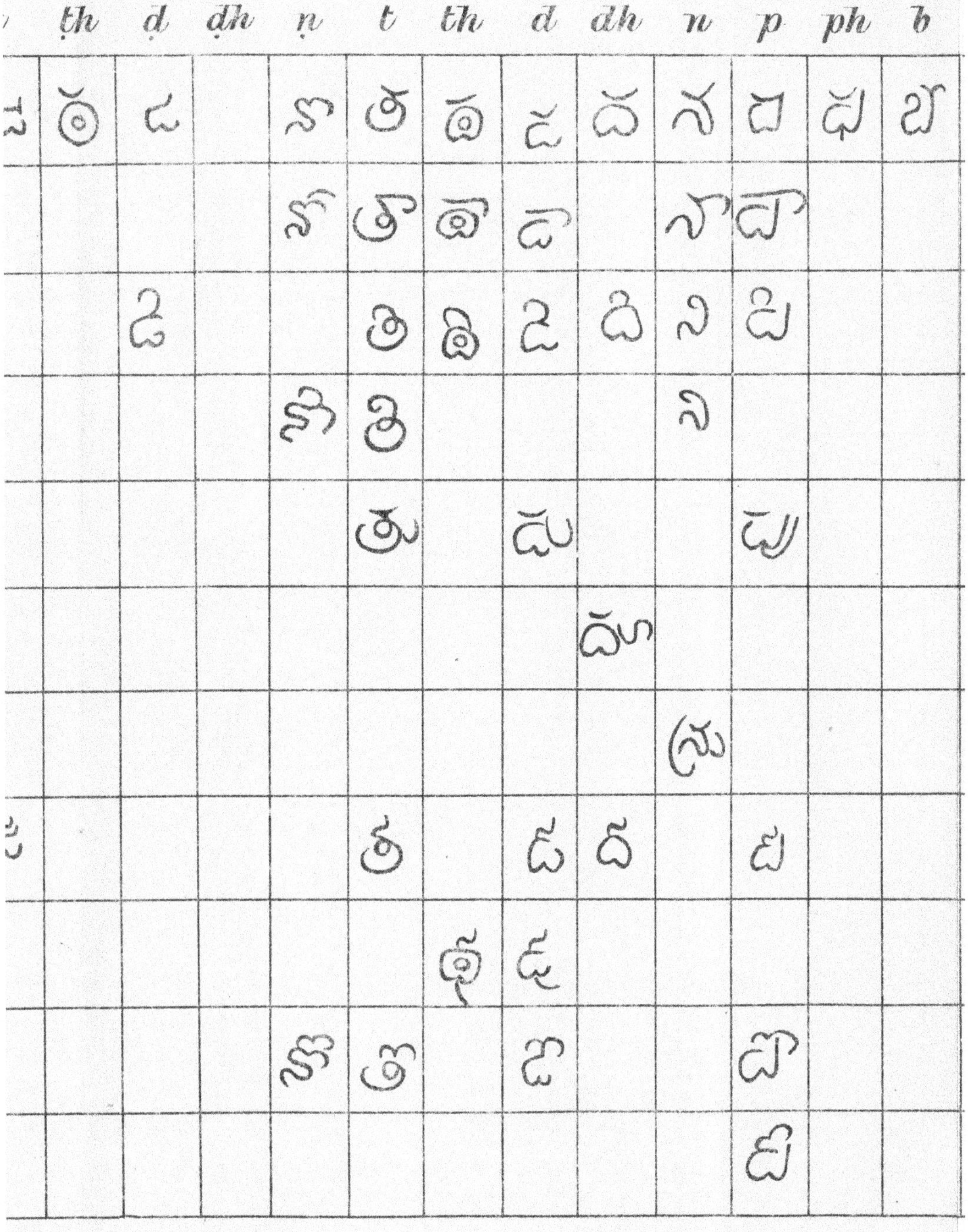
ṭh
ḍ
ḍh
ṇ
t
th
d
dh
n
p
ph
b

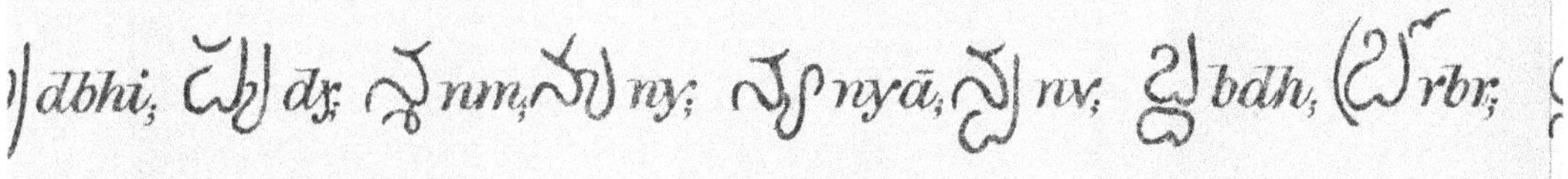
dbhi;
dy;
nm;
ny;
nyā;
nv;
bdh;
rbr;

OLD TELUGU, d. 1356 A.D.

(*From an inscription on Copper plates*)

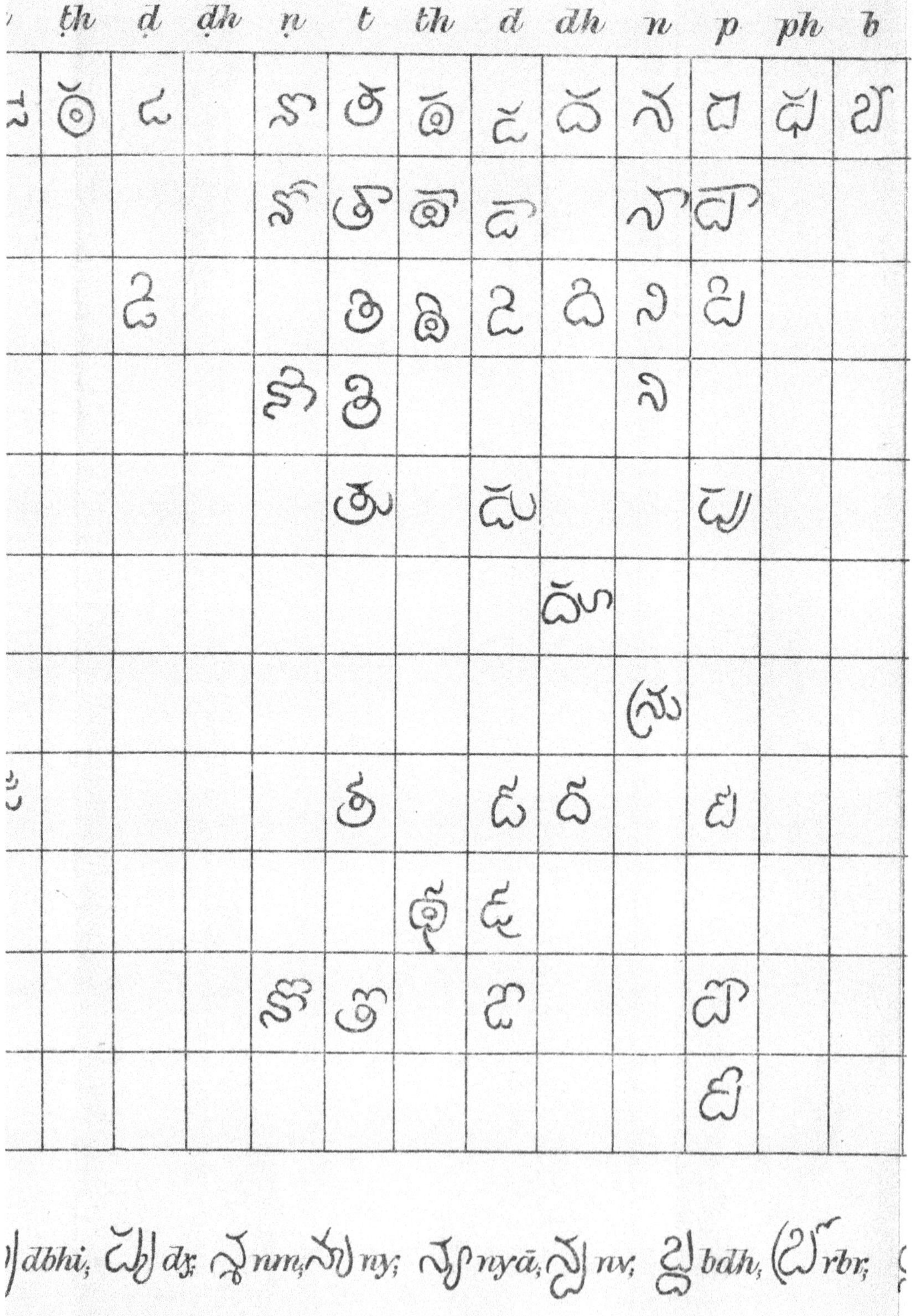
ṭh ḍ ḍh ṇ t th d dh n p ph b
dbhi; dy; nm; ny; nyā; nv; bdh; rbr;

D.

	bh	*m*	*y*	*r*	*l*	*v*	*ç*	*sh*	*s*	*h*	*ḷ*	*x*
	భ	మ	య	ర	ల	వ	శ	ష	స	హ	ళ	క్ష
	భా	మా	యా	రా	లా	వా	శా	షా	సా	హా	ళా	క్షా
	భి	మి	యి	రి	లి	వి	శి			హి		క్షి
	భు	ము		రు				షు	సు	హు		క్షు
	భూ			రూ								
	భృ											
			యె	రె		వె		షె	సె			క్షె
							శై		సై			
		మో	యో	రో	లో	వో	శో		సో	హో		
		మౌ							సౌ			

ల్లు *ll*, శ్చి *çci*, ష్ఠా *shṭhā*, హ్ని *hni*.

IX.

HAḺA-KANNA

(From a pa

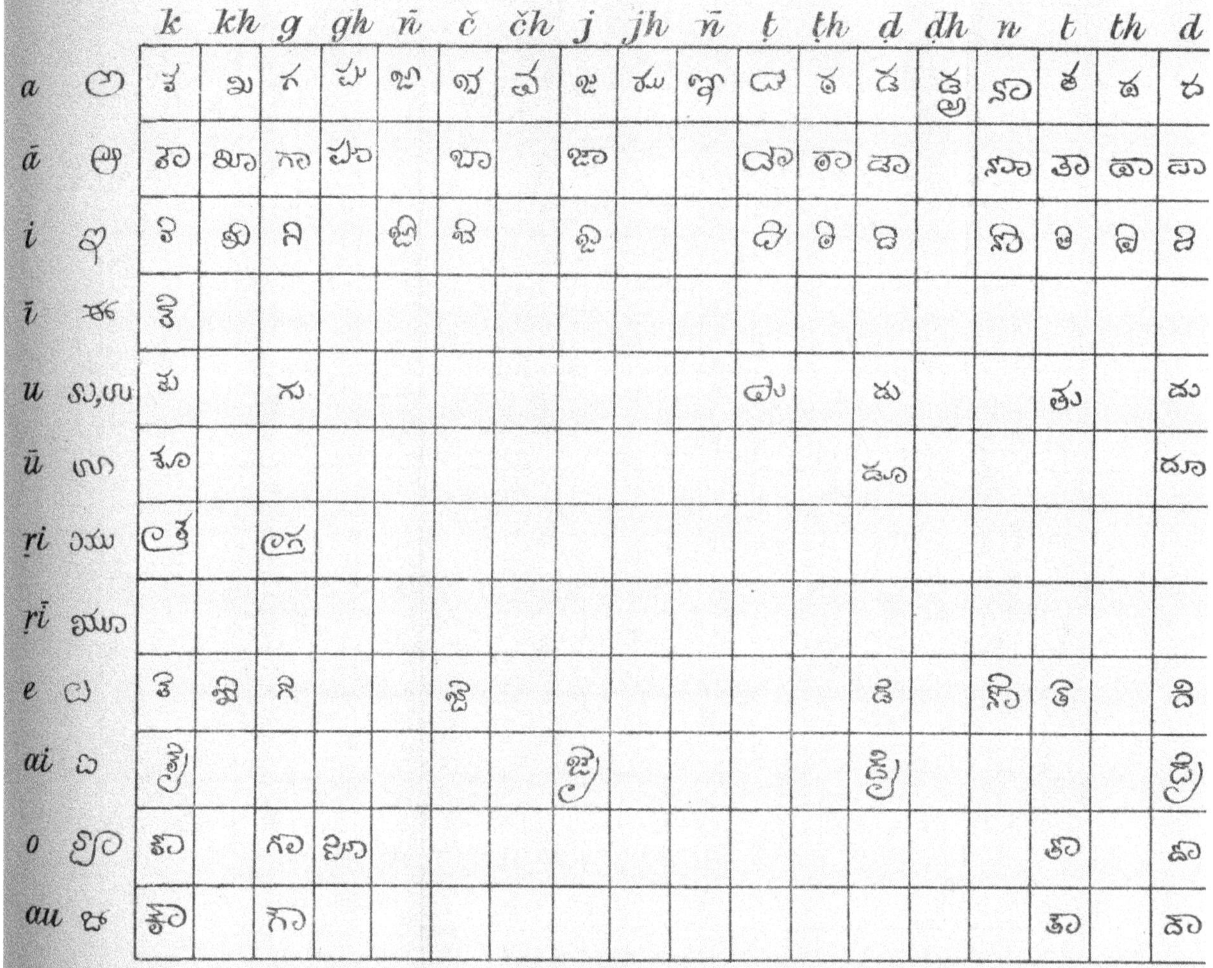
k kh g gh ñ č čh j jh ñ ṭ ṭh ḍ ḍh ṇ t th d
a ā i ī u ū ṛi ṛī e ai o au

Compounds kt; ktr; ky; kr; ččh; jñ; ṭṭ; tk; tth; or sth.

NADA, 1428 A.D.

palm-leaf MS.)

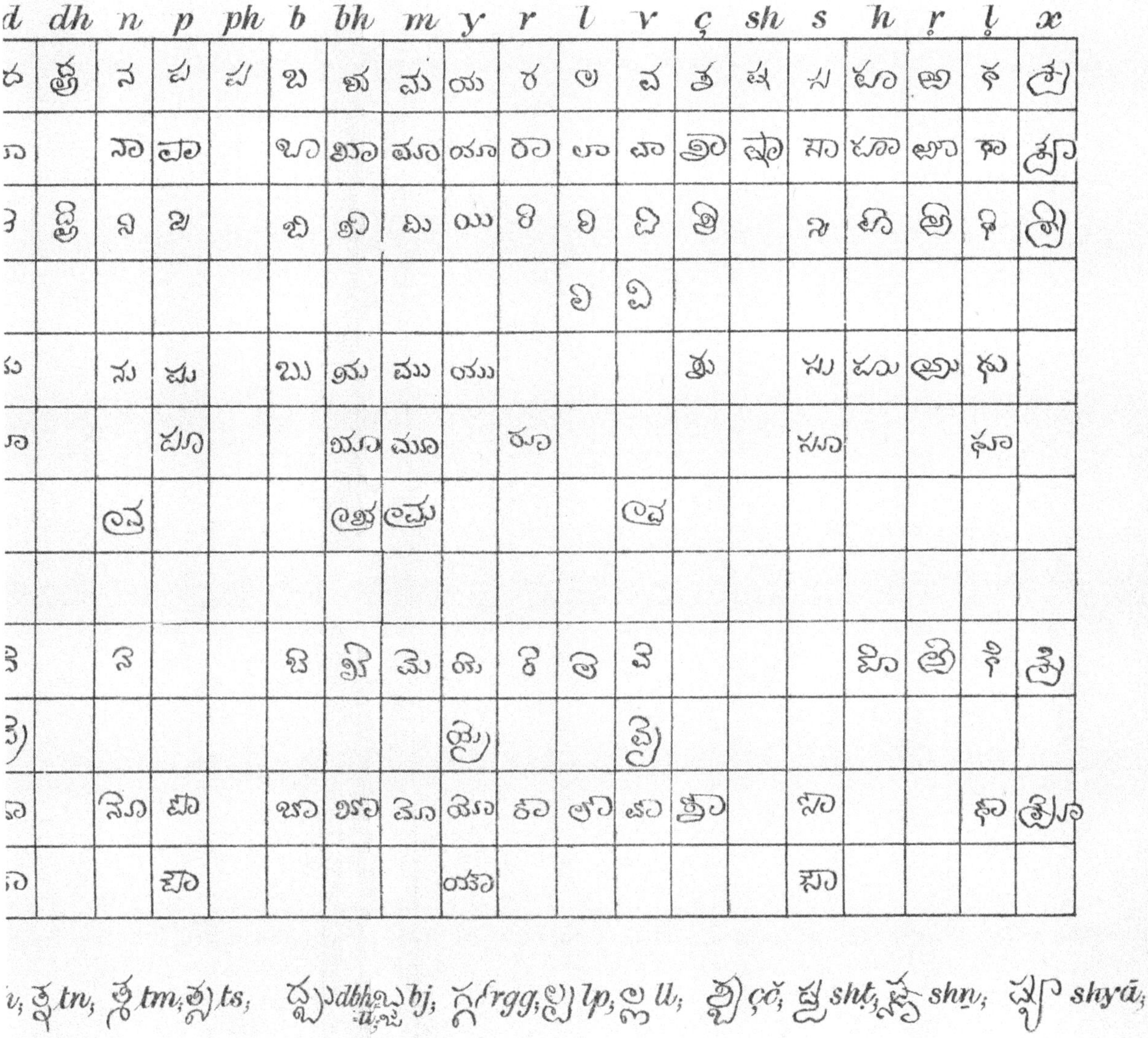

X.

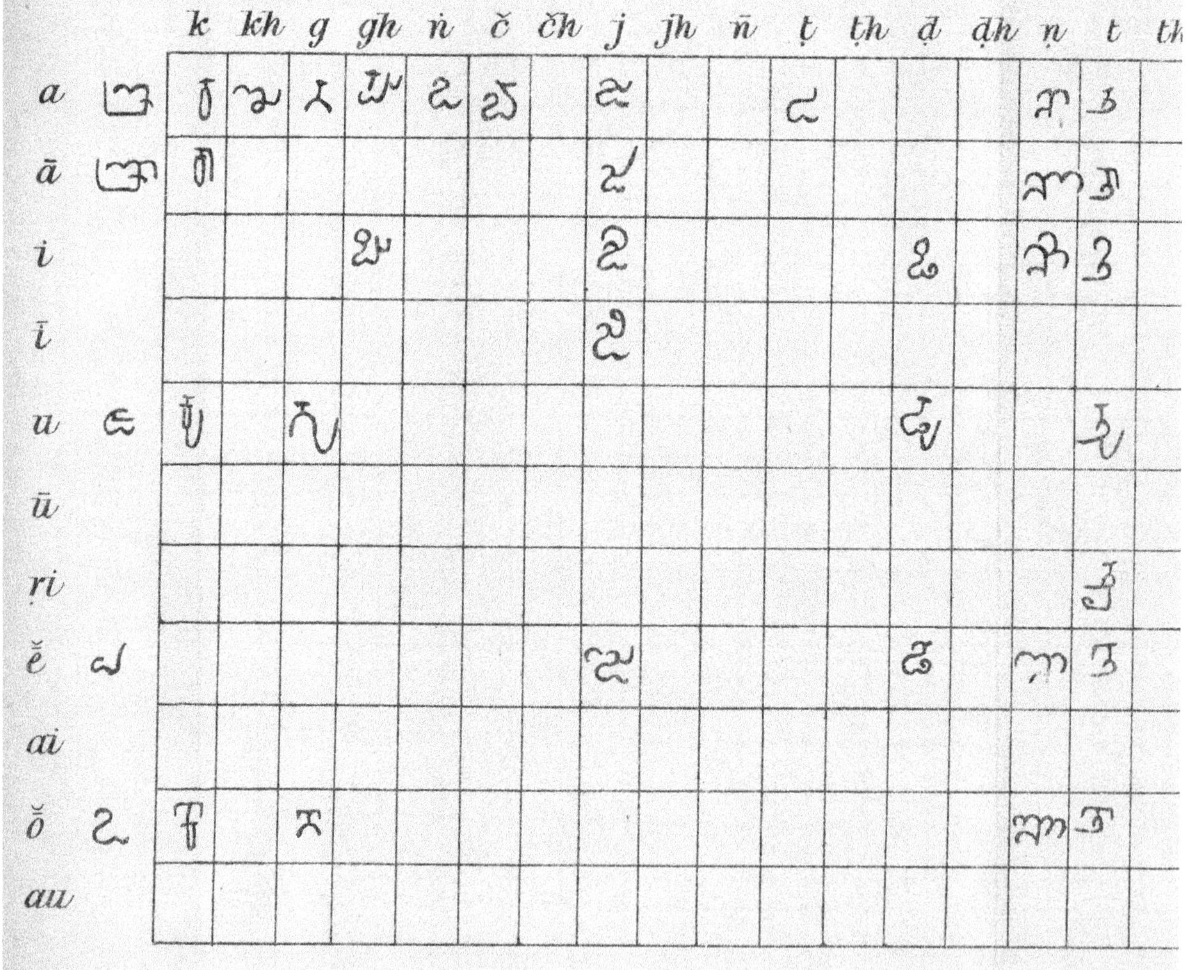
k kh g gh ṅ č čh j jh ñ ṭ ṭh ḍ ḍh ṇ t th
a
ā
i
ī
u
ū
ṛi
ĕ
ai
ŏ
au

Compounds etc.

ṅg; ṭṭ; ṉḏ; tt; tth; tp;
nā

7 A. D. (but of the 10th c.)

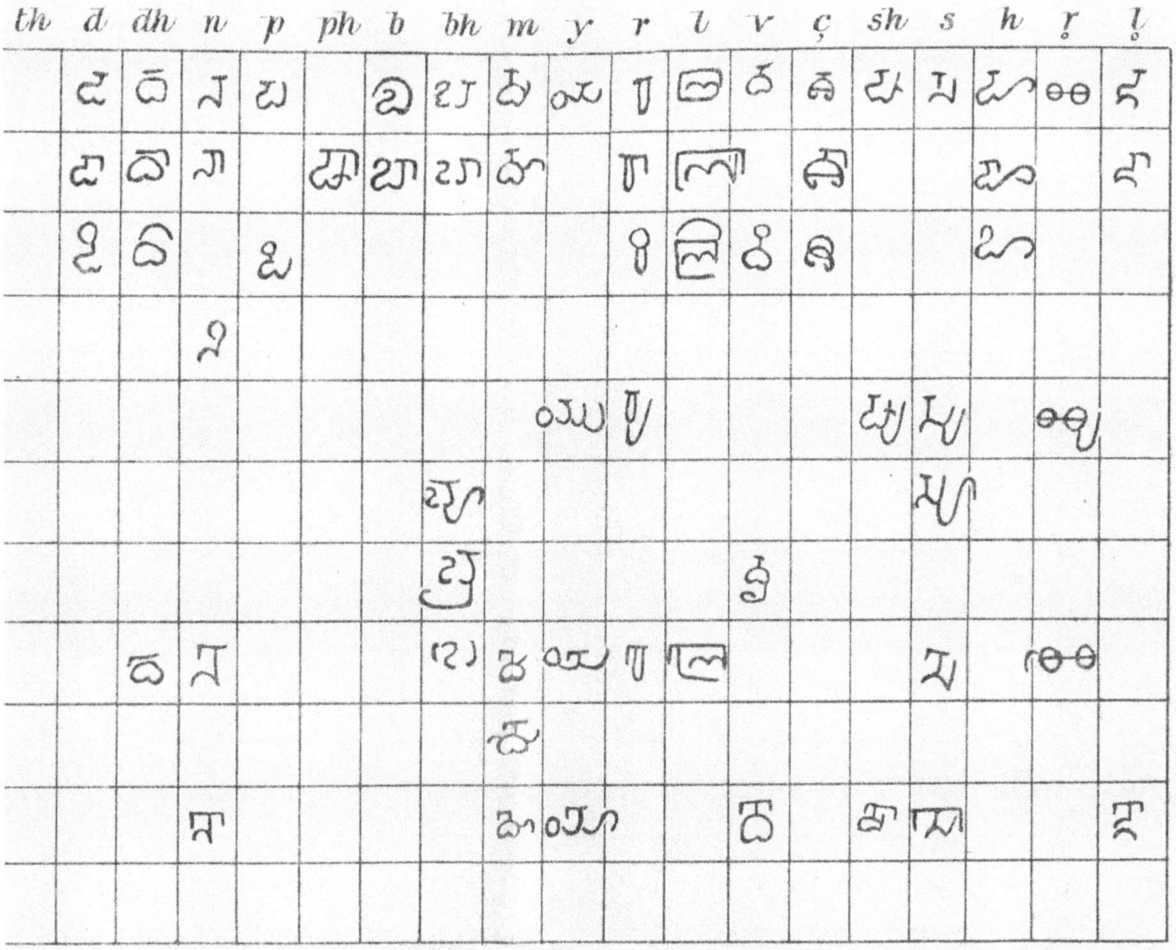

ts; d̄hye; nko; ndr; nvā; mbh; rk; rmm; st; hn; nām; traḫ;

EAST

Pl. XI

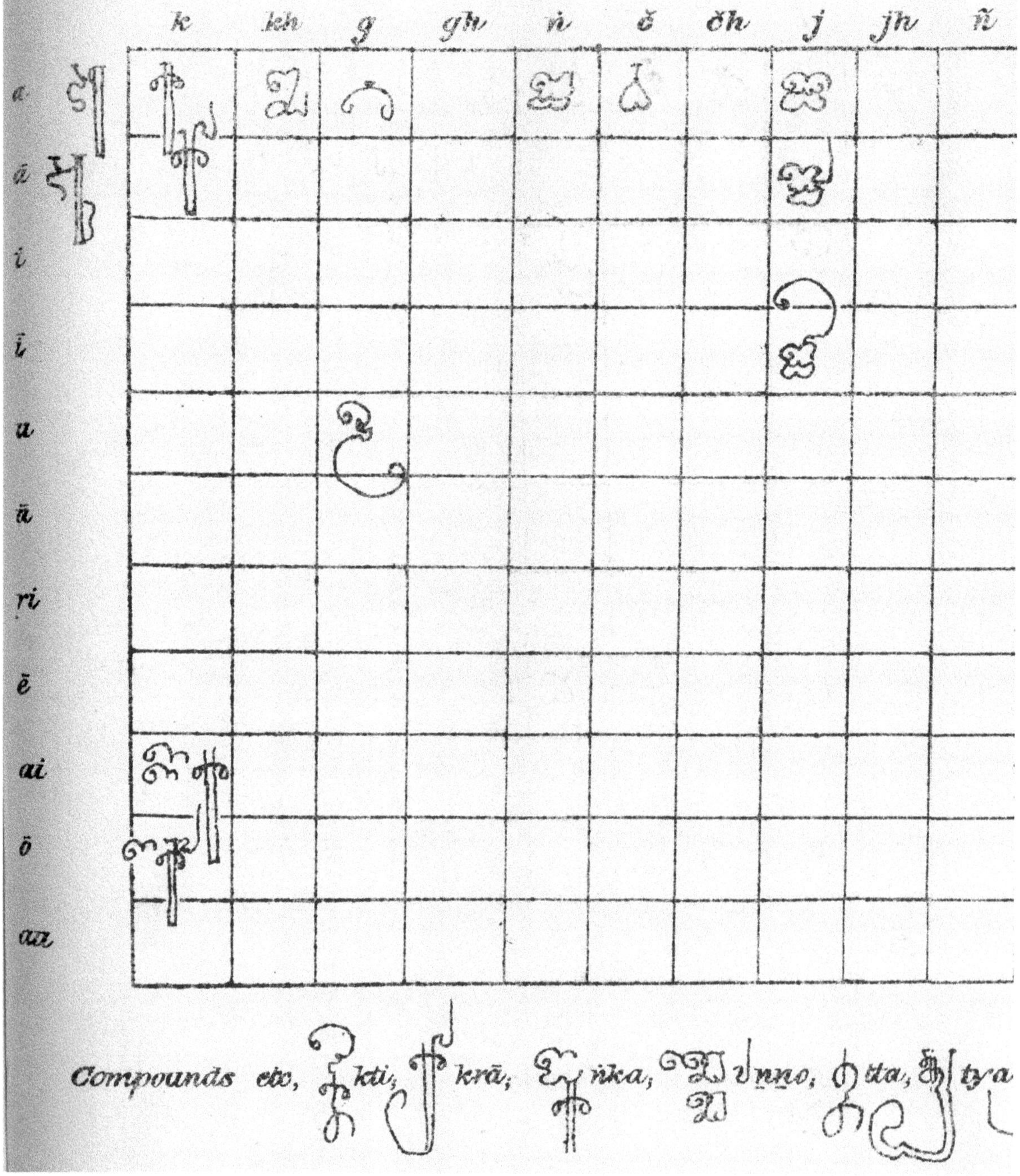
k
kh
g
gh
ṅ
č
čh
j
jh
ñ
a
ā
i
ī
u
ū
ṛi
ē
ai
ō
au
Compounds etc,
kti;
krā;
ṅka;
nno;
tta;
tya

ASTERN ČÊRA (TRANSITIONAL) c 700 A.D.

from an Inscription on stone at Seven Pagodas (reduced)

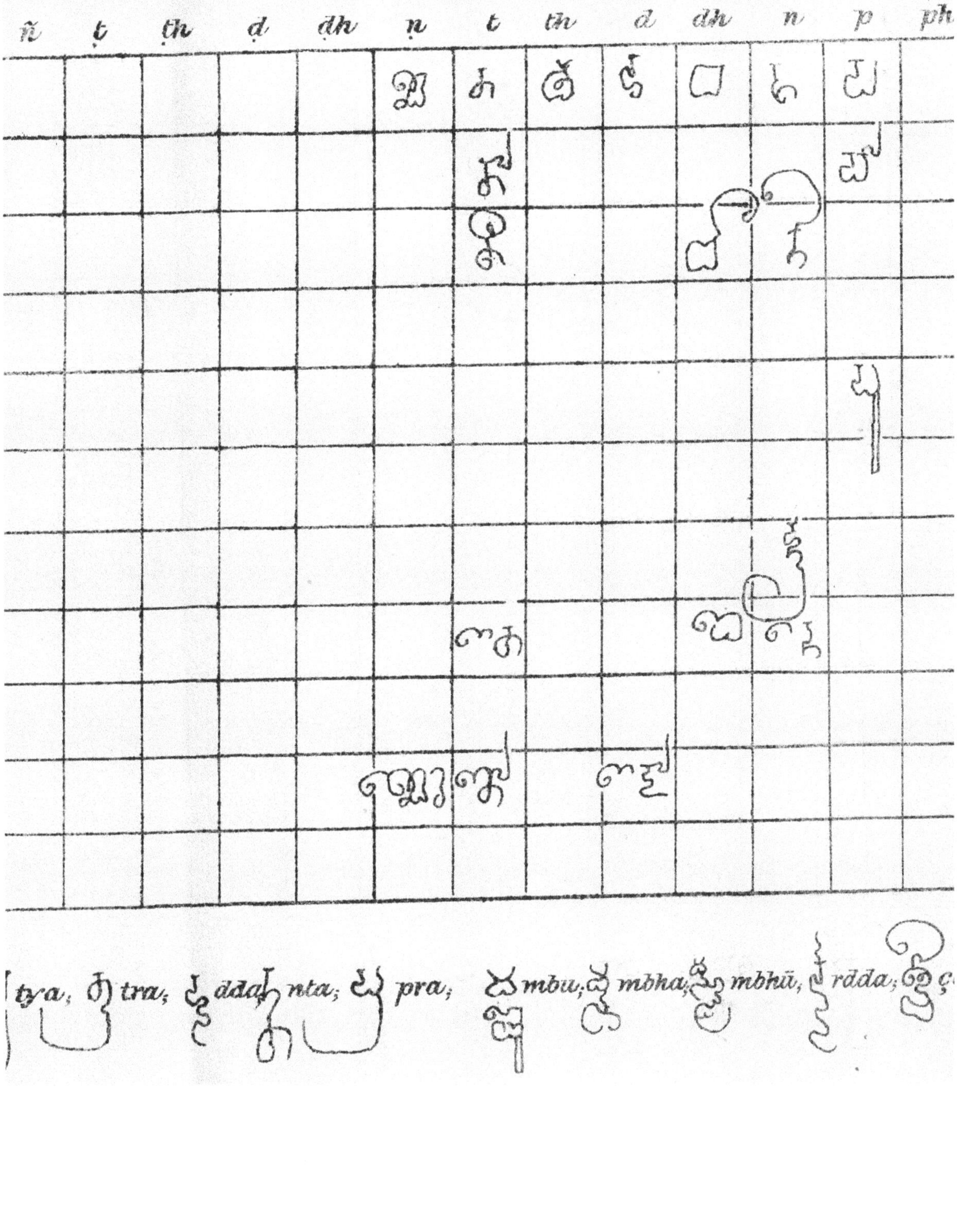
ñ ṭ ṭh ḍ ḍh ṇ t th d dh n p ph
tya, tra, dda, nta, pra, mbu, mbha, mbhū, rdda, ç

ASTERN ČĒRA (TRANSITIONAL) c 700 A.D.

from an Inscription on stone at Seven Pagodas (reduced)

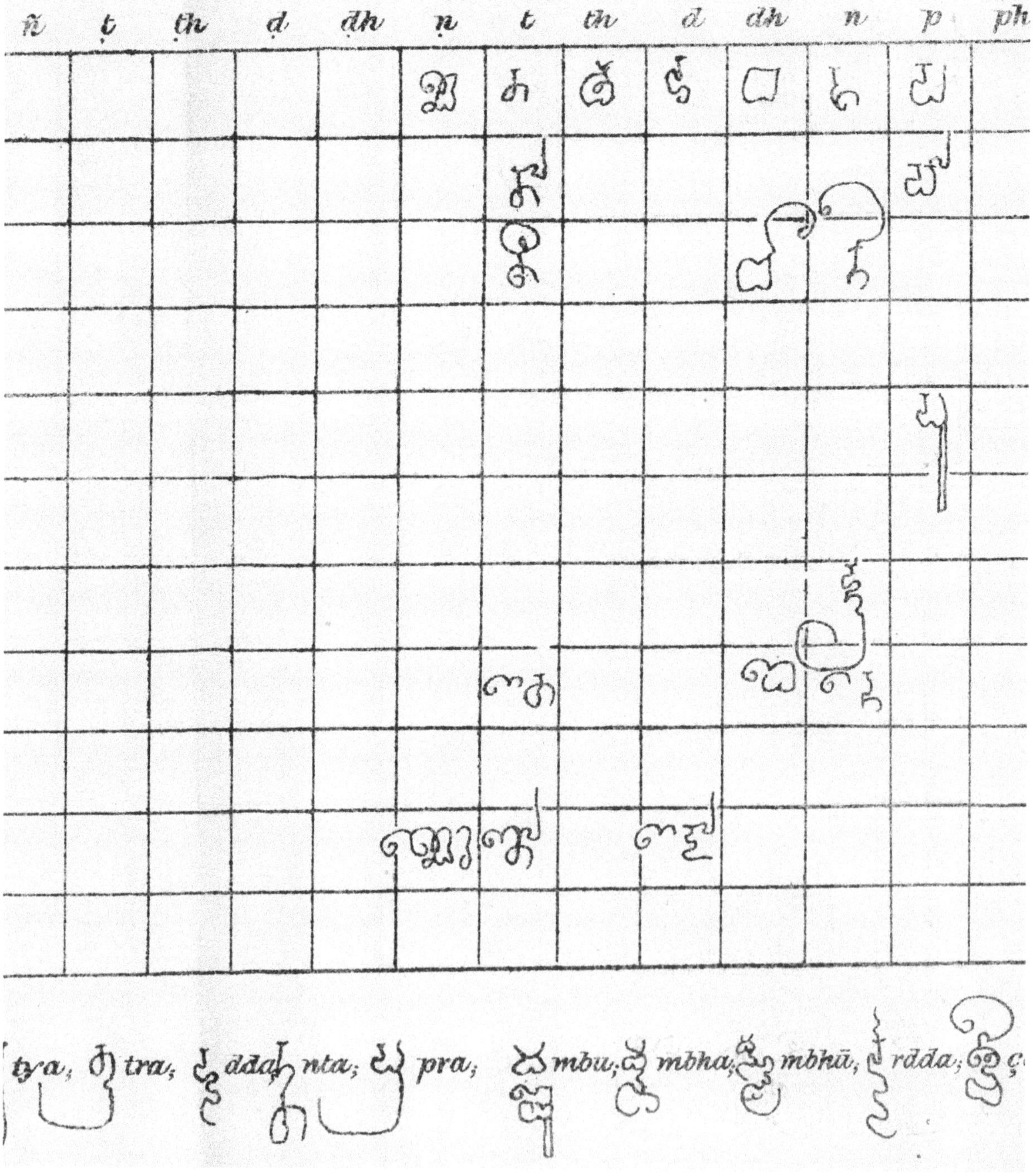
ñ ṭ ṭh ḍ ḍh ṇ t th d dh n p ph
tya; tra; ḍḍa; nta; pra; mbu; mbha; mbhā; rḍḍa; ç

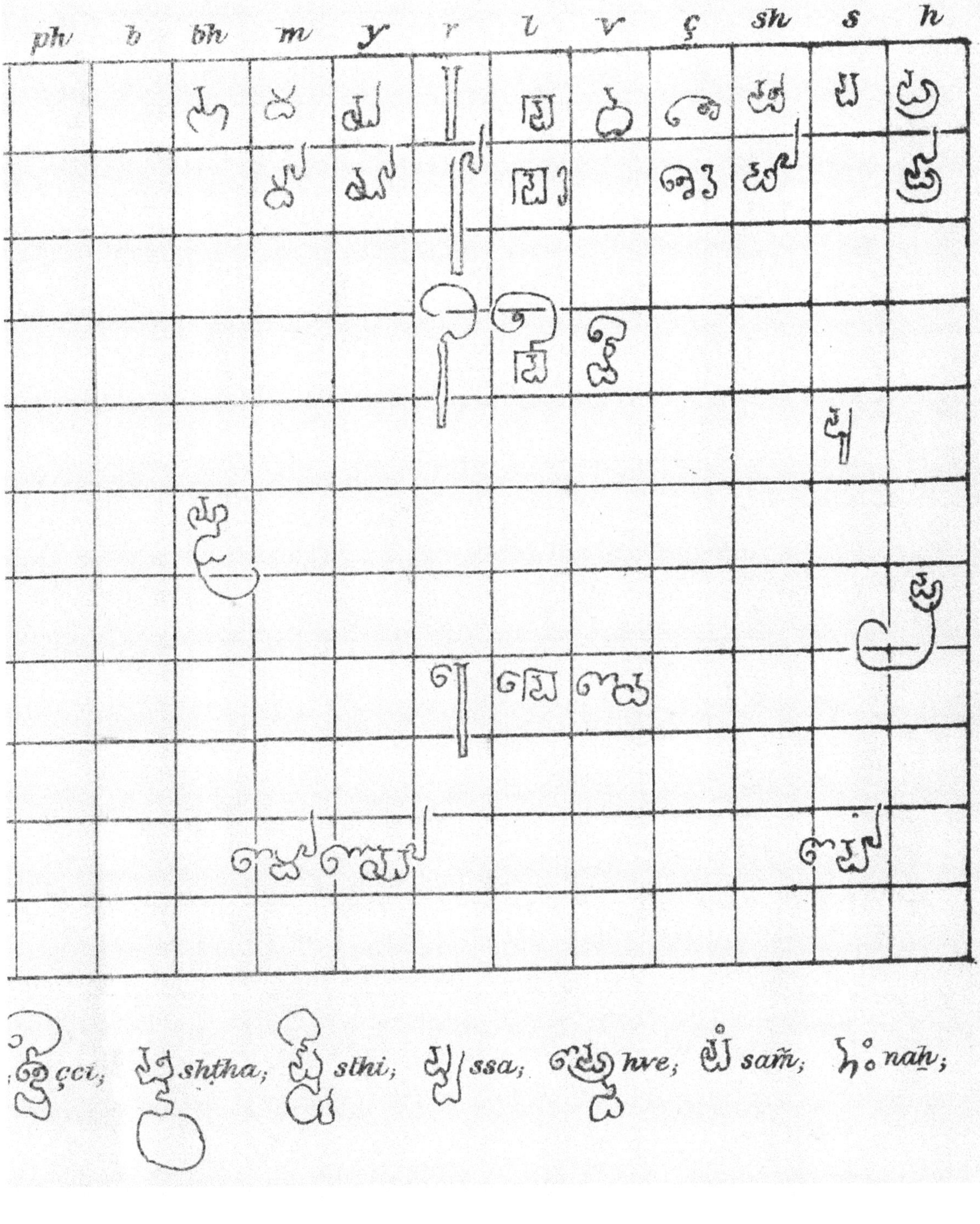
ph b bh m y r l v ç sh s h
çci; shṭha; sthi; ssa; hve; saṁ; naḥ;

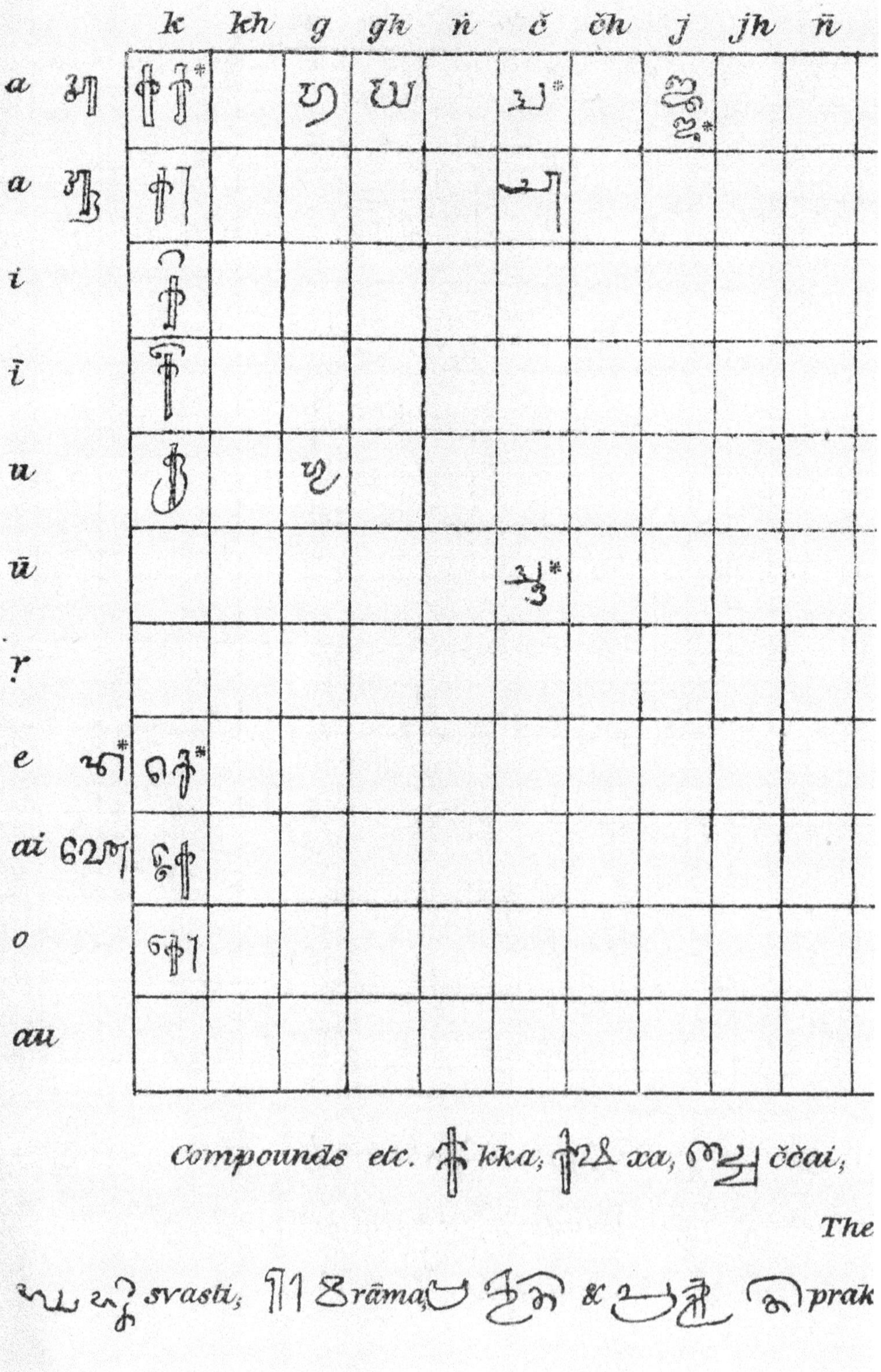
k kh g gh ṅ č čh j jh ñ
a
ā
i
ī
u
ū
ṛ
e
ai
o
au
Compounds etc. kka; xa, ččai;
The
svasti; Srāma; & prak

ČŌLA-GRANTHA (11th cent.)

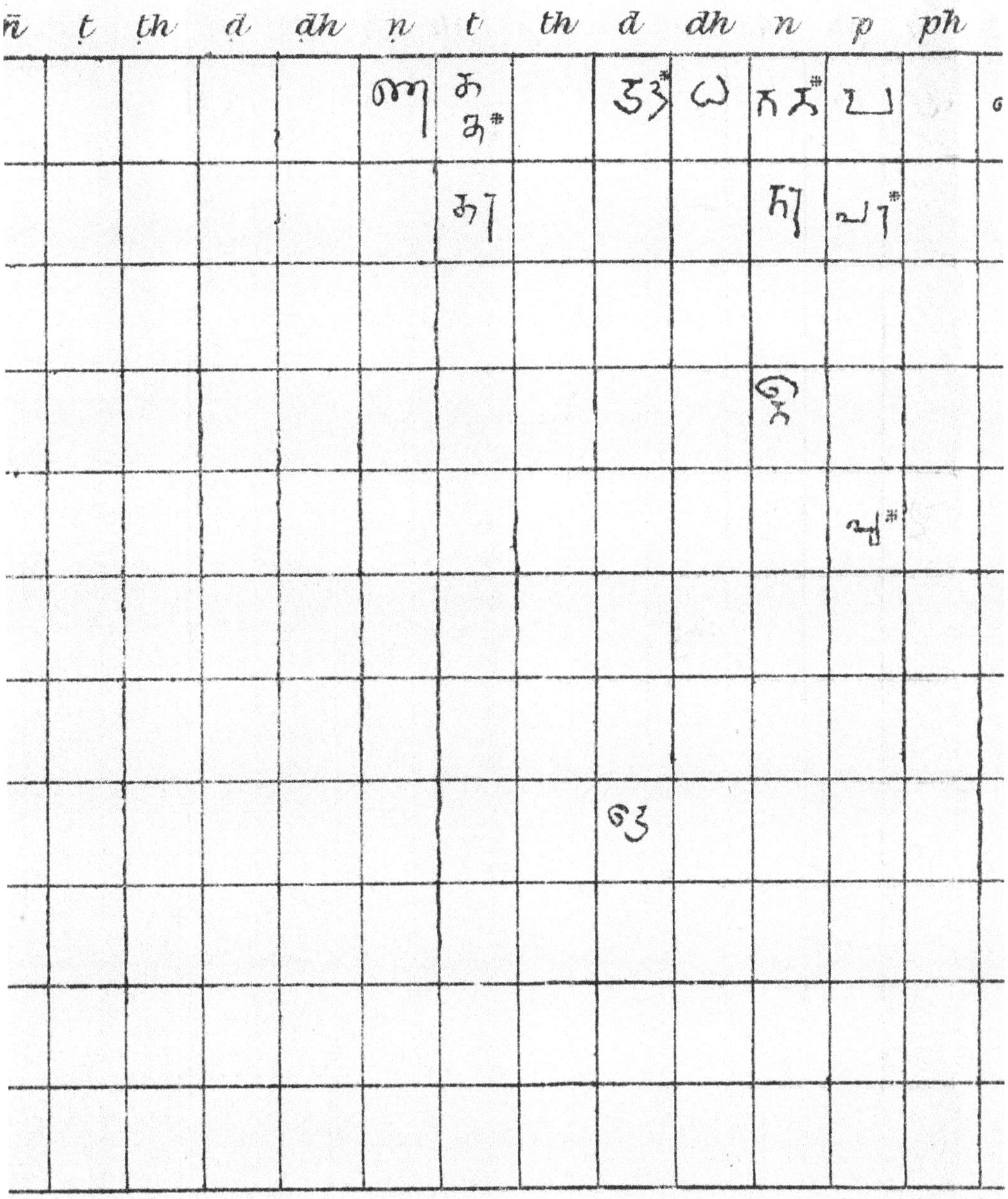

ñ ṭ ṭh ḍ ḍh ṇ t th d dh n p ph

ri; ṇḍa; nto; pra; lla; shka; shṭ

The following occur in the Syrian grant B (9th cent.)

prakṛiti; piriçāsa; i. e. praçāsa; taris

ČŌLA-GRANTHA (11th cent.)

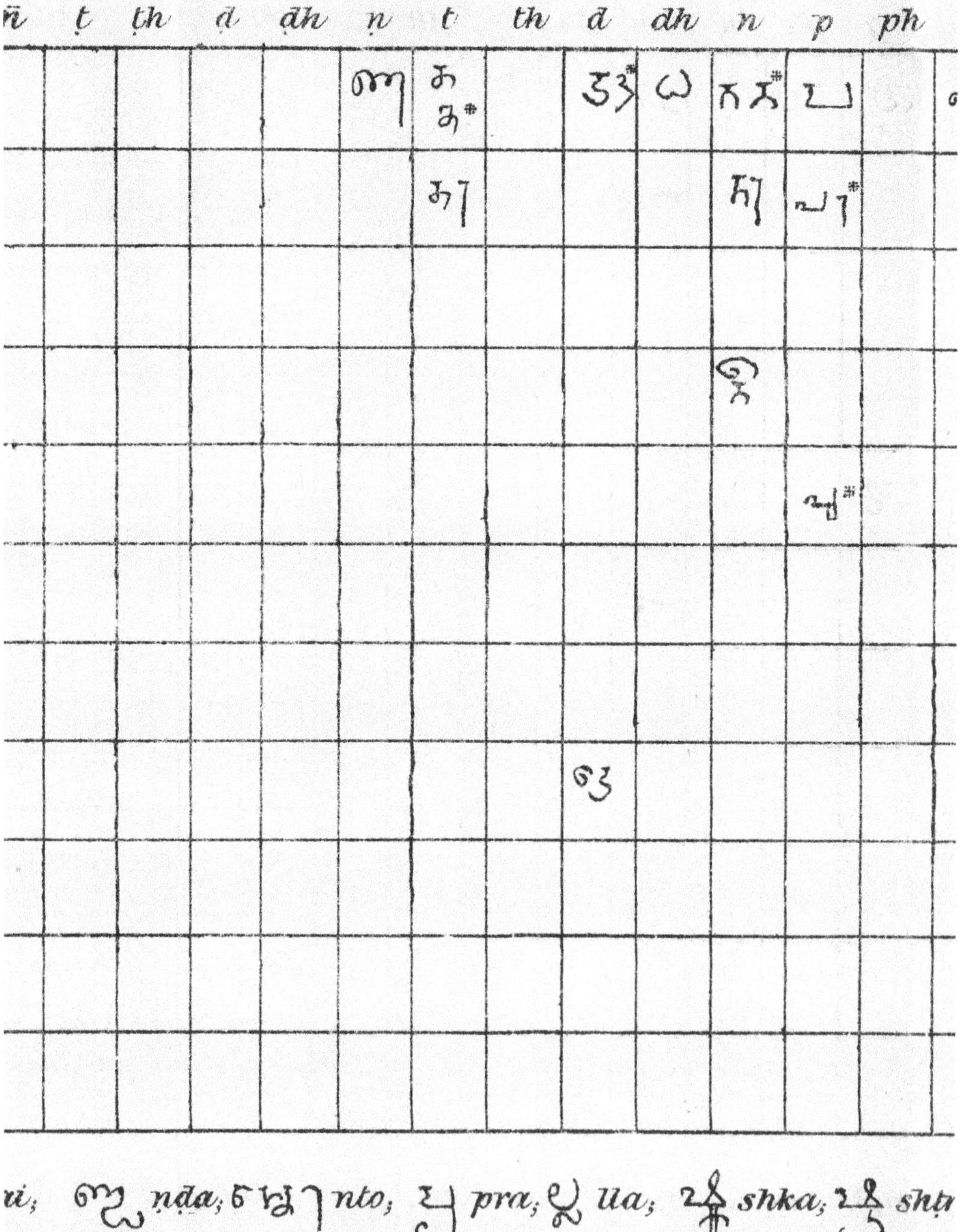

ñ ṭ ṭh ḍ ḍh ṇ t th d dh n p ph

ui; ṇḍa; nto; pra; lla; shka; shṭr

The following occur in the Syrian grant B (9th cent.)

prakṛiti; pitiçāsa; i.e. praçāsa; taris

ph b bh m y r l v ç sh s h

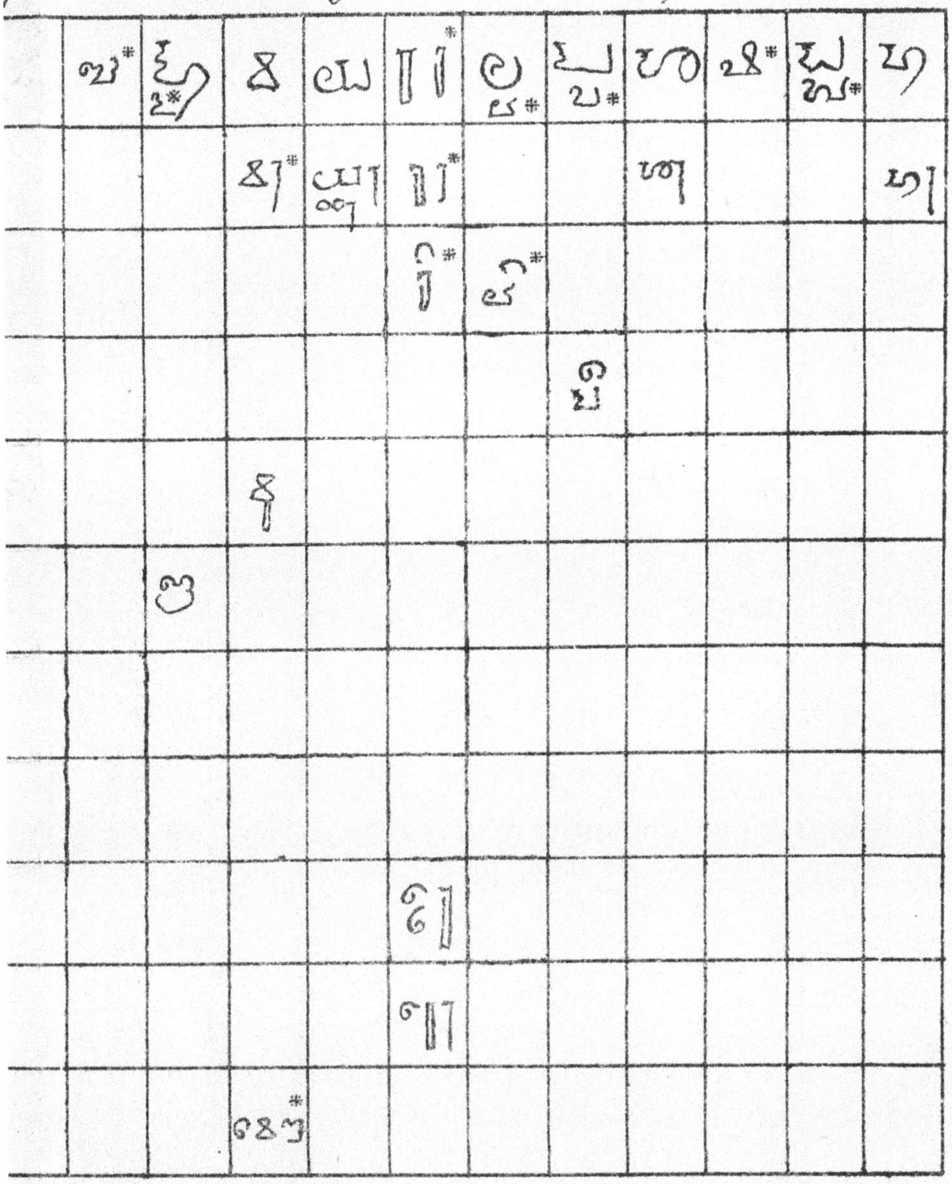

shṭra; sva; m;(final) o = m̃; ḥ.

tarisā; sapiriço; bhūmi ssu.

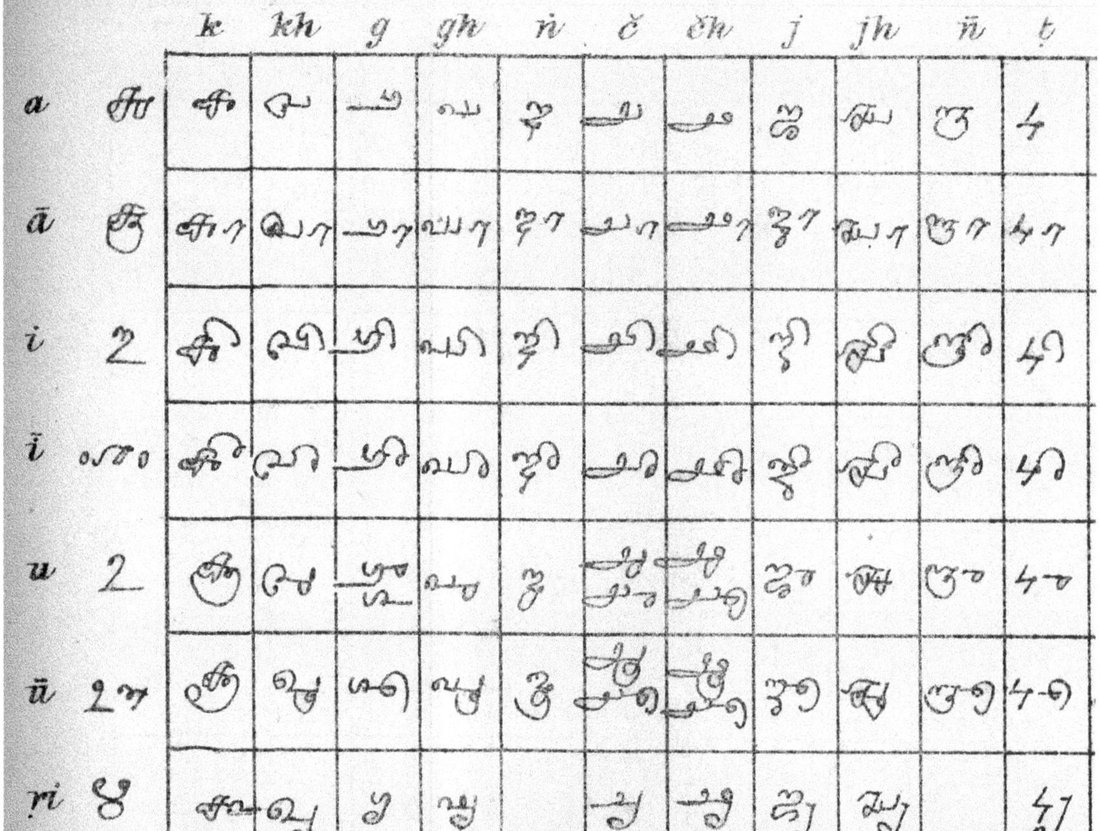
k kh g gh ṅ č čh j jh ñ ṭ
a
ā
i
ī
u
ū
ṛi
ē
ai
ō
au
Compounds & Various Forms; a; ā; & ṭri;
ṭ (with Virāma); ṭta; tya; ntra; nda; nma;

IODERN GRANTHA- 19th cent

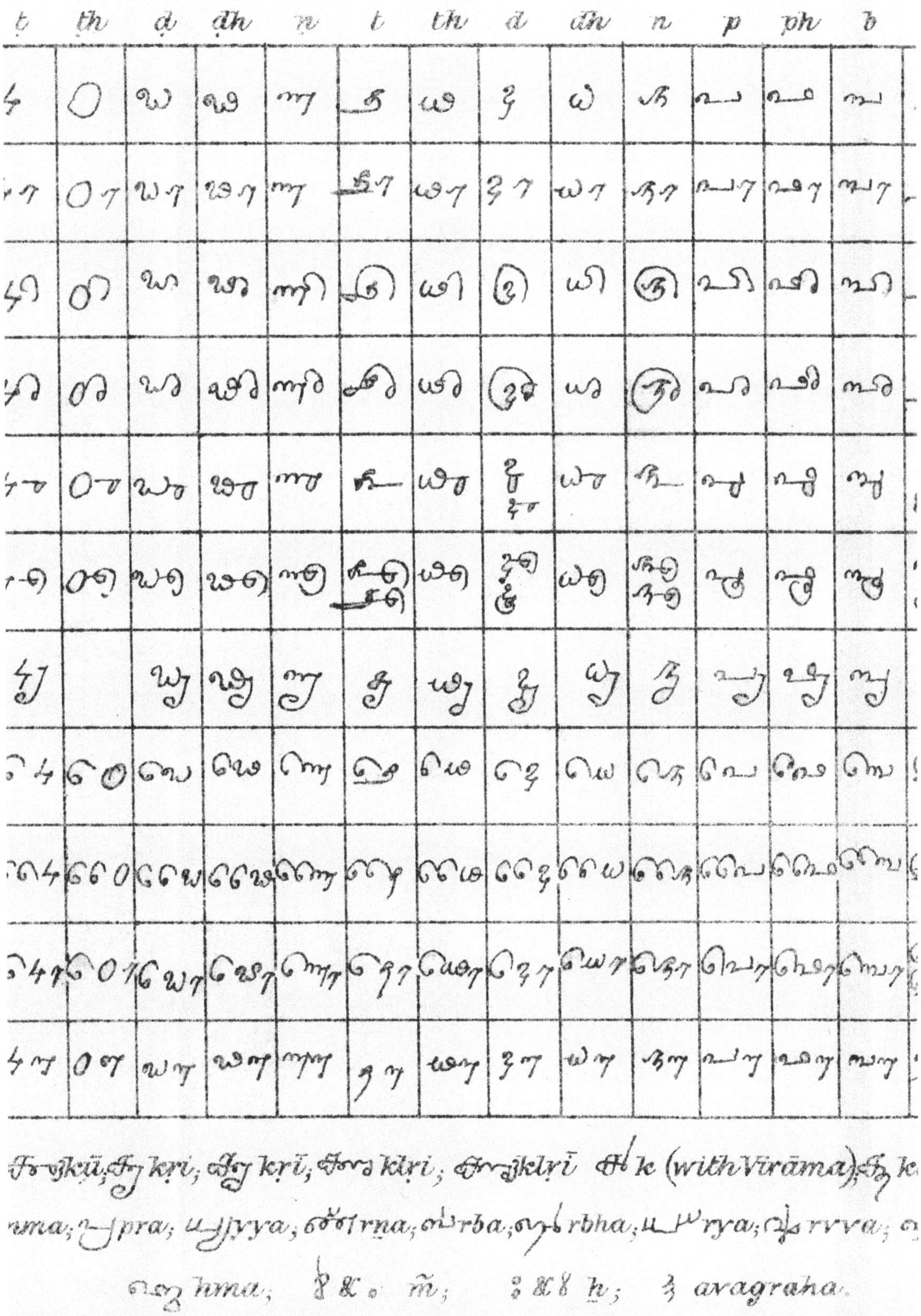
ṭ ṭh ḍ ḍh ṇ t th d dh n p ph b
kū, kṛi, kṛī, klṛi, klṛī
k (with Virāma)
nma; pra; yya; rṇa; rba; rbha; rya; rvva;
hma; ṁ; ḥ; avagraha.

IODERN GRANTHA- 19th cent

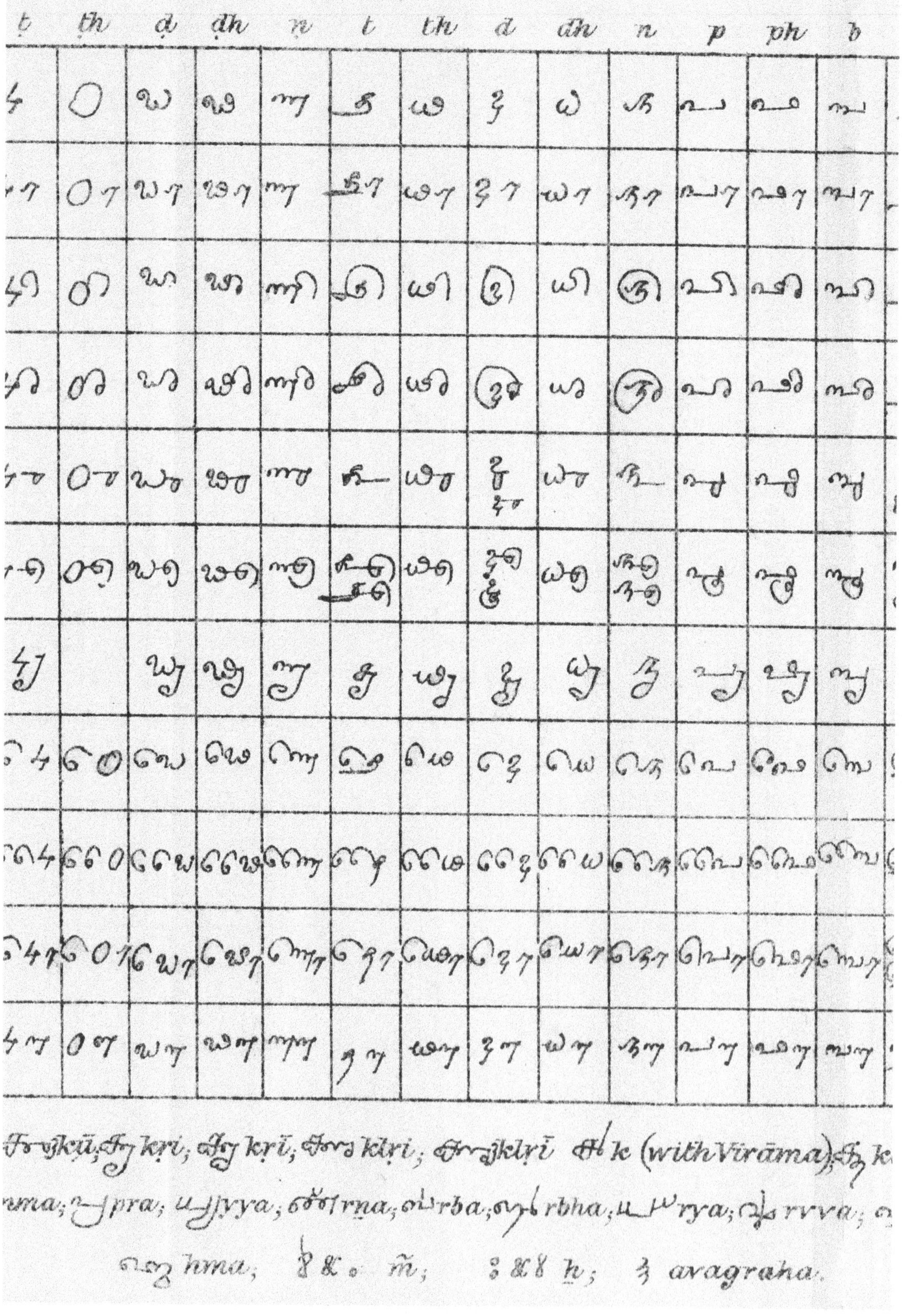

ṭ ṭh ḍ ḍh ṇ t th d dh n p ph b
kū; kṛi; kṛī; klṛi; klṛī
k (with Virāma)
ma; pra; yya; rṇa; rba; rbha; rya; rva
hma; ṁ; ḥ; avagraha.

nt.

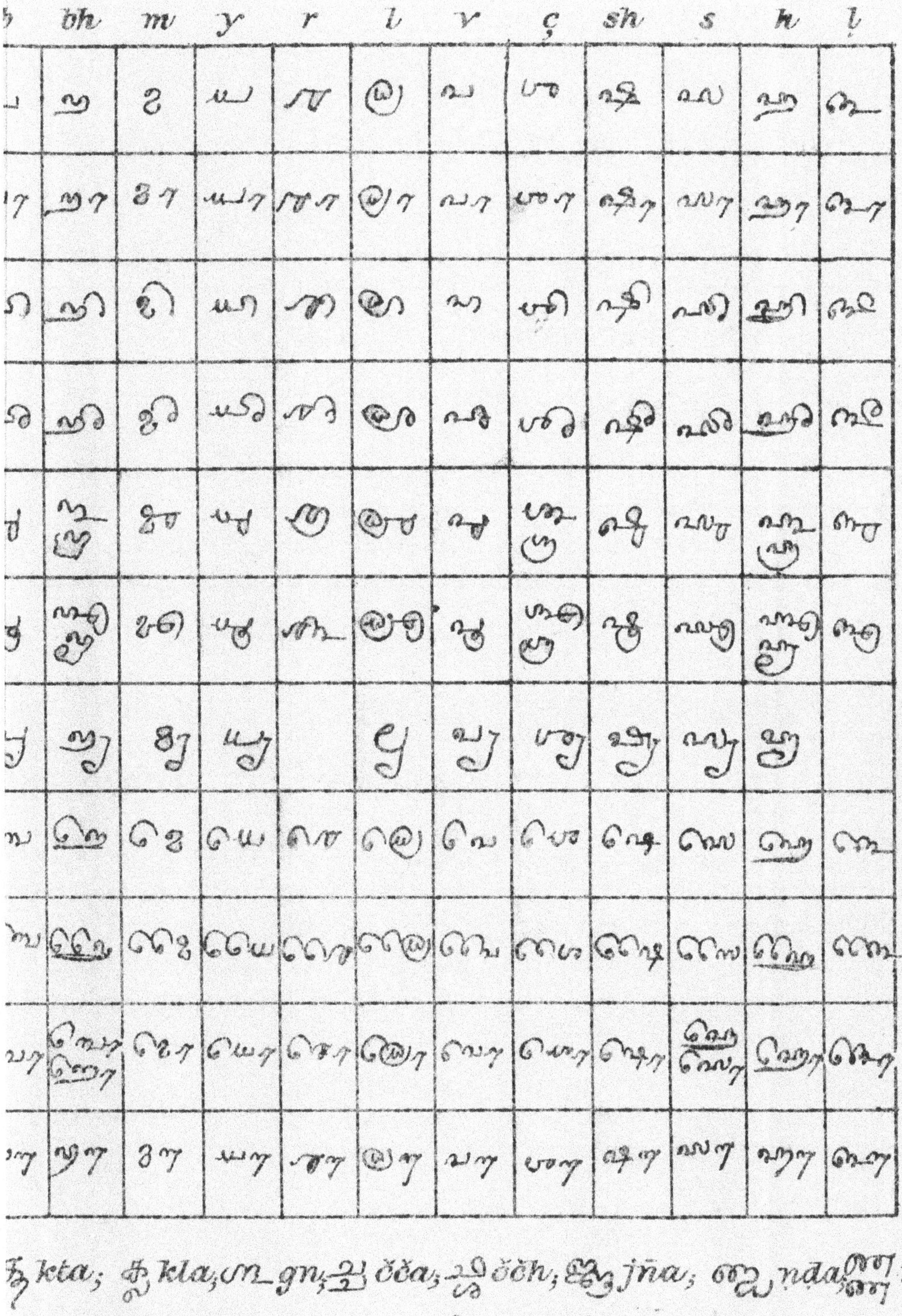

kta; kla, gn; čča; čch; jña; ṇḍa, ṇṇa;

; rha; çča; çça; shṭa; shṭha; sya; ssa;

XIV.

TULU, 19

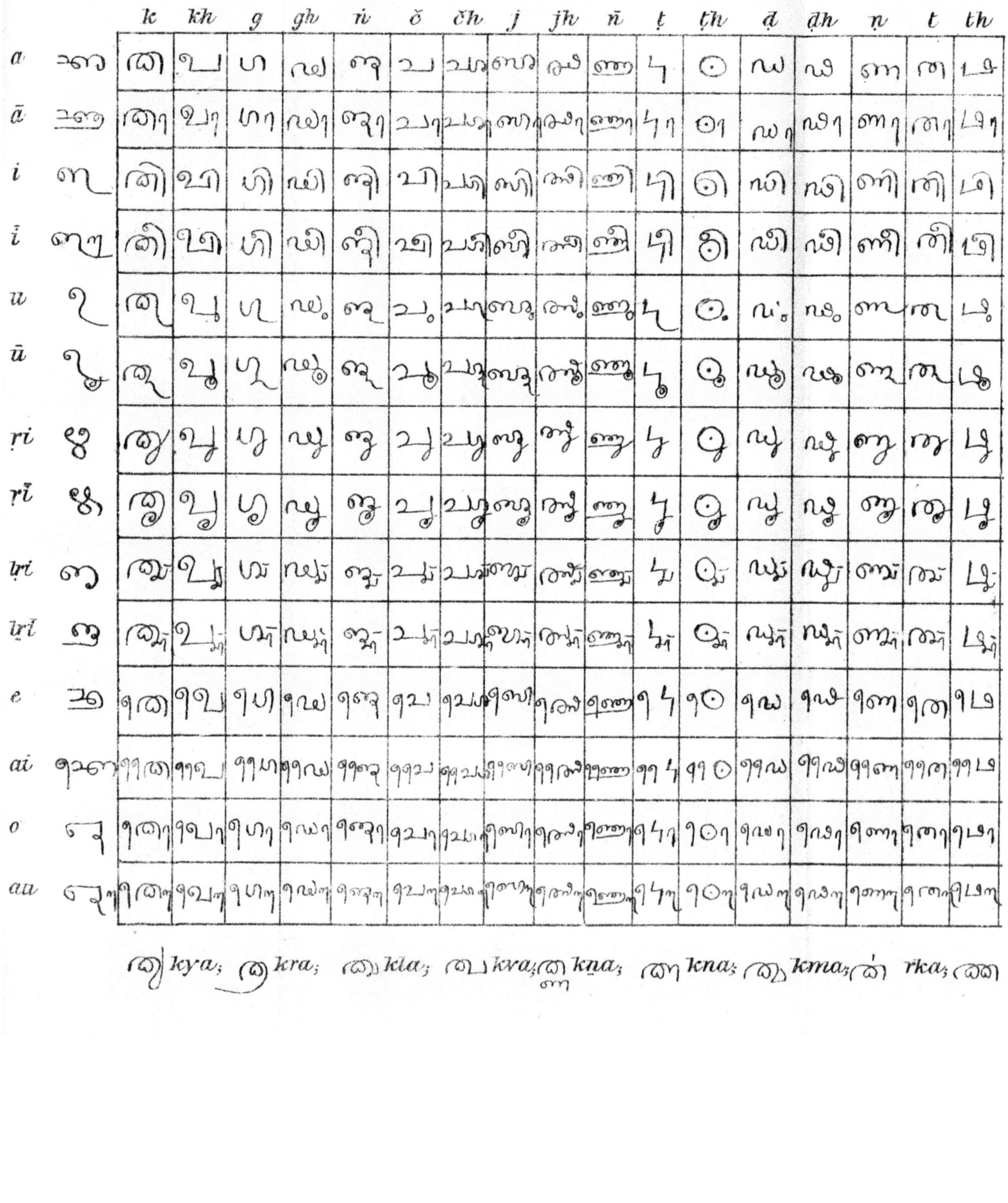
k kh g gh ṅ č čh j jh ñ ṭ ṭh ḍ ḍh ṇ t th
a
ā
i
ī
u
ū
ṛi
ṛī
ḷṛi
ḷṛī
e
ai
o
au
kya; kra; kla; kva; kṉa; kna; kma; rka;

TH CENT.

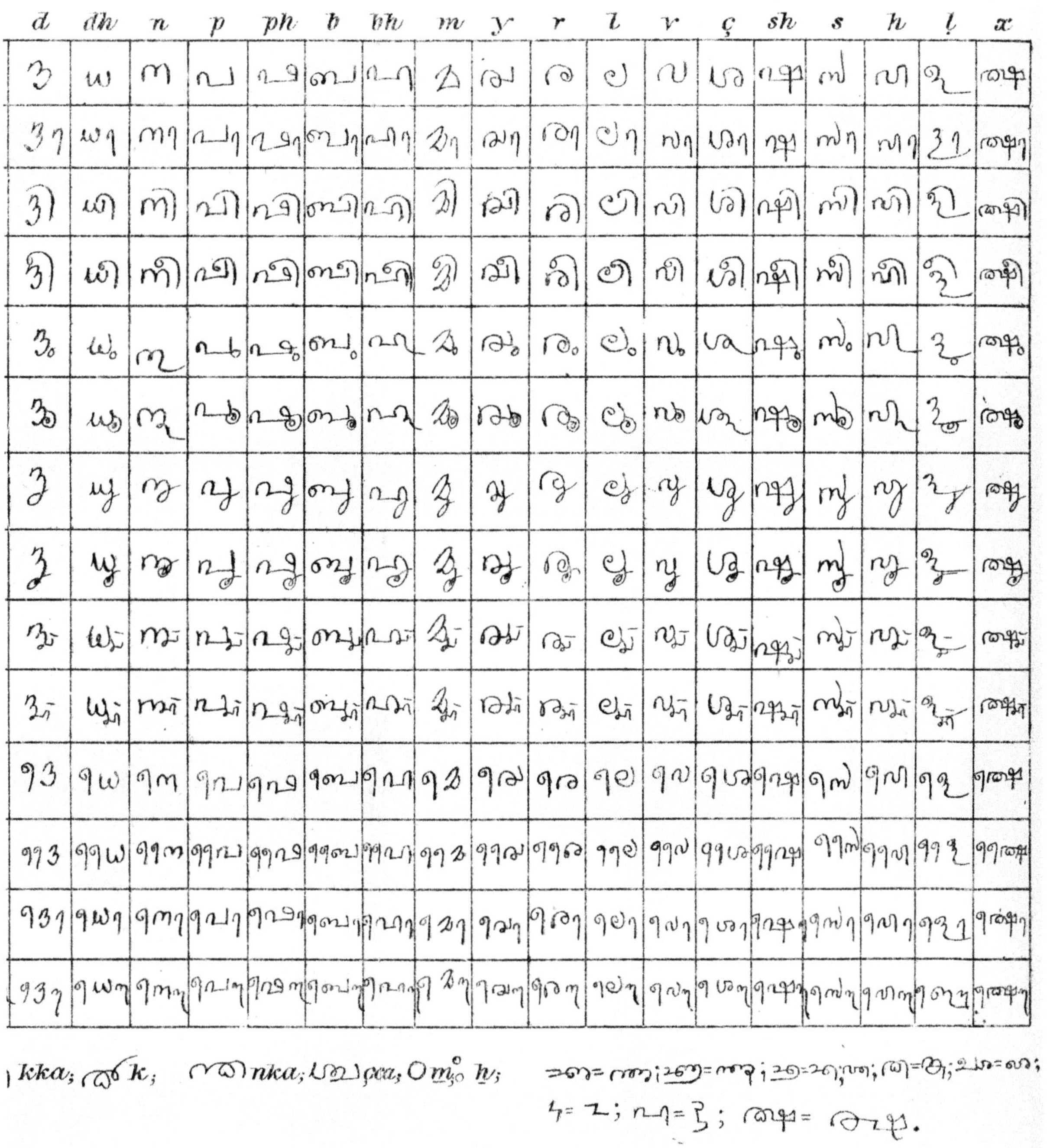
d dh n p ph b bh m y r l v ç sh s h ḷ x
kka; k; nka; ca, m h;

XV

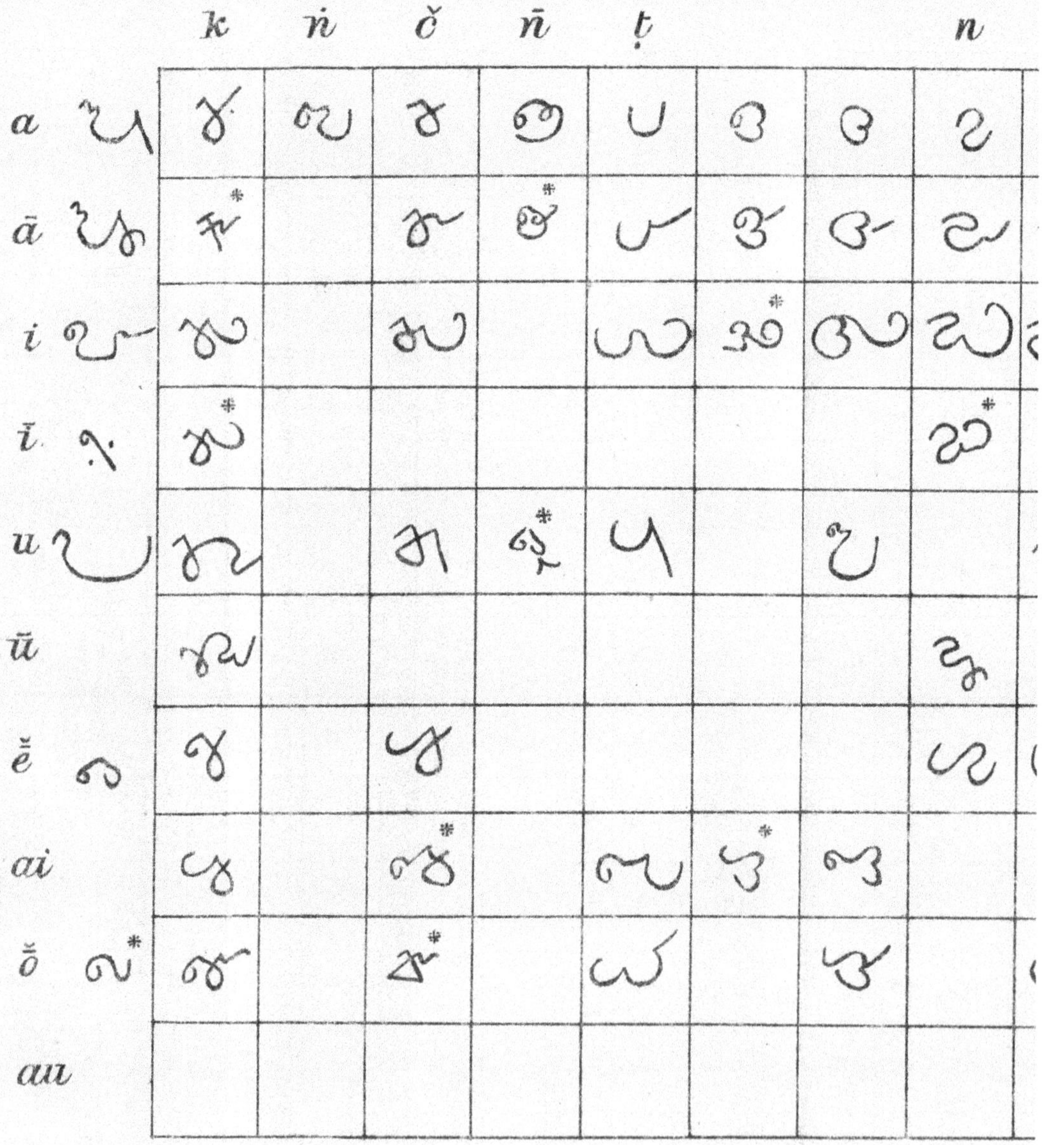

The above letters are taken from
*except those marked * which are from the*

In B also — = *ī*; = *u*; = *o*; = *k*; = *po*;

ḶUTTU, 8th Century A.D.

m the grant (C) to the Jews,
e second grant (B) to the Persians (9th cent?)

; & =mo; =y; =ḻu; & =ṉ; In C— also=ḻu.

TAMIL – 1073 A.D.

From an Inscription round the base of the shrine of the great Temple at Tanjore.

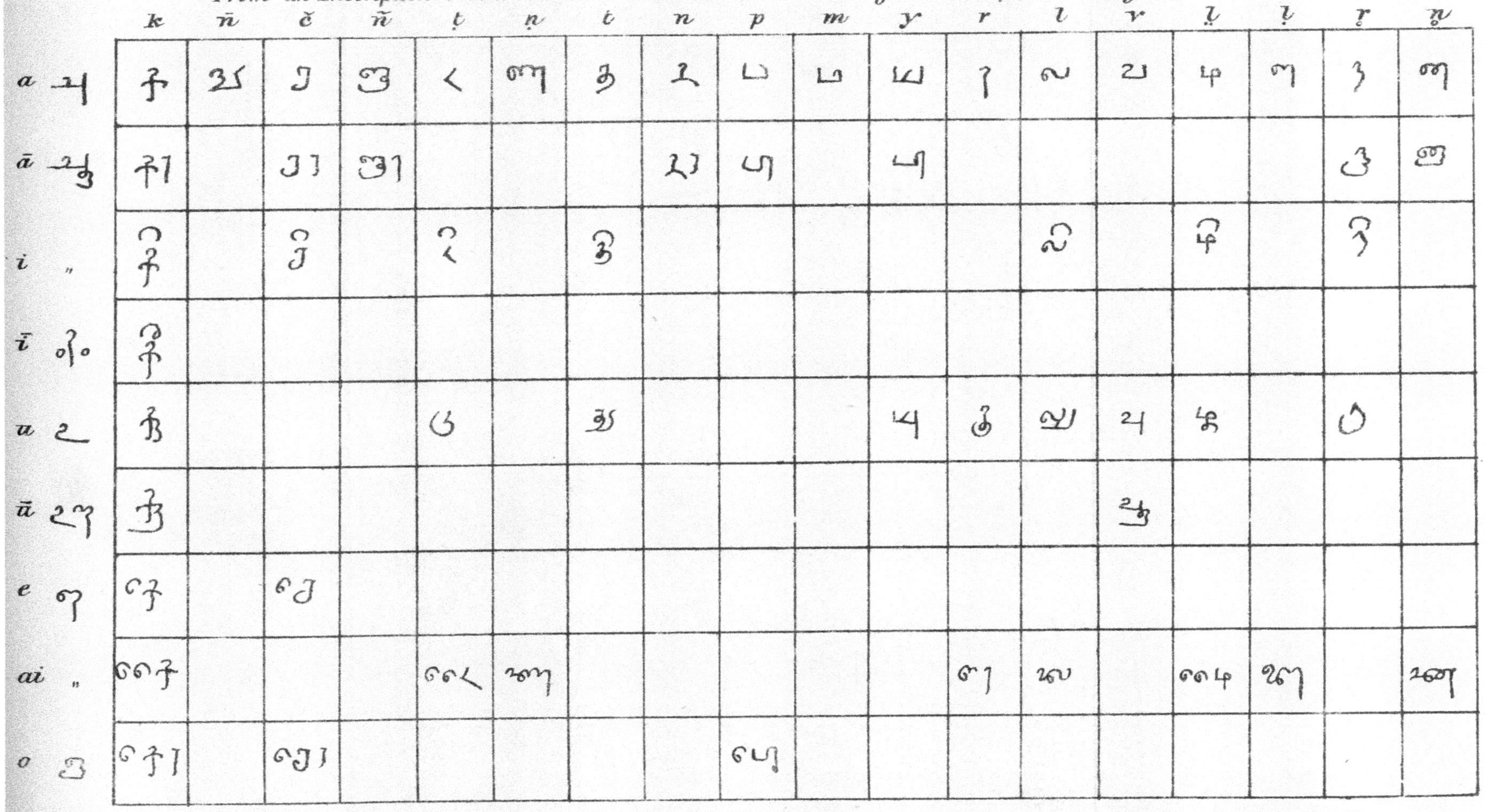
k n̄ č ñ ṭ ṇ t n p m y r l v ḻ ḷ ṟ ṉ
a
ā
i
ī
u
ū
e
ai
o

3 & G occur for *i* in Inscriptions of about the same date.

		k	kh	g	gh	ṅ	č	čh	j	jh	ñ	ṭ	ṭh	ḍ	dh	ṇ	t
a	अ	फा	र	ग	प		व		ज			र		३		ण	त
ā	आ	का		ग			वा		ज			ए				ला	ता
i		कि															लि
ī		की								जी		टी					
u	उ	कु		गु										उ			
ū		कू							ज								
ri		कृ															
e	∇	के		गे			वे										
ai		कै															
o		को		गो	गे		वो										
au				गे													कै

Compounds etc.   क्क kk.   क्र kr.   ख्य khy.   त्त tt.   त्र tr.

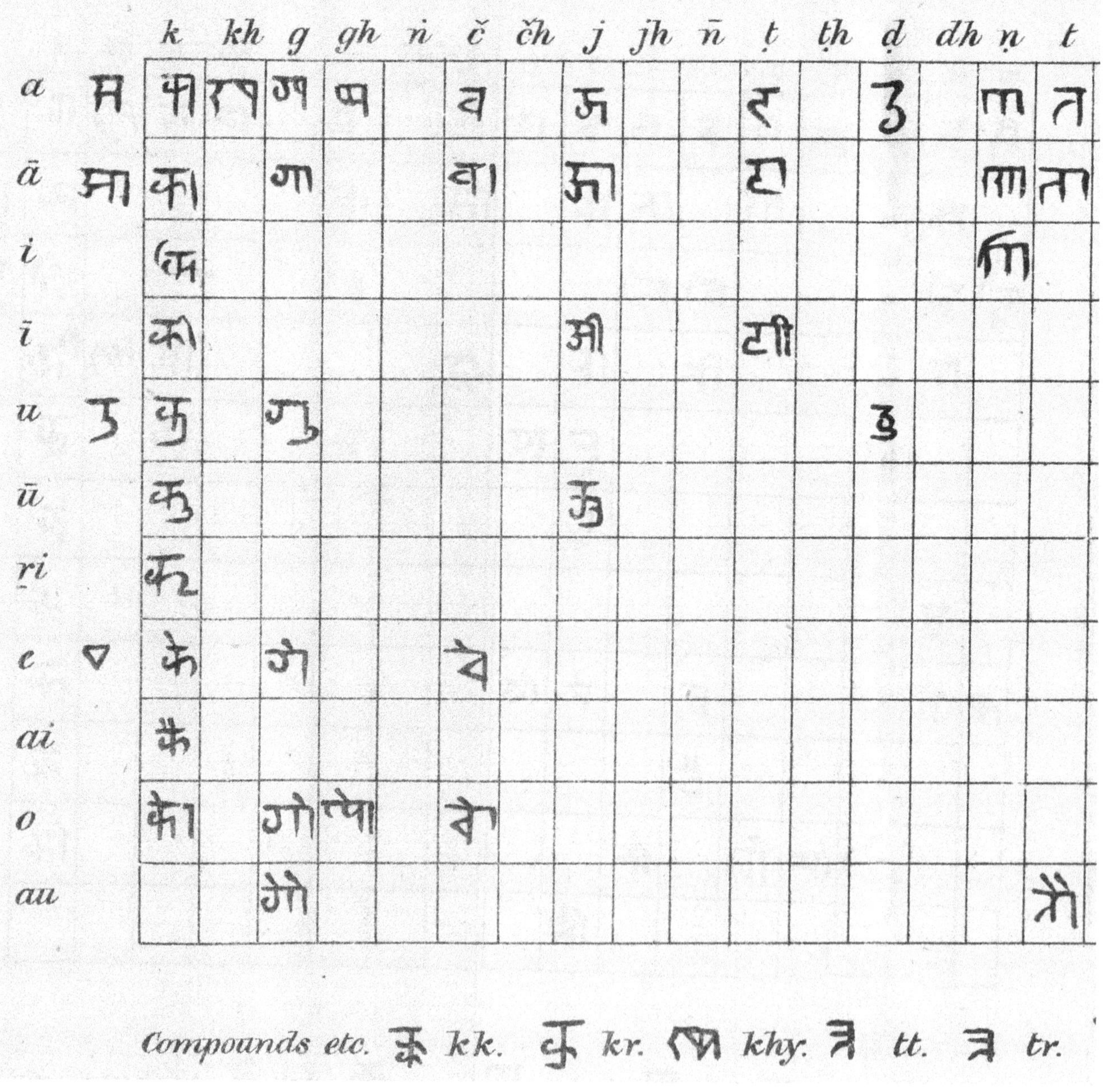

BY HARIHARA, D. 1399 A.D.

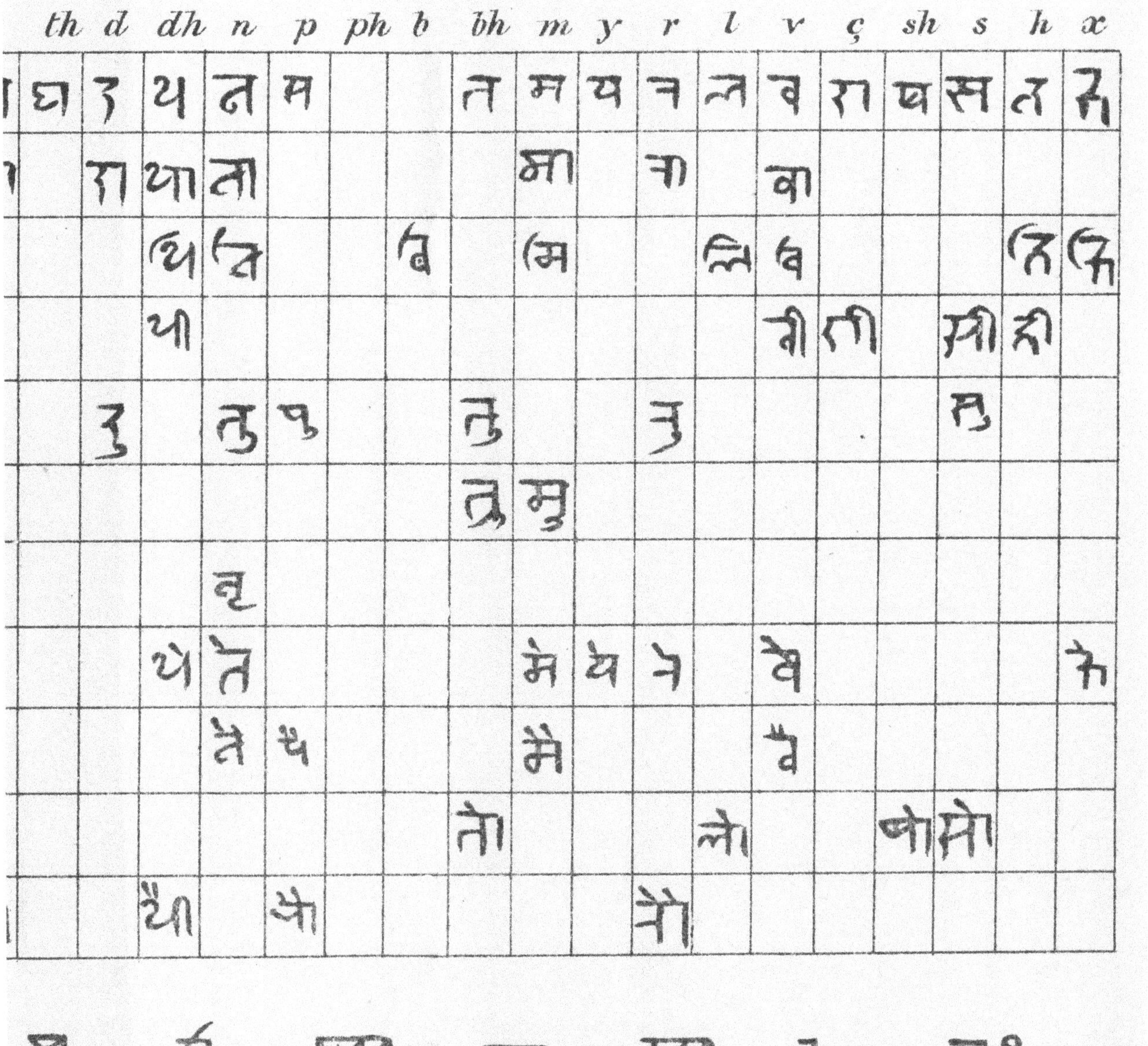

th d dh n p ph b bh m y r l v ç sh s h x
pr. rm. shy. sm. sy. dam. mah.

NAND

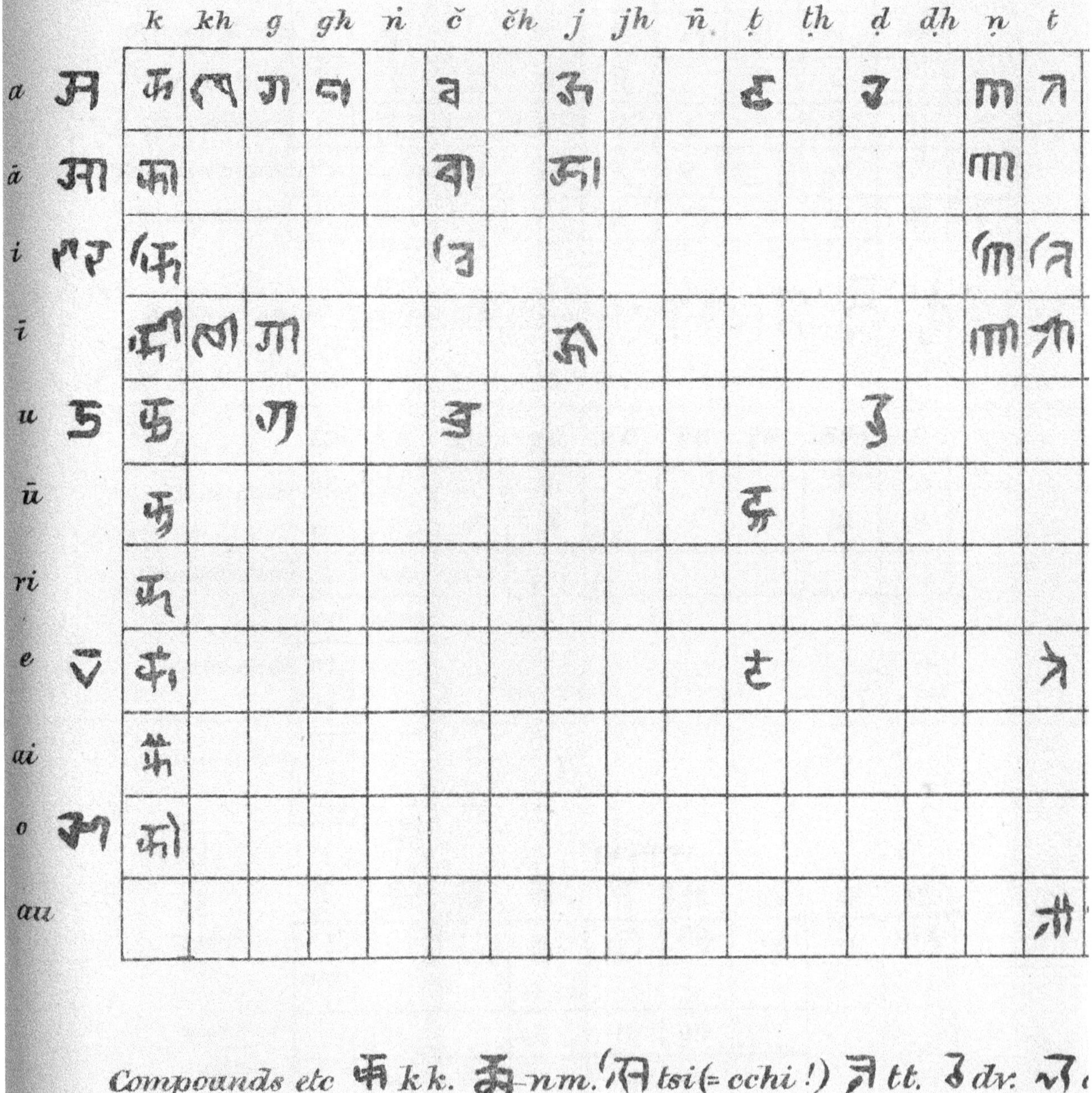
k kh g gh ṅ č čh j jh ñ ṭ ṭh ḍ ḍh ṇ t
a
ā
i
ī
u
ū
ri
e
ai
o
au
Compounds etc kk. nm. tsi (= cchi !) tt. dv.

NÂGARÎ, 1601 A.D.

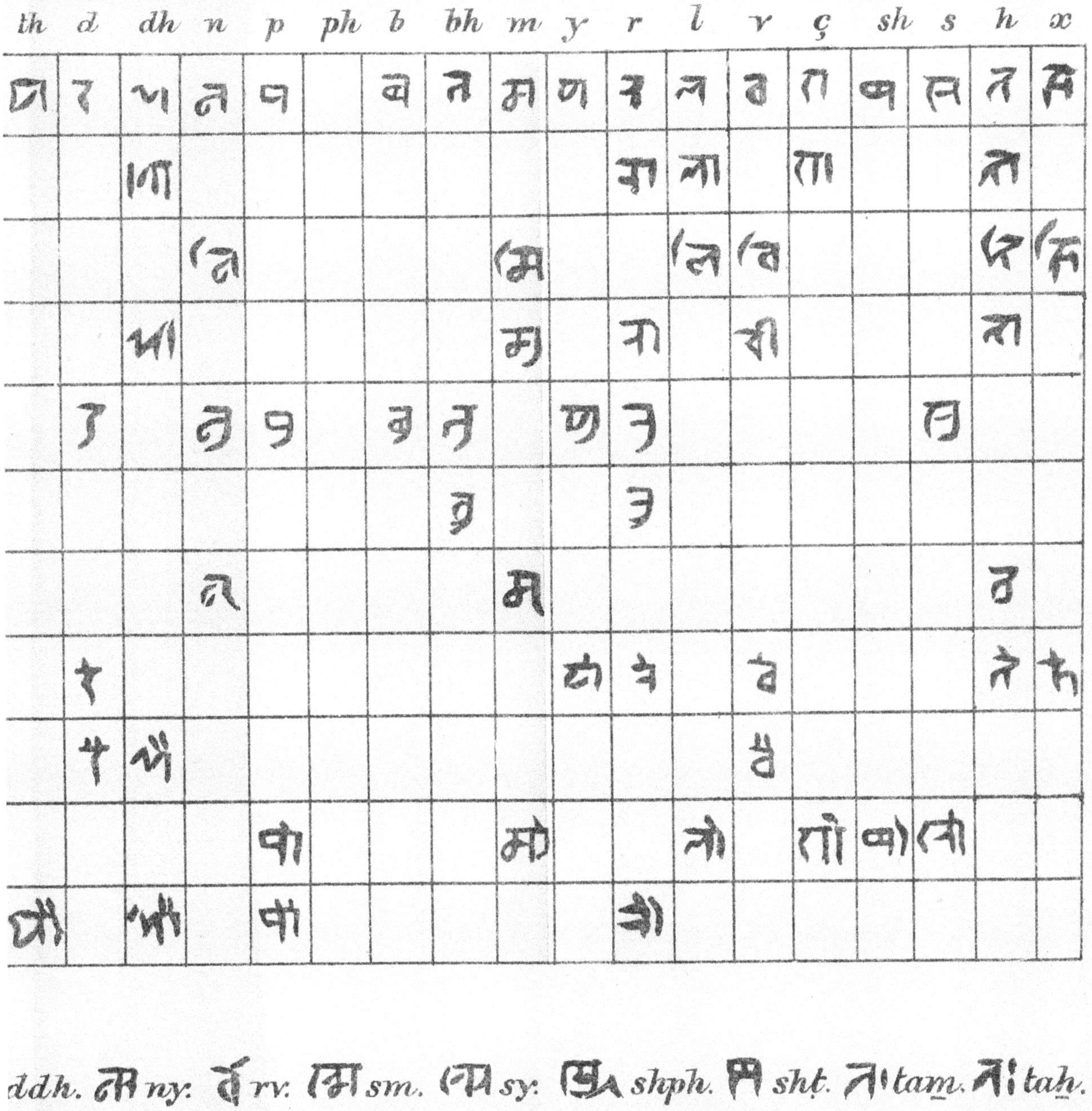
th d dh n p ph b bh m y r l v ç sh s h x
ddh. ny. rv. sm. sy. shph. sht. tam. tah.

Numerals.

	1	2	3	4	5	6	7	8	9	0
Cave char.										
Grantha-Tamil.										
Devanāgarī (10th c.)										
Gobar.										
Telugu-Canarese.										
Malayālam.										

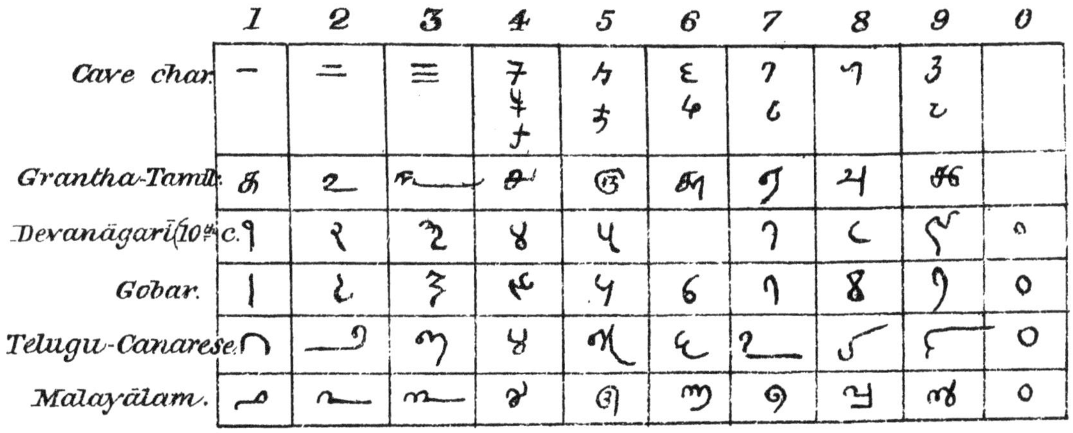

In the grant of Vijayananti Varmā (4th c.?)   = 1; 2; 3; 4.

	10	20	30	40	50	60	70	80	90
Cave char.									
Grantha-Tam.									

	100	1000
Cave char.		
Grantha-Tam.		

Fractions.

	$\frac{1}{16}$	$\frac{2}{16}$	$\frac{3}{16}$	$\frac{4}{16}$	$\frac{8}{16}$	$\frac{12}{16}$	$\frac{1}{20}$	$\frac{1}{80}$	$\frac{1}{320}$
Tamil									
Mal.m									
Tel.									
Can.									

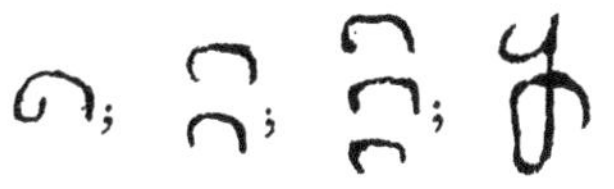

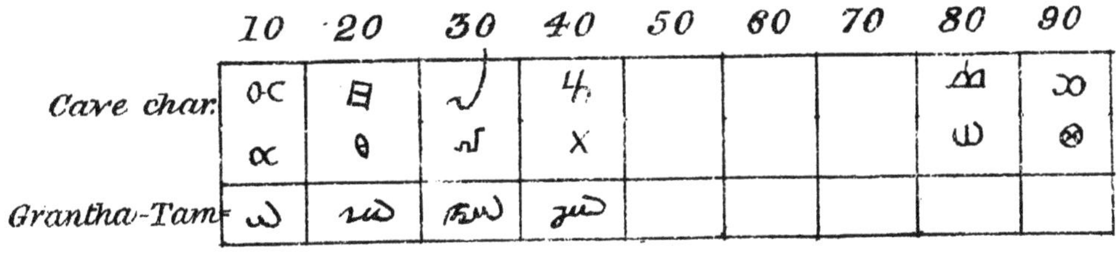

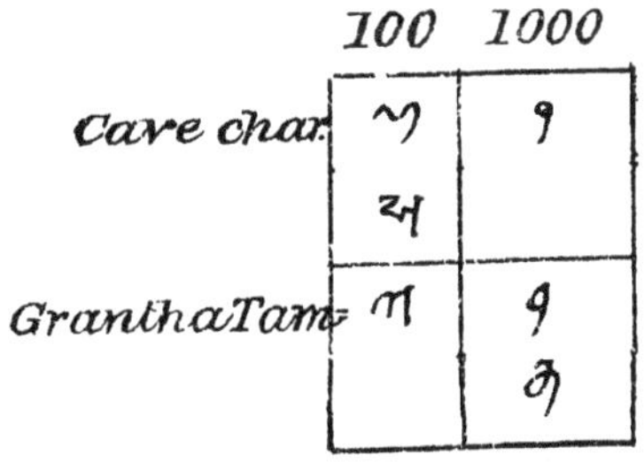

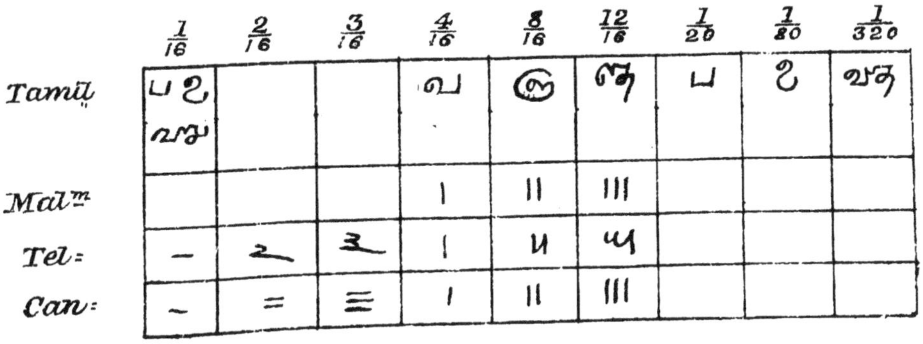

Grant of Vijayanandi Varmmā, ca 4th cent. A.D.

1

2

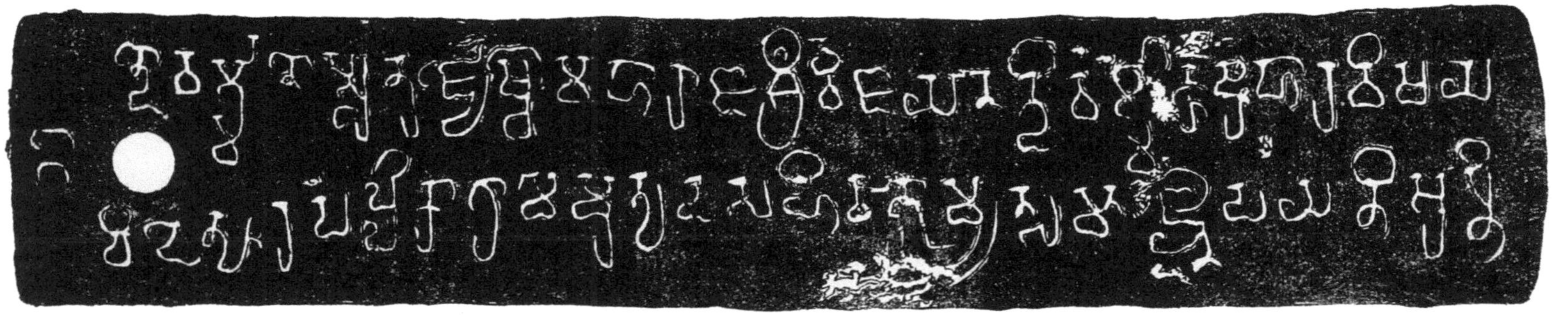

3

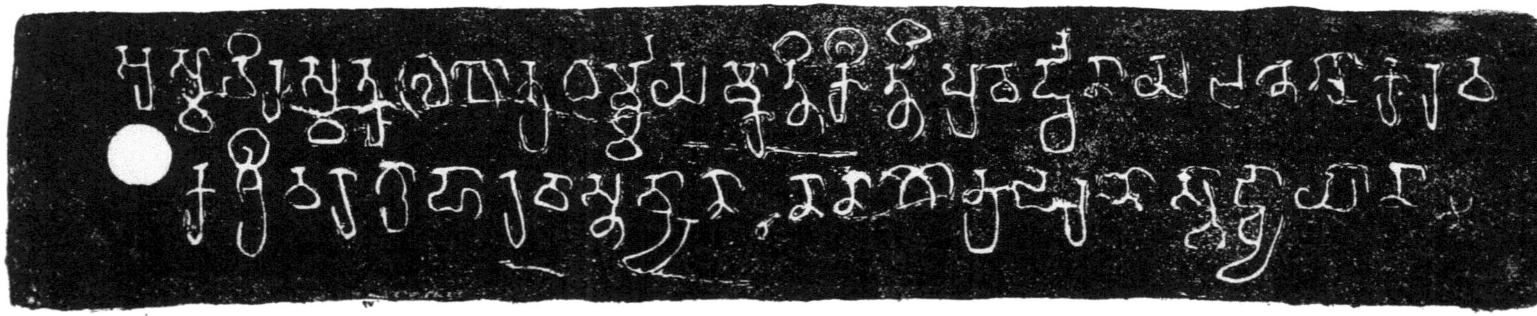

4

5

6

XXII

WEST (KALYĀṆA)

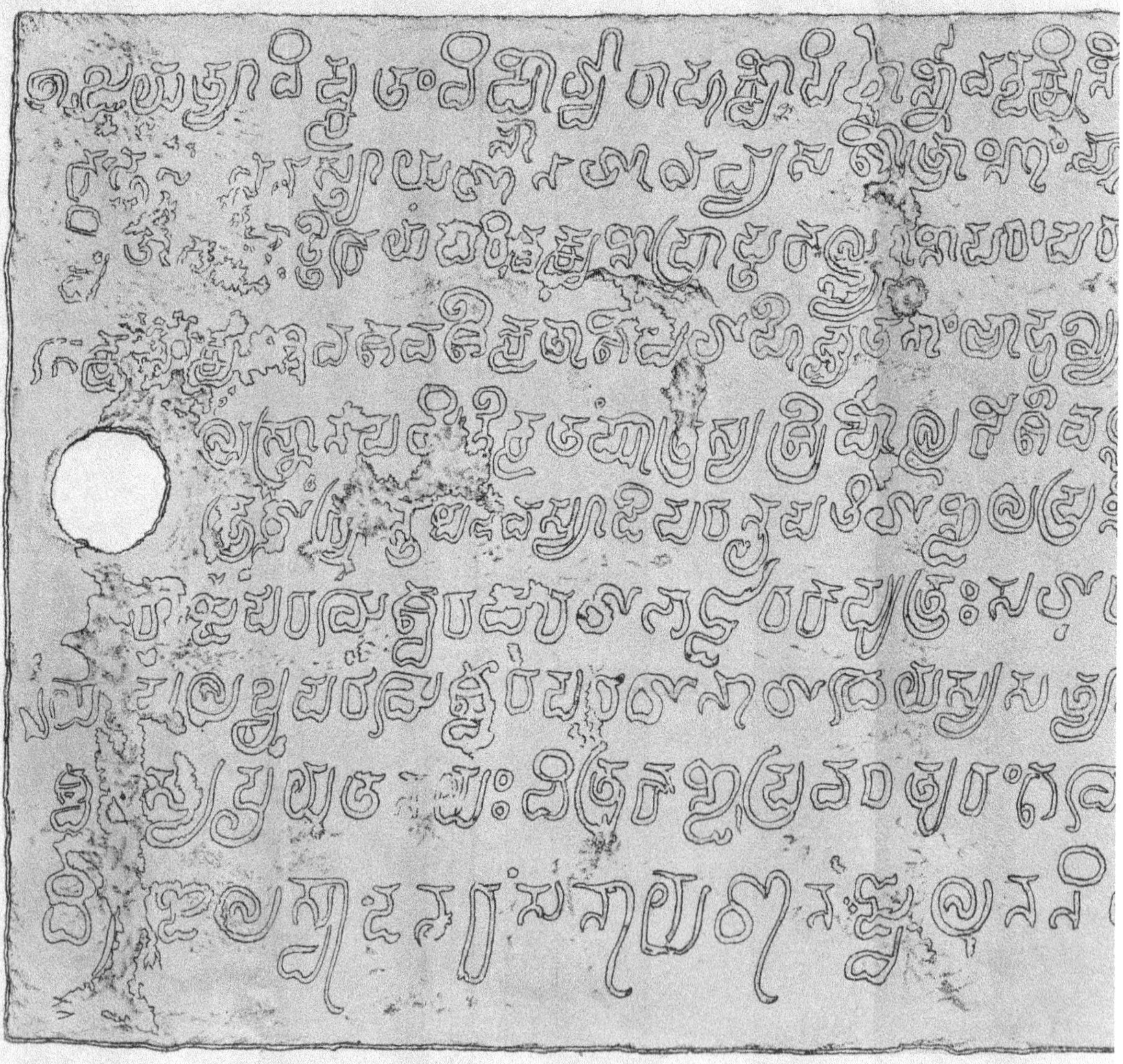

ČĀLUKYA OF 608 A.D.

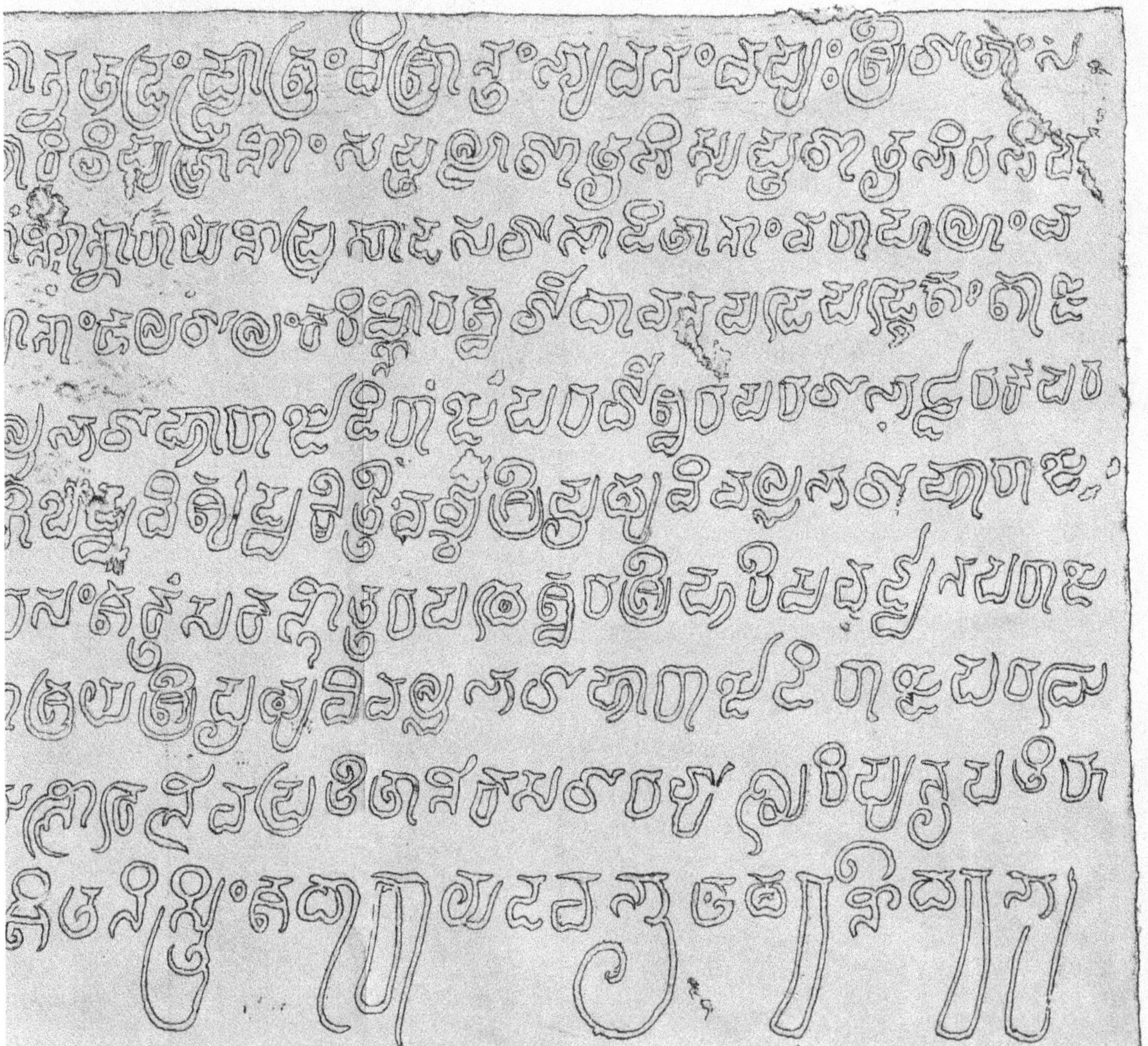

1

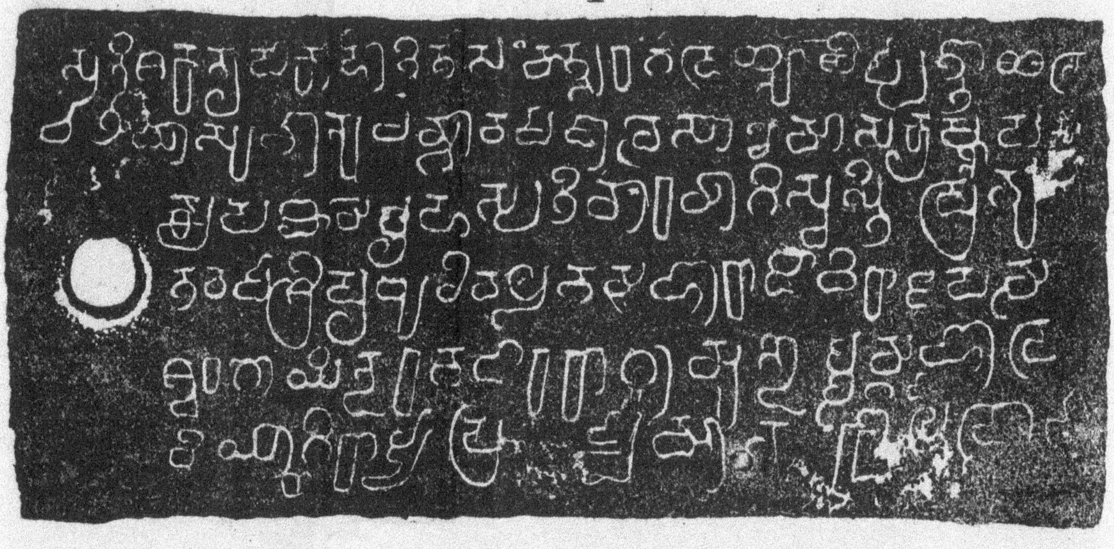

3

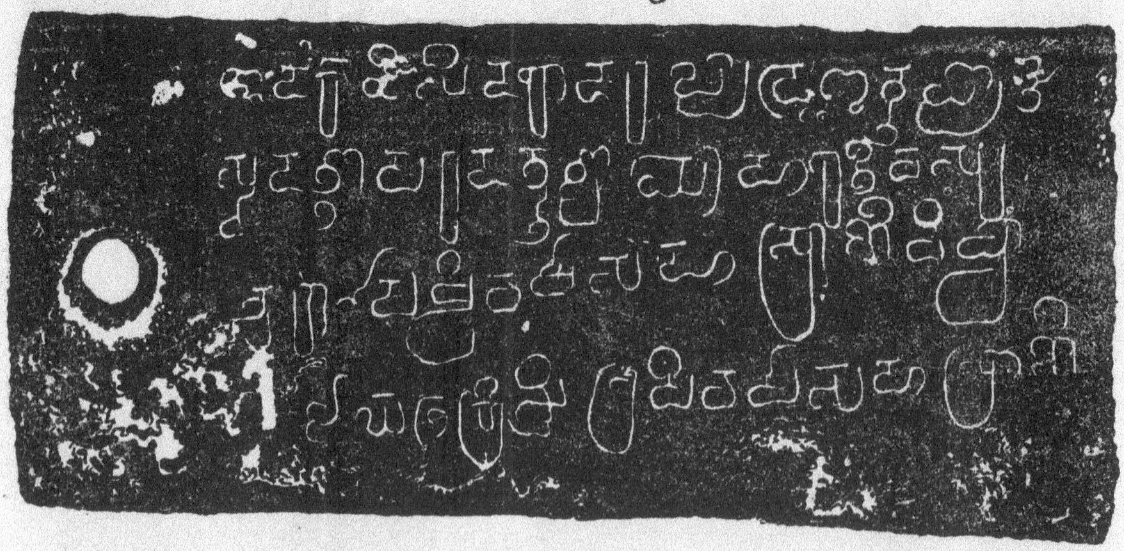

804 A.D.

2

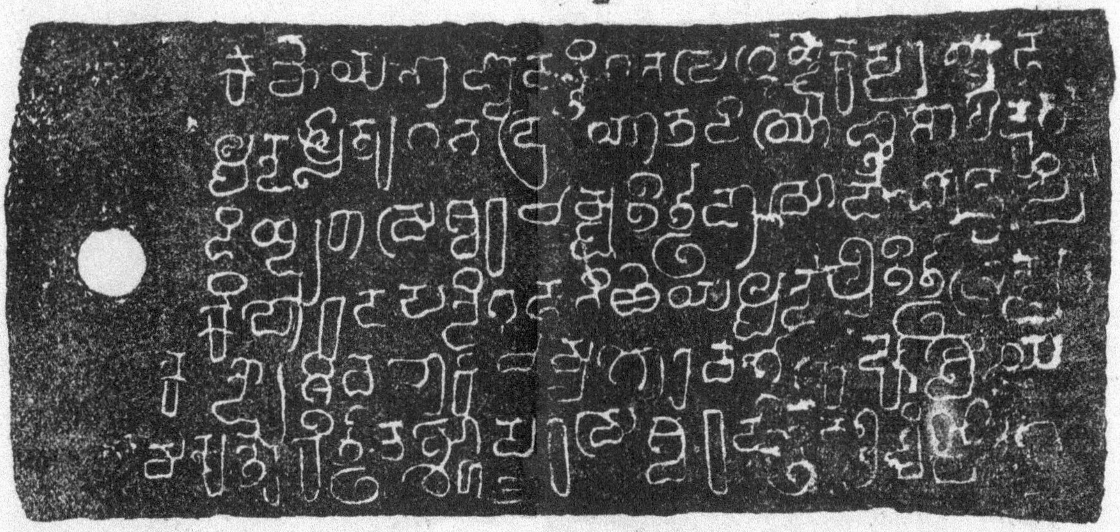

4

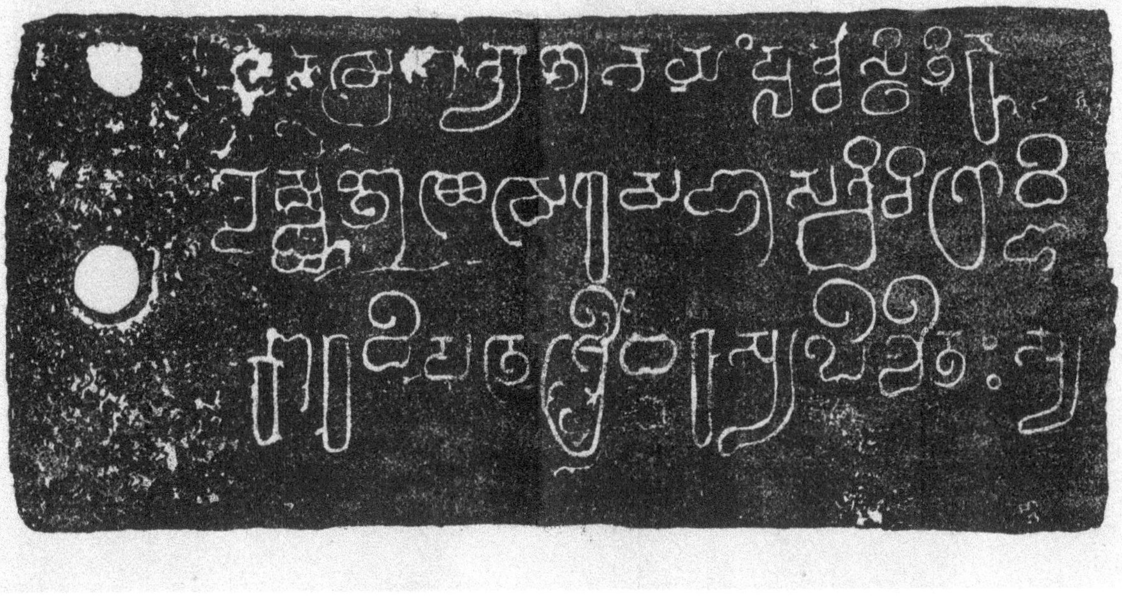

Pl. XXIV.

EASTERN ČĀLUKYA-(7th cent A.D.)

Grant by Vishṇuvardhana.

1

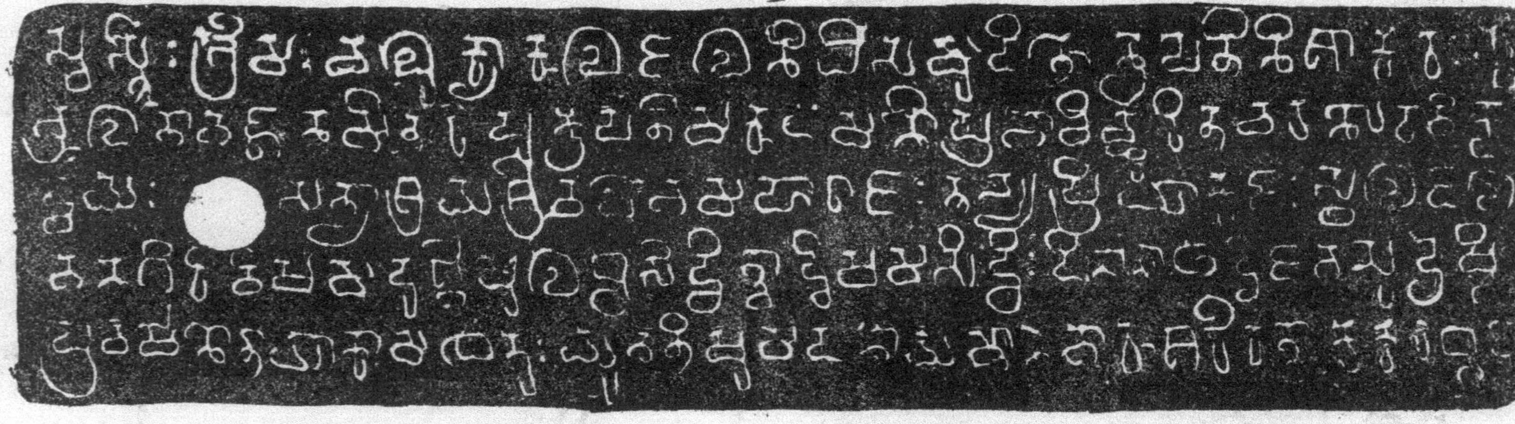

2

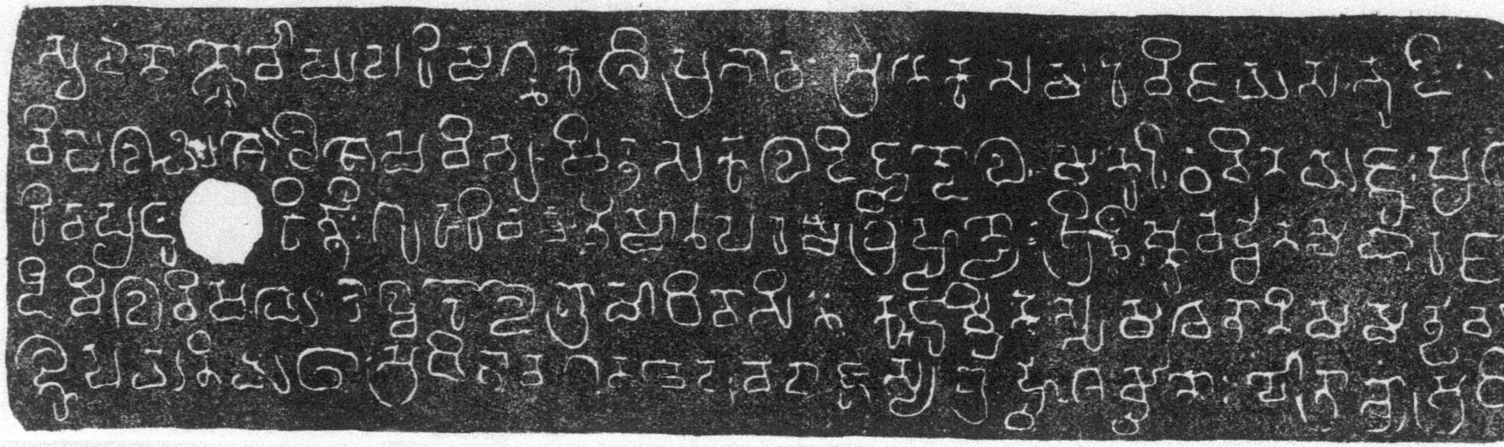

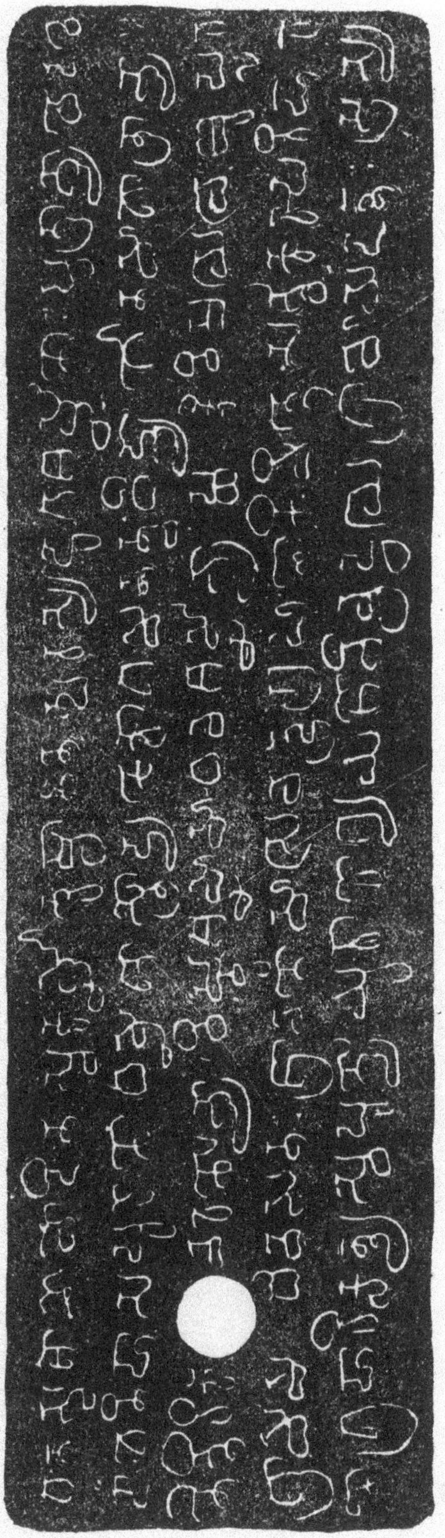
3

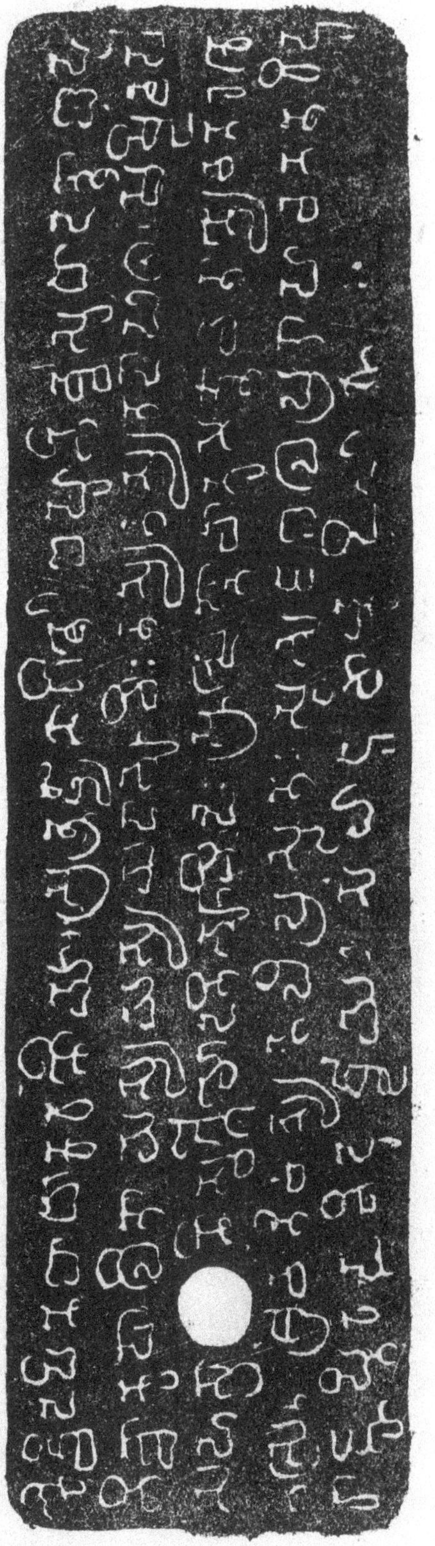
4

XVI

EAST (KALIṄGA) ČĀLUKYA OF 945 A.D.

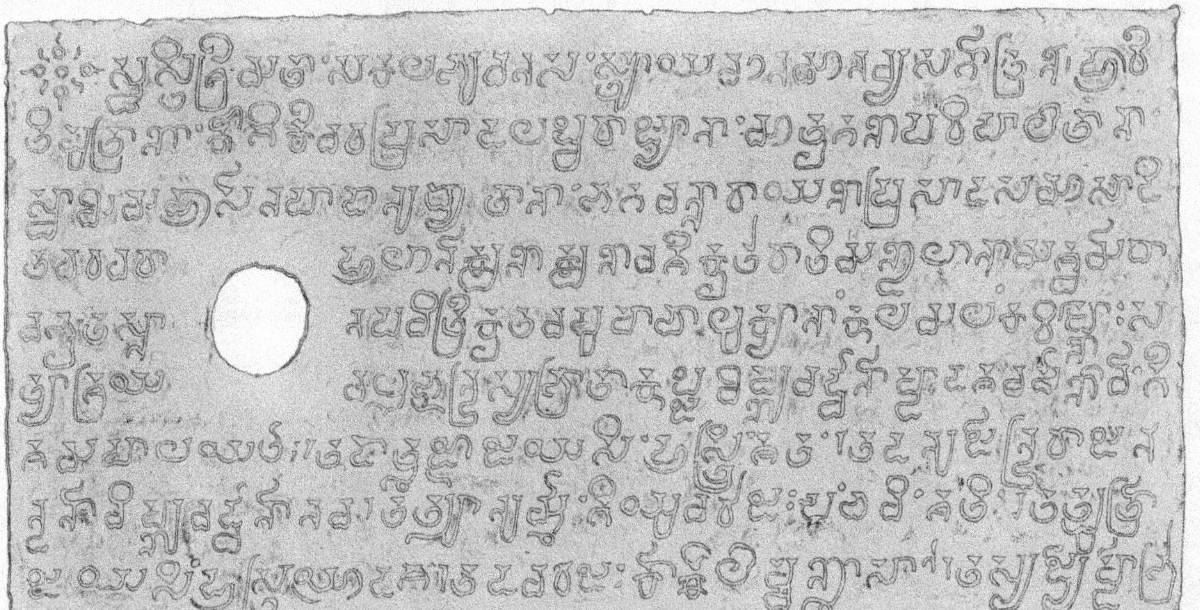

XXVI.

E. ČĀLUKYA (TRANSI

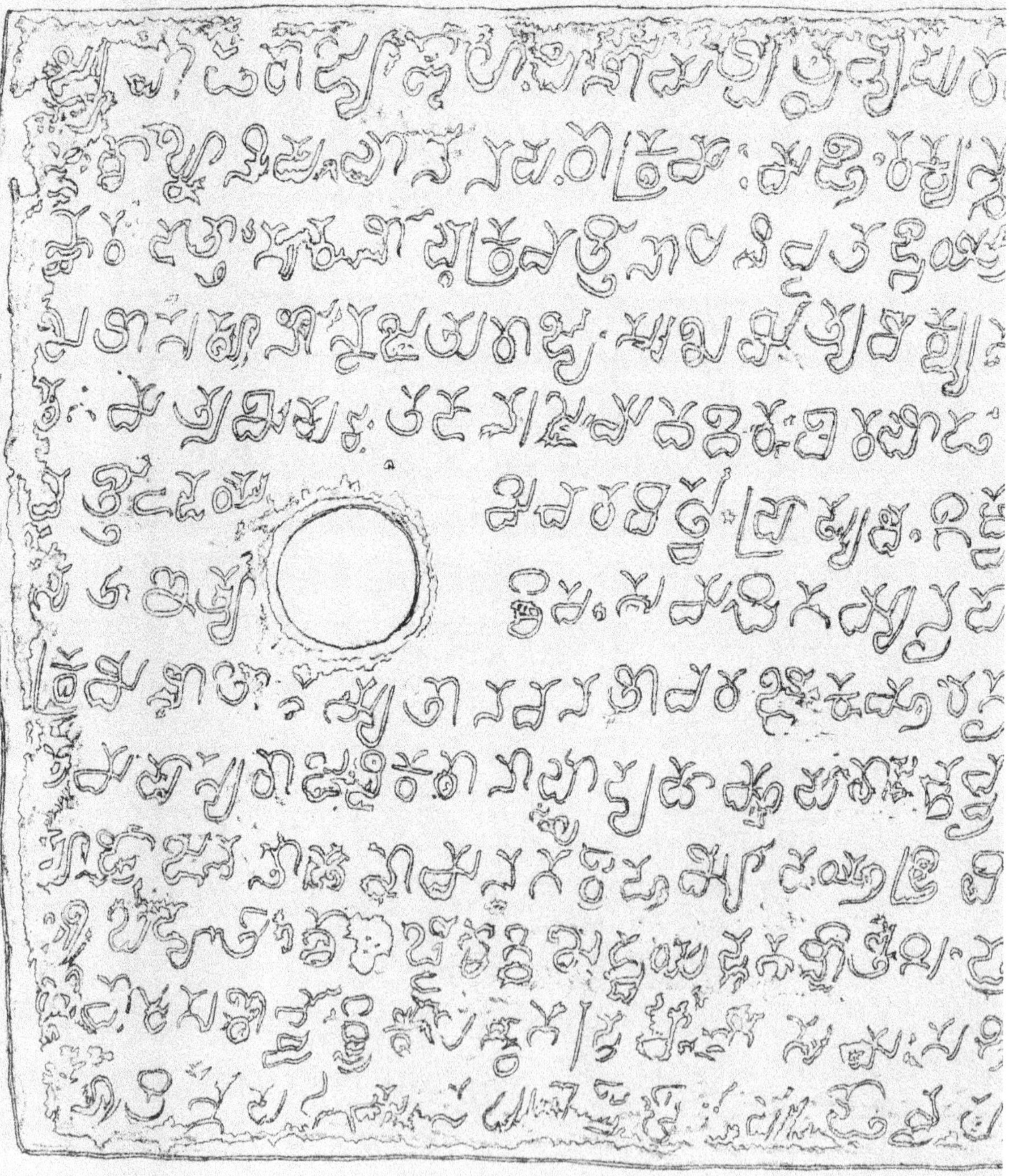

ISITIONAL) d. 1079 A.D.

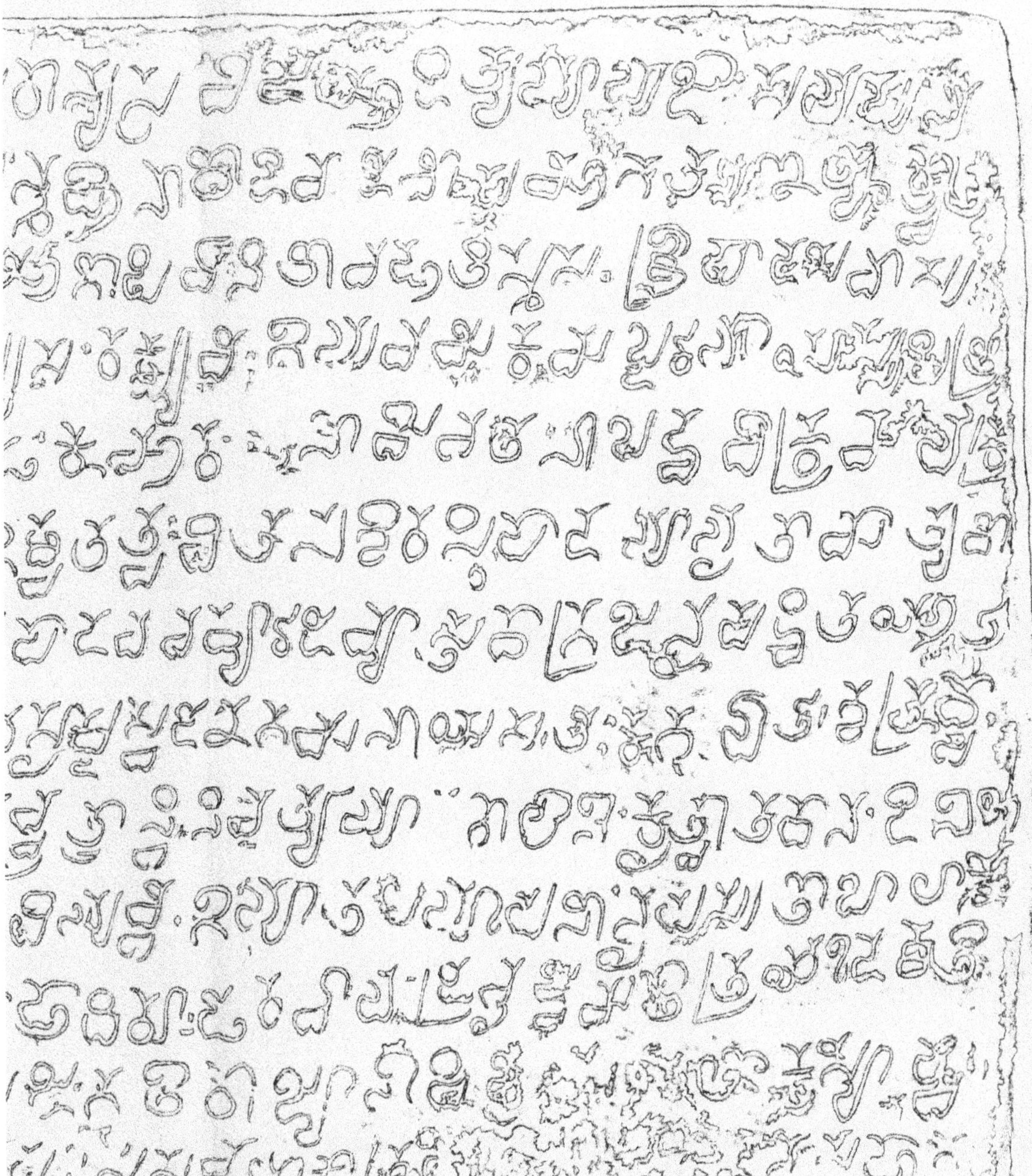

VIJAYANAGARA 1399 A.D.

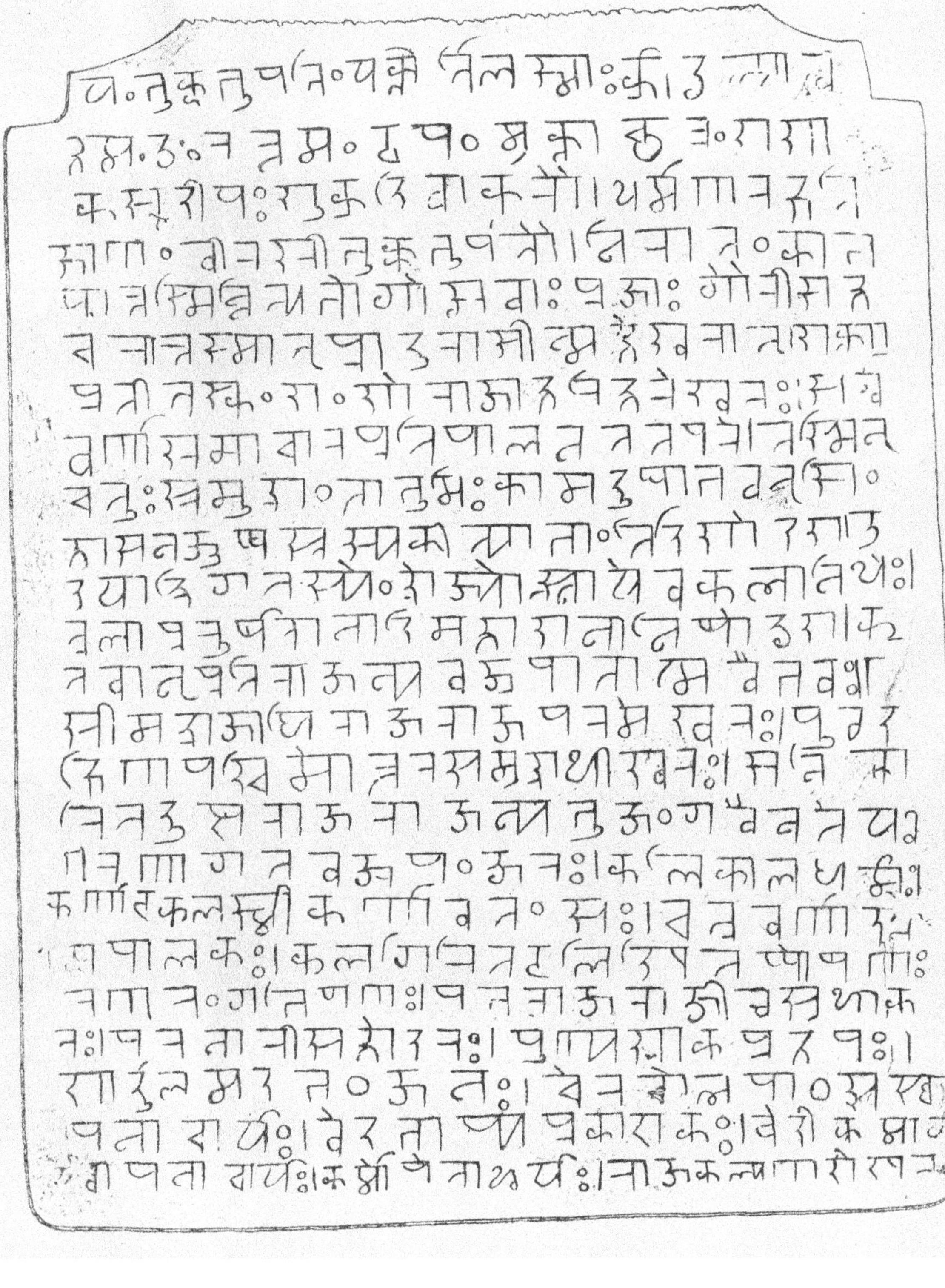

XXVIII.

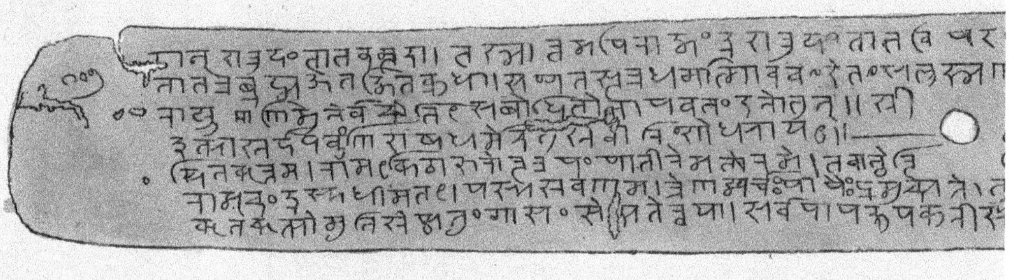

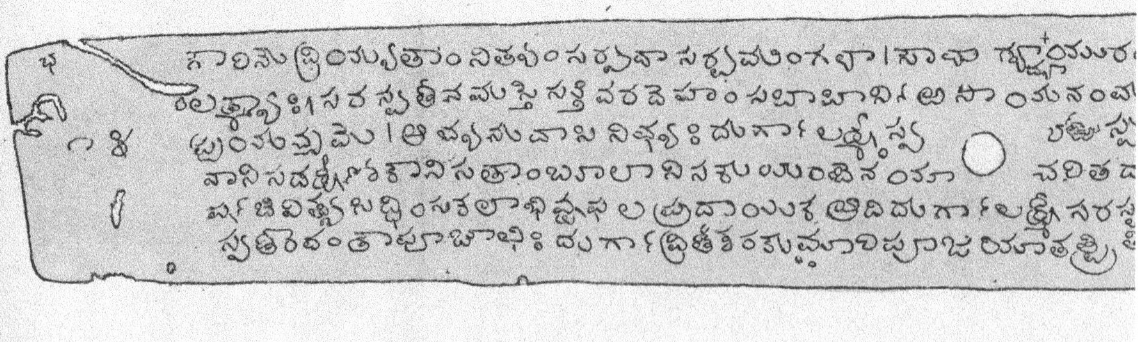

NANDINĀGARĪ (c. 1550) from Tanjore № 11894.

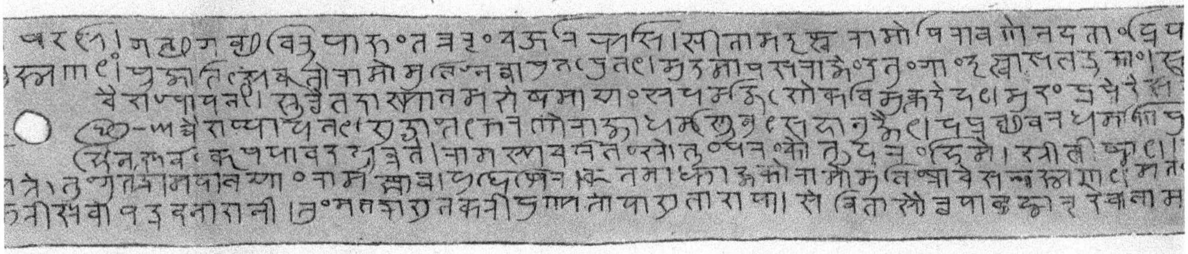

TELUGU (c. 1670); from Tanjore № 9531.

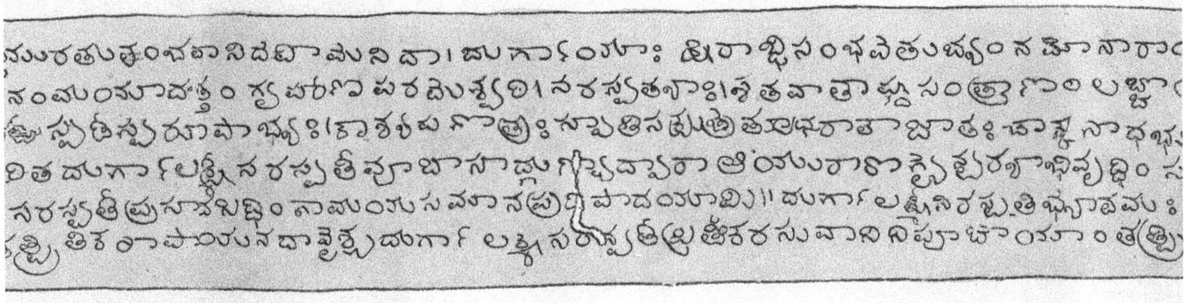

NANDINĀGARĪ (c. 1550) from Tanjore № 11894.

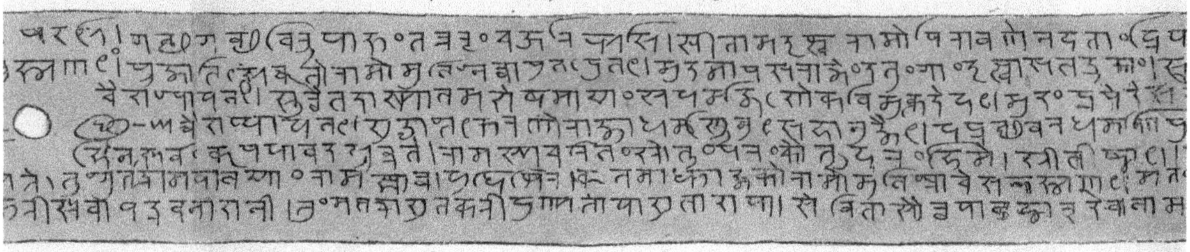

TELUGU (c. 1670); from Tanjore № 9531.

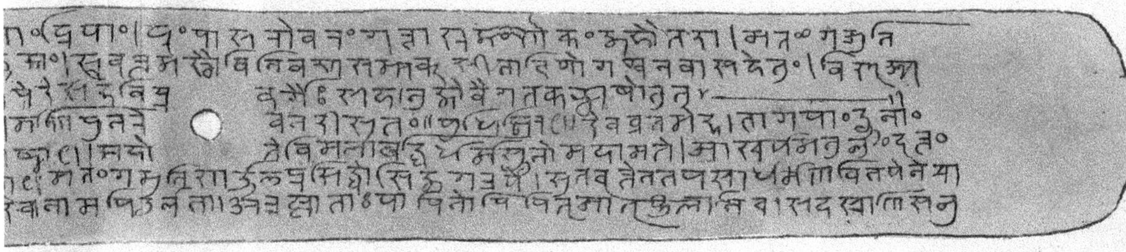

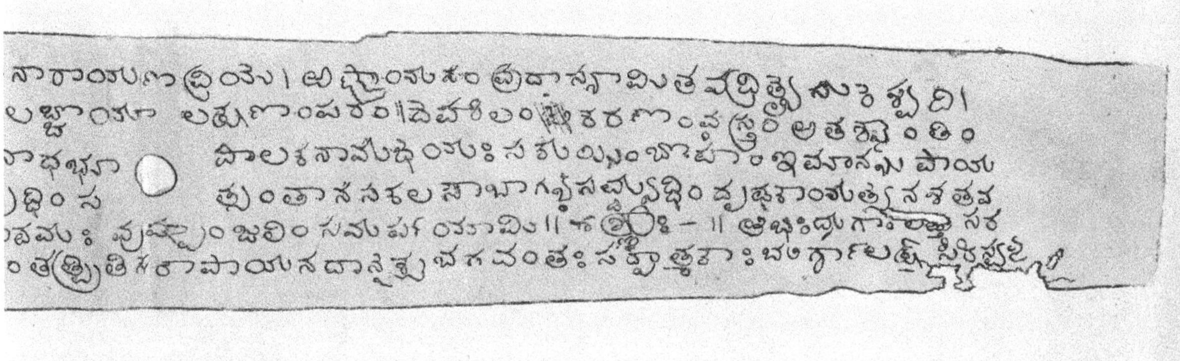

XXIX.

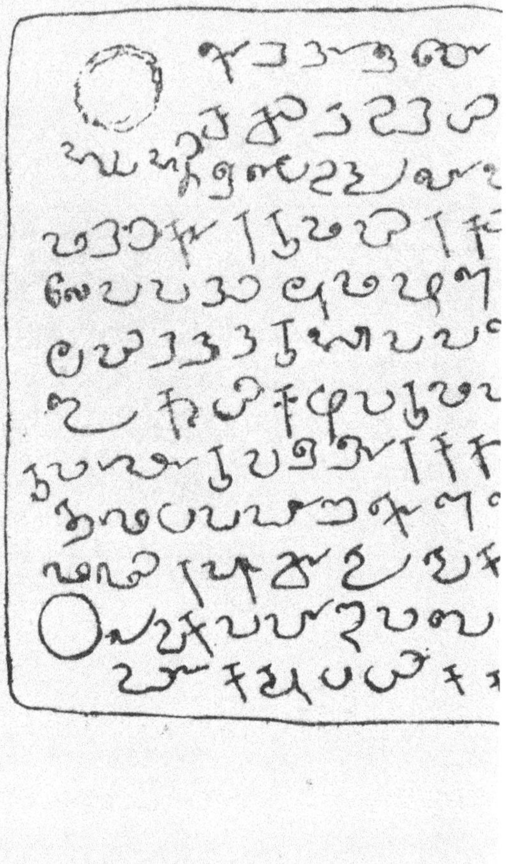

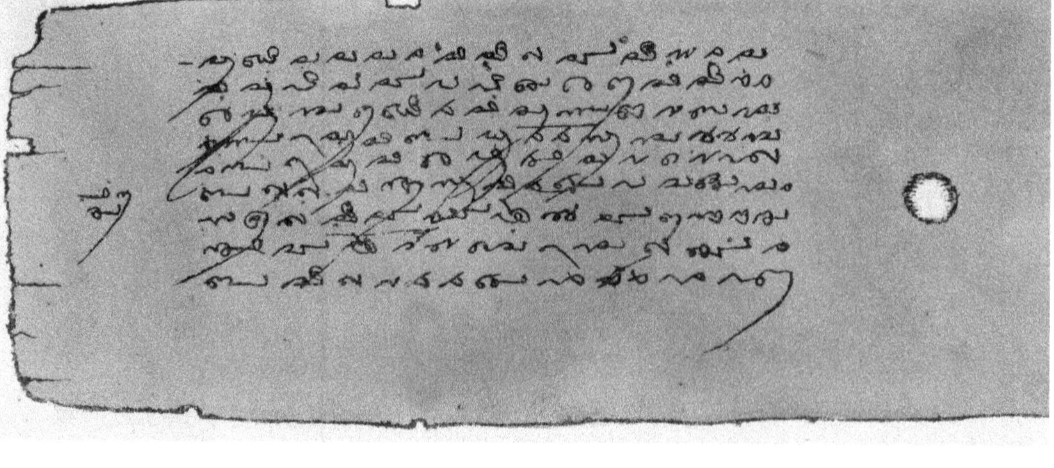

VAṬṬEḶUTTU.

1 of Syrian grant (B) c. 825 A.D.

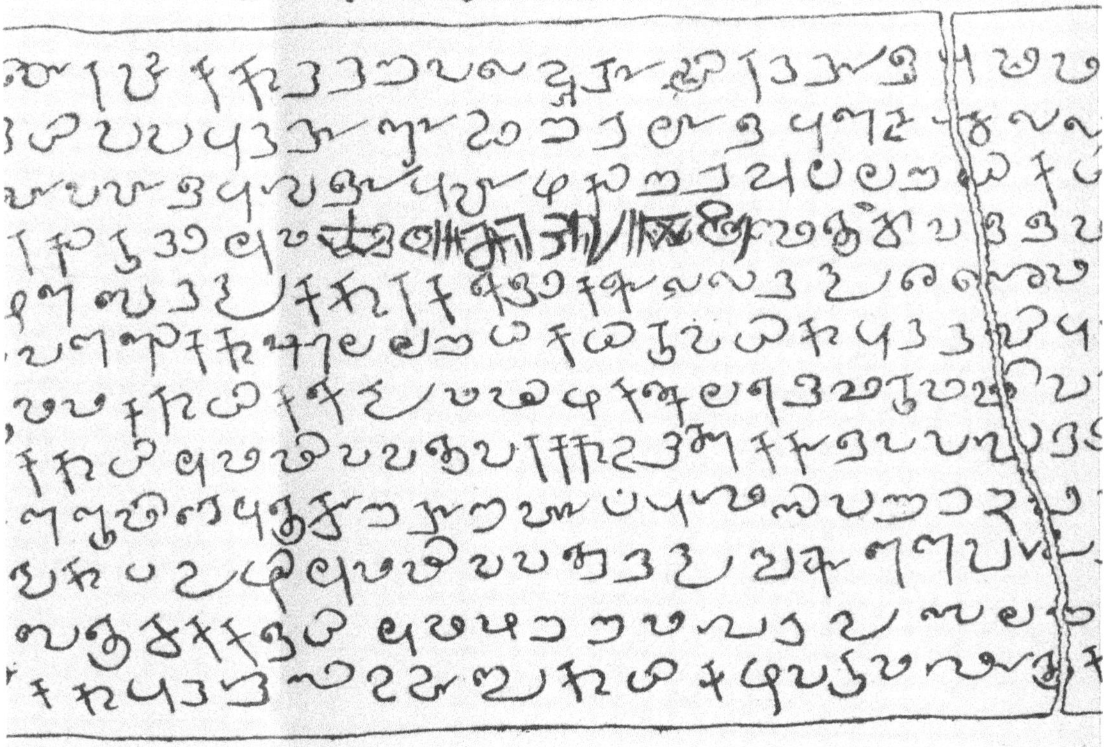

KŌLEḶUTTU – 1724 A.D.

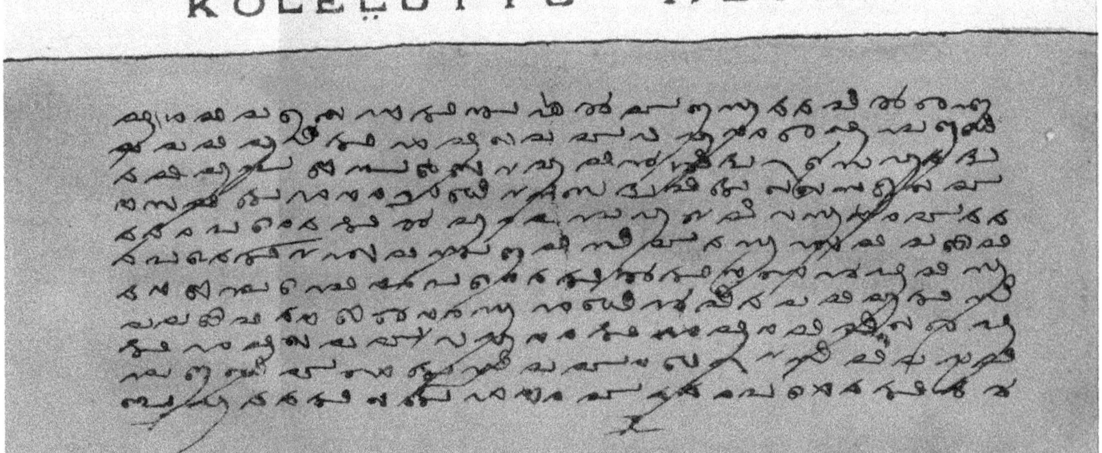

VAṬṬEḶUTTU.

1 of Syrian grant (B) c. 825 A.D.

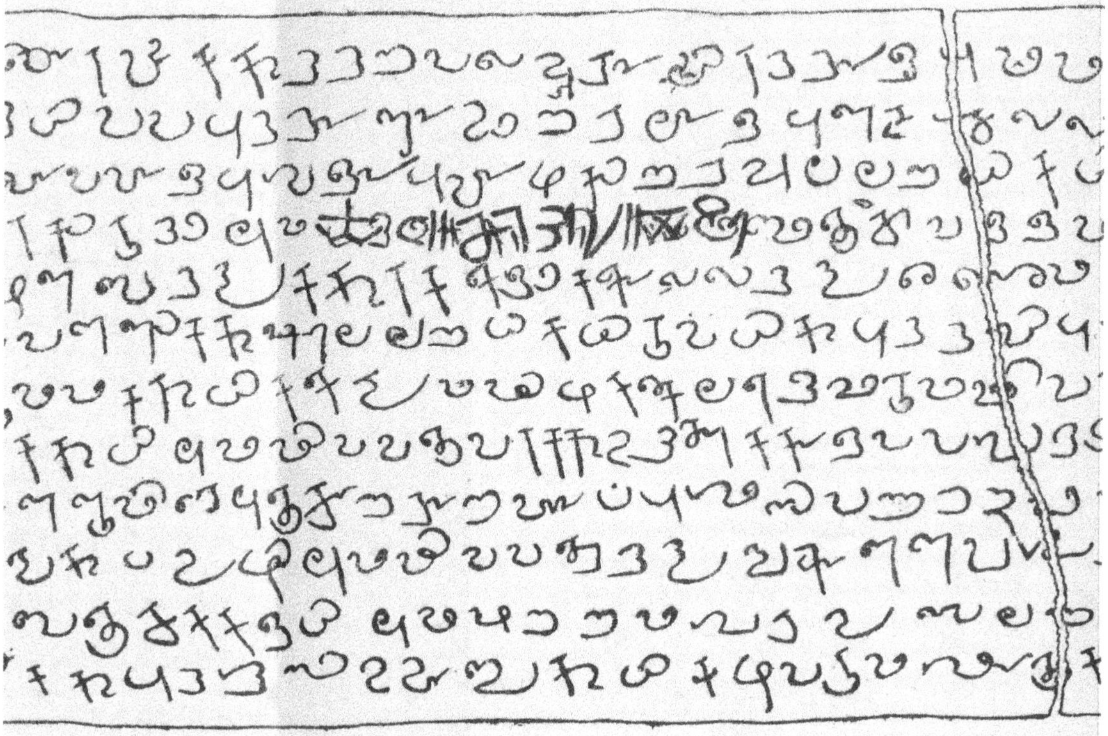

KŌLEḶUTTU – 1724 A.D.

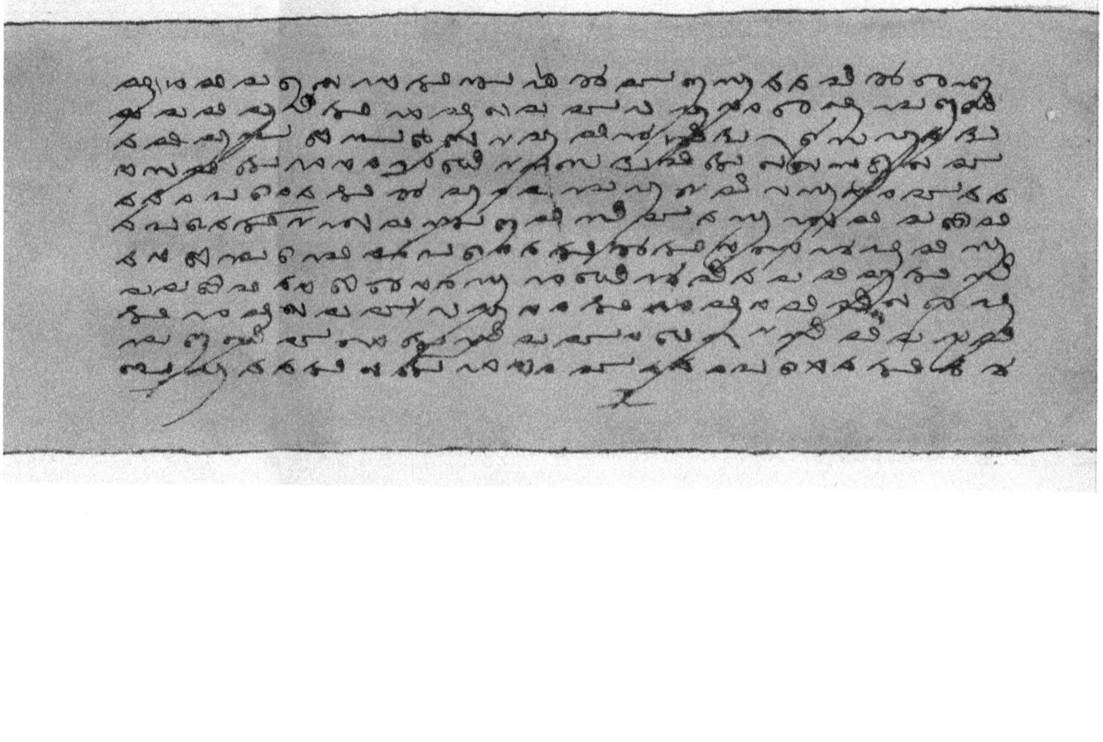

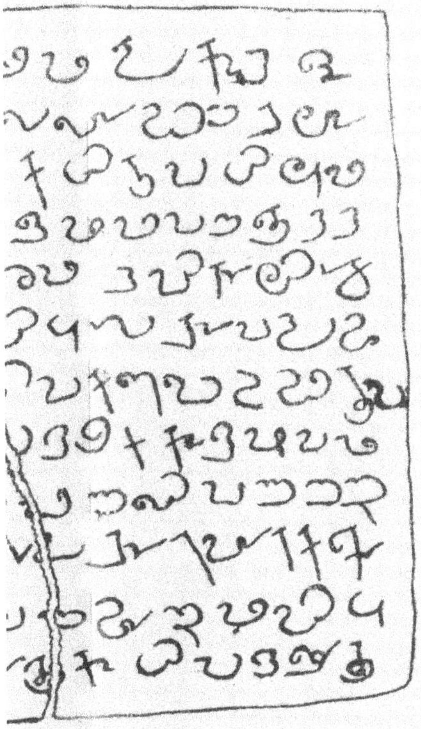

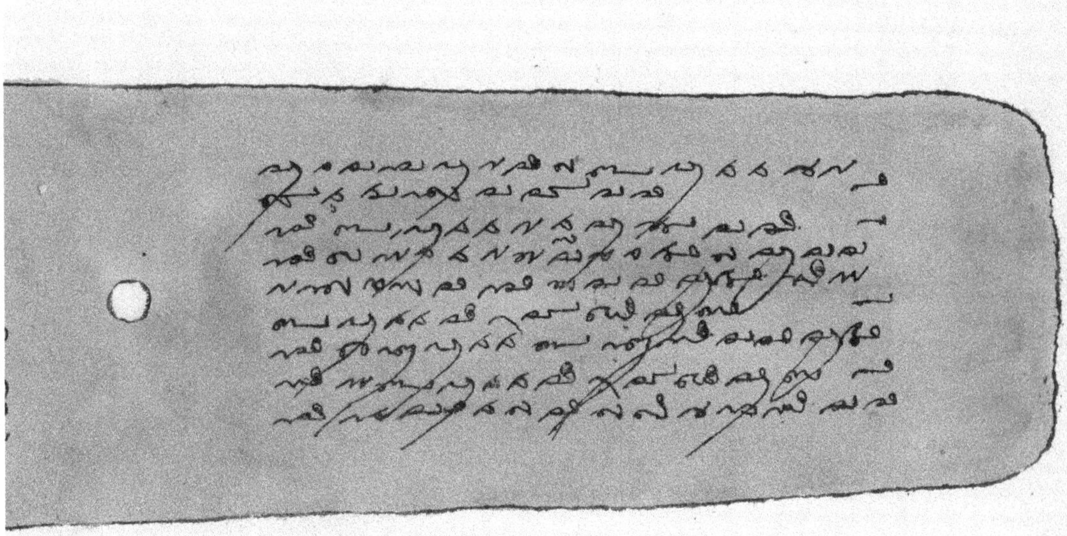

XXX.

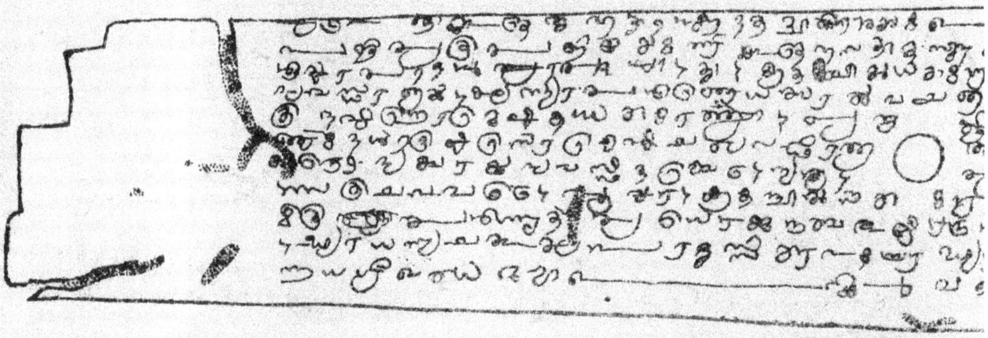

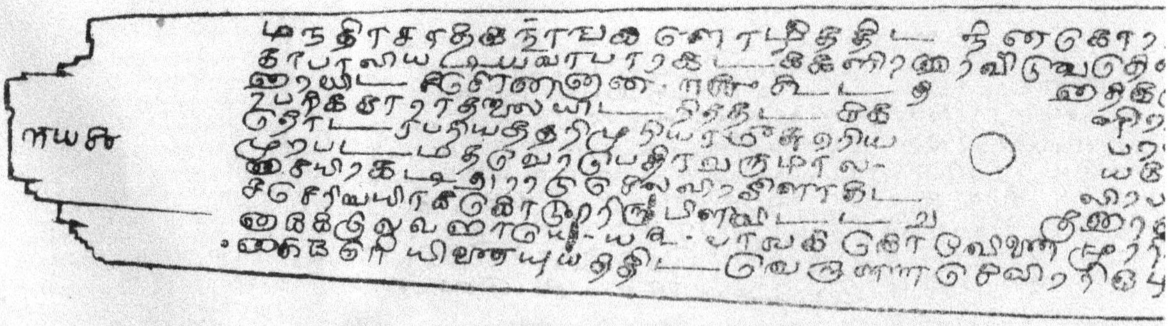

GRANTHA, c. 1600.

from Tanjore № 8594.

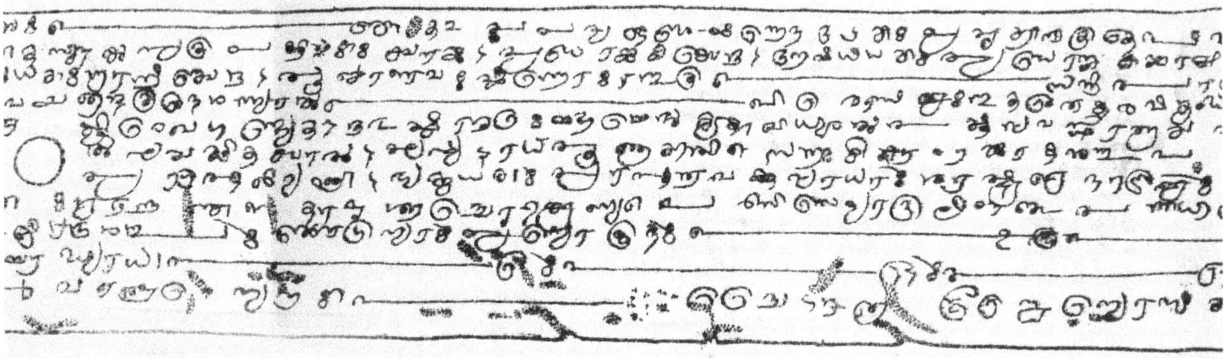

TAMIL, c. 1600.

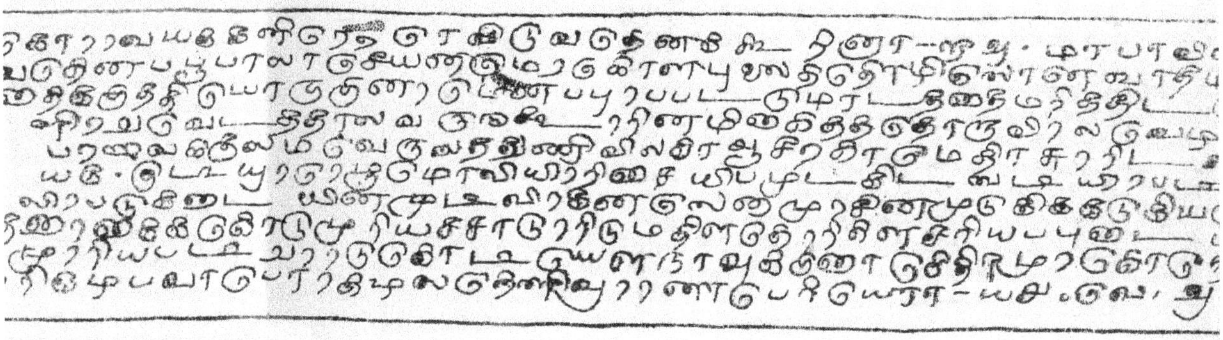

GRANTHA, c. 1600.

from Tanjore Nº 8594.

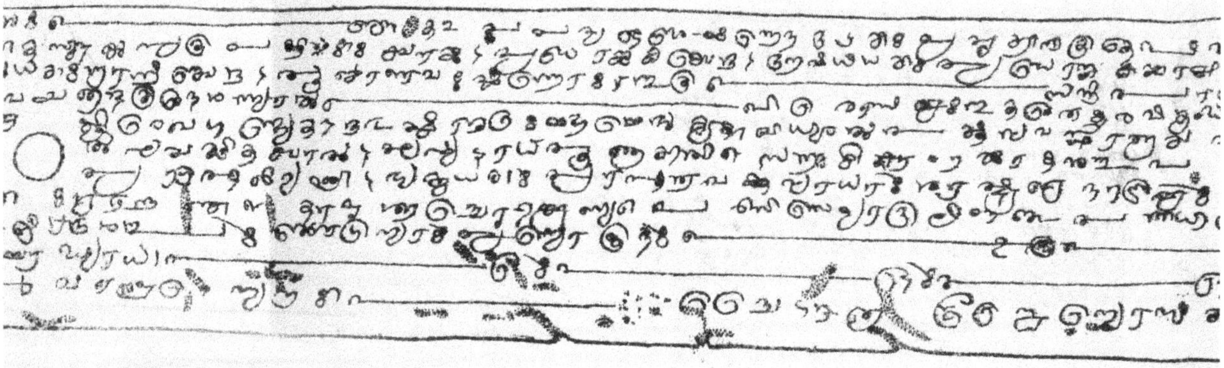

TAMIḶ, c. 1600.

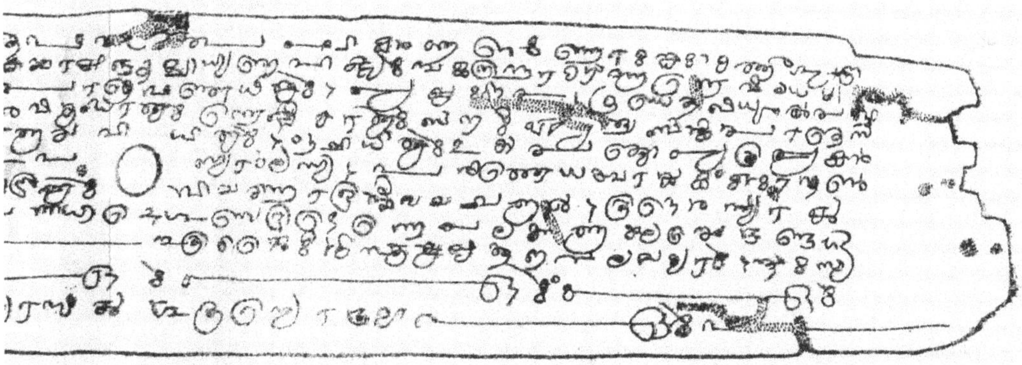

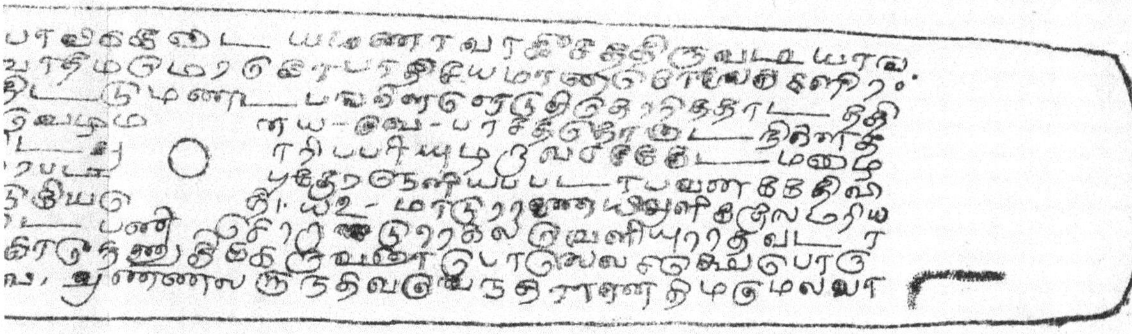

For EU product safety concerns, contact us at Calle de José Abascal, 56–1°,
28003 Madrid, Spain or eugpsr@cambridge.org.

www.ingramcontent.com/pod-product-compliance
Ingram Content Group UK Ltd.
Pitfield, Milton Keynes, MK11 3LW, UK
UKHW050455190625
459647UK00035B/2852